HAROLD *and Me*

HAROLD and Me

MY LIFE, LOVE, AND HARD TIMES
WITH HAROLD ROBBINS

JANN ROBBINS

A TOM DOHERTY ASSOCIATES BOOK
NEW YORK

HAROLD AND ME: MY LIFE, LOVE, AND HARD TIMES WITH
HAROLD ROBBINS

"A Week in the Port of St. Tropez" (pages 191–211), excerpted from Harold Robbins' unpublished autobiography, *After the Tropic of Cancer*, originally appeared in
the January 1996 edition of *Playboy* magazine under the title "The Stallion" and is
reprinted by permission of *Playboy* magazine.

"The Lives They Lived: Harold Robbins; Smutty Plots, Clean Prose" (page 299)
originally appeared in *The New York Times Magazine* on January 4, 1998, and is
reprinted by permission of Wayne Koestenbaum.

A Forge Book
Published by Tom Doherty Associates, LLC
175 Fifth Avenue
New York, NY 10010

www.tor-forge.com

Forge® is a registered trademark of Tom Doherty Associates, LLC.

Library of Congress Cataloging-in-Publication Data

Robbins, Jann.
    Harold and me : my life, love, and hard times with Harold Robbins / by
Jann Robbins.
        p.   cm.
    "A Tom Doherty Associates book."
    ISBN-13: 978-0-7653-0003-4
    ISBN-10: 0-7653-0003-6
    1. Robbins, Harold, 1916–1997.   2. Authors, American—20th century—
Biography.   3. Robbins, Harold, 1916–1997—Marriage.   4 Robbins,
Jann.   5. Authors' spouses—United States—Biography.   I. Title.
PS3568.O224Z88   2009
813'.54—dc22
    [B]
                                                               2008034732

First Edition: December 2008

Printed in the United States of America

0   9   8   7   6   5   4   3   2   1

To Robert Gleason with thanks for his unwavering suppport
through the years
and for understanding the heart and soul of the man,
Harold Robbins.

With thanks and gratitude to Junius Podrug for his dedication,
loyalty, and great work.

ACKNOWLEDGMENTS

With gratitude and thanks to:

Matt Cimber
Kyle Avery
Eric Raab
Melissa Frain
Patty Garcia

And to the millions of readers who have kept Harold Robbins'
works alive.

HAROLD *and Me*

CHAPTER ONE

1982

*T*his was a day I would never forget. I'd just received a phone call from a friend telling me I had a job interview with world bestselling novelist Harold Robbins.

Not only did I desperately need a job, but I had moved to LA intending to become a writer myself. I had, coincidentally, spent the last night before leaving Oklahoma City, my hometown, with Harold Robbins. I stayed up all night reading his novel *The Pirate*.

I arrived in Los Angeles from Oklahoma City with my résumé, my advertising portfolio, my awards, and my ambition. The LA ad world was singularly unimpressed, and I had been unemployed since my arrival. In the LA market, the fact that I had written television, radio, and print commercials and won regional awards was insignificant. On every interview I was told I was "overqualified" or "underqualified." Well, at least, it contained the word "qualified." I kept getting rejections, but I was determined to stay in LA. From the moment I stepped off the plane into the balmy breezes on Christmas Day I knew I had found my home.

When the call came to interview with Harold Robbins for a temporary job, my two cats and I were living on dry Post Grape-Nuts and we were desperate. On the morning of my interview, I dressed meticulously, choosing a cream silk blouse, soft lilac linen skirt, proper, all the while wondering what Harold Robbins would be like. Intellectual? Terse? No-nonsense? Crazy? Or like the characters in his book? He wrote about sex, drugs, power, and seduction in his books. Would he try to seduce me? My friend who arranged the appointment had told me Harold Robbins was as "wild" as his books but also a very nice person. I remembered his image from pictures I had seen in magazines: black Stetson cowboy hat, dark, heavy sunglasses, looking like he owned the universe.

Harold Robbins had sold over 750 million novels in his career and been translated into forty-two languages throughout the world. That fact was blazoned on the backs of all his books, and I had read most of them.

The Carpetbaggers was racy, wild, and provocative. It had made a hidden progression from my grandmother, to my mother, to my aunt, and even though I wasn't old enough to read it, I suspected it was somehow wicked since it was passed in a brown paper bag. In fact, they only read it at night.

*M*y diesel Peugeot puttered like a sewing machine as I entered Beverly Hills, passing beautiful mansions tucked among the trees and hills surrounded by walls of privacy. I followed my directions to 1501 Tower Grove Road and gave my name to the guard at the large black wrought-iron gates, and he let me through. The driveway was a half mile of plush greenery and surreal landscaping.

After I parked my car in the circular driveway, Rick, the majordomo, greeted me. Entering the large and elegant gray two-story home, I followed him over plush carpeting up a winding staircase.

At the double doors in the hallway the majordomo knocked and then opened both doors in a sweeping gesture. We stepped up one stair and entered a huge, sprawling bedroom. Cream satin drapes from ceiling to floor, cream satin walls, smoke-mirrored ceiling, and a huge king-size bed. It looked like the ultimate seduction chamber, straight out of a Harold Robbins novel.

In the middle of the bed, a man wearing jet-black sunglasses sat cross-legged with a cigarette in his hand, smoke curling into the air, sipping coffee out of a mug emblazoned with the inscription "Too Much Sex Blurs Your Vision." The last three words blurred. He was wearing a white T-shirt and red jockey briefs.

This was my introduction to Harold Robbins.

I had always had a slight limp. Most people, seeing me walk for the first time, fixate on that limp. I'm overly sensitive about this, but as I walked toward Harold he never took his eyes off mine. He hadn't noticed the limp and I could have kissed him.

He put his hand out to me. "Hi, I'm Harold Robbins."

I shook his hand and smiled back at him. "I'm Jann Stapp."

"Pull up a chair," he said, and motioned to the ecru satin chair in the sitting area near the bed. I turned the chair toward the bed and handed him my résumé. At the time, I was naive enough to think that it was your résumé that counted. In the world of Harold Robbins I discovered that shapely legs, a pertinent derriere, and a come-fuck-me smile were all that mattered.

"You're a very pretty girl," he said, looking at me and smiling.

"Thank you."

He kept on his black sunglasses and I couldn't see his eyes. I wondered if he always wore them. I wondered if he did all of his interviews sitting in bed, drinking coffee out of a mug that said "Too Much Sex Blurs Your Vision" . . . in red jockey briefs. I wondered if the Hollywood stories were true about the casting couch or, in this case, the author's bedroom.

He briefly glanced over my résumé and grinned broadly. "I went to Oklahoma once. Tulsa. I had chicken-fried steak with gravy and biscuits, the best! Almost as good as eating pussy." His deep voice rasped with a rough New York accent.

Now that was the Harold Robbins from one of his characters in a blockbuster novel!

"How do you like California?"

"I moved here on Christmas Day and don't want to leave," I said. A red bedside intercom light blinked and a beep sounded from the telephone as I spoke.

He smiled at me. "What do you want, Linda?" he bellowed into the speaker.

Linda's voice filled the room. "Dr. Cooper is running late; he'll be here in about fifteen minutes."

Harold took off his sunglasses for the first time. "Does that mean I can charge him for my time?" he quipped, and laughed at his own joke.

"You'll have to ask him about that," Linda said, and hung up the phone, laughing.

He had a penetrating stare and had never yet taken his eyes off of me. "Linda is Grace's secretary, not mine. She's a pain in the ass. My head got fucked up a few weeks ago; she and everybody else are driving me crazy. I've got to get rid of her."

I wondered if Grace was here. My friends had told me she traveled quite a bit.

"I had an accident the day my married . . . Caryn."

I looked at him, a little confused, but said nothing.

"Goddammit, that's what I mean. My sentences get fucked up," he said in frustration. "I slipped . . . shower. Fuck it . . . it's all screwy. Crazy . . . I can see the sentence in my head. . . . It comes out . . . wrong. It's driving . . . crazy. You don't understand me and I don't know it's wrong."

He was very frustrated but would not explain what had happened. I smiled at him. "It's okay, Mr. Robbins."

My smile seemed to break his frustration and he smiled back at me.

"I went crazy the other night when I was downstairs in the kitchen. I was trying to tell Rick." He glanced at me. "He's the one who brought you up here. I was telling him what I wanted for dinner and he and Linda kept finishing my sentences. I threw the pans all over the kitchen. Christ, they all try to help, but I need to do it on my own. I sent Grace to fucking Cannes to get her out of here. She was driving me crazy. I told her that she could go to the Cannes Film Festival and she's over there pissing money away like . . ." He shook his head when he couldn't complete the sentence.

"In the hospital the doctors said I'd bruised my head during a fall and I had aphasia. I slipped in the shower on the morning of Caryn's wedding. I hired Dr. Cooper, a speech pathologist, to help me get out of this shit. We work together every day, two hours in the morning, two hours in the afternoon. I'm exhausted after I finish. You'll meet him."

Again the intercom interrupted him. "Dr. Cooper is here."

"Send him up," Harold said.

"Cooper says this fuckup in my head can be corrected. But I'll have to work my ass off." He laughed. "My head's always been fucked up; that's why my books are crazy."

I understood Harold's dilemma. I, too, had faced battles. When I was born the doctors told my parents I might never walk. My father refused to accept this and came home from work early each day and for months forced me to walk up and down the sidewalk, like a Marine Corps drill instructor. Finally, I took steps on my own with only a slight limp remaining. That battle I fought every day of my life, taking physical therapy throughout my life. I knew Harold was facing a similar battle and I knew intuitively that he would never give up.

"Mr. Robbins," I said. "You'll do just fine. You're a strong person."

He looked at me curiously, a mischievous glint in his eye. "Yeah?"

I nodded.

Dr. Cooper, a tall, athletic-looking man with a balding head and gray hair fringed around his temples, entered the room. Cheerful and energetic, he looked at Harold. "What are you doing up here with this bombshell blonde?"

"She's my new assistant," Harold said proudly.

I did a quick double take. "I got the job?" I asked.

He looked at me, a little surprised. "Isn't that why you're here?"

He never looked at my résumé or questioned my office skills. I assumed this was how moguls and superstars did things in Hollywood. Still, I had no idea how much I would be paid, when I would work, and what if I couldn't do the job that he needed? But I was already hooked. I had a job and I liked Harold Robbins.

Chapter Two

Linda, the secretary, showed me around the house. "You'll like working for Harold," she said as we walked through the spacious and beautiful rooms. She pointed out the paintings on the dining room walls as being Marc Chagall's four-canvas medley titled *The Seasons*. As we walked through the foyer, she pointed out a caricature of Harold in pen and ink, signed *A Mon Ami, Picasso*.

As we sauntered through her tour chatter I wondered if she knew that Harold wanted to get rid of her. She seemed like a nice girl but never stopped talking. She filled in the blanks for everyone, not just Harold. She led me up the stairs and into the study where Harold worked. A dramatic and impressive room with black textured walls, black ceiling, and black Roman shades. The only other colors in the room were red and a touch of white, a red bedcover on a queen-size bed pushed flush against the wall. I'm not sure why, but this room reminded me of a volcano. An explosion of creativity. The black walls gave an "aloneness" feeling against the red flares of ideas erupting scenes that seared the pages of Harold Robbins novels.

The black carpeting was plush, the black sheen walls tastefully textured, and the black credenza highly varnished and opened into the tools of his trade. Piles of scripts, paper, pens, and a small television monitor. On the black varnished built-in desk was his black IBM Selectric typewriter sitting ominously silent. On the desk were a red ceramic ashtray, with a red and white with black print package of Lucky Strike cigarettes. White unlined typing paper stacked on top of onionskin carbon pages were neatly piled to the right of the typewriter.

A sexy naked female mannequin knelt in a corner of the painted deep red and black room. Her rouged, pouty lips were open slightly, with long, chicly tangled blond hair falling provocatively over one eye. Her naked derriere faced the open door of the bathroom tiled in black and white with sheen-varnished red walls. When the black drapes were lowered, the room was pitch-dark, other than the pin light that haloed down above Harold Robbins's typewriter.

When we left the office and walked back across the landing to the stairs Linda stopped and pointed out another oil painting. "This one is an original by Bernard Buffet, *Les Pines*."

I felt like I was in a museum. "These are all very beautiful."

"They have a house in France," Linda chatted. "Harold knew Picasso from the South of France. They walked their dogs together before Picasso died. He got those paintings downstairs in the dining room from Mrs. Chagall. Paid her under the table. They have stacks of paintings by Dalí sitting in their closets," Linda said casually. "Do you know Grace?"

"No, I don't," I said.

"She's a real trip," Linda said, rolling her eyes as we went downstairs and into the kitchen.

Harold buzzed the intercom in the kitchen. "Jam, are you down there?"

"Did you say 'Jam'?" I asked.

"Yeah, that's your name! Strawberry Jam!"

"Okay," I said. I didn't know Harold well enough yet to know that he was kidding me. I would soon realize he wanted a provocative answer. And I certainly didn't know him well enough to correct him. He could call me anything he wanted as far as I was concerned.

"Get up here; Cooper wants to talk to you about the flowers in Oklahoma. He thinks you're a farm girl!"

Dr. Cooper was standing on the balcony outside the sliding doors with Harold when I came into the bedroom. They called me outside.

"Do you see those white flowers down there?" Cooper asked.

The view from where we were standing was magnificent, overlooking Los Angeles and beyond to one side, looking into the lush and beautiful Benedict Canyon with hills, and looking down I saw the well-manicured grounds of the Harold Robbins estate. I pinpointed the flowers. "Yes, I see them."

"I told Robbins they looked like mistletoe blooms and I said that you were a farm girl from Oklahoma who would know what they are."

I looked up at Cooper and laughed. "The only thing I know about mistletoe is getting kissed if it's over your head. I'm a city girl, Dr. Cooper, and besides, I made a D minus-minus in botany at Oklahoma University!"

Harold cracked up with laughter. "Cooper, I told you she was no farm girl." He stepped back and patted my ass. "With an ass like that!"

I laughed and moved out of his reach.

We went back inside after a few moments and the doctor and Harold began his therapy. Harold held the telephone up to his ear, repeating words and sentences that Dr. Cooper was giving him. I sat down and watched. The exercises lasted about an hour.

When they were finished, Harold turned to me. "You ready for lunch?"

"Sure," I answered.

"The Oklahoma kid," Dr. Cooper said, laughing. "Have you ever had bagel, lox, and cream cheese?"

"I don't think so," I answered. "But I'm sure I'll like it."

"She knows about 'southern-fried' . . . ," Harold said, teasing.

I looked back at him and smiled.

As he looked at me, he said in almost a whisper, but loud enough for Dr. Cooper and me to hear, "Southern-fried pussy, the best, Cooper."

"Robbins, give her a break; she's just a kid," Cooper said.

Harold chuckled.

We went down the back stairway and through the kitchen, where Rick was preparing lunch for us, and into the dining room. The meal was elegantly served on the twelve-foot-long dining room glass-beveled tabletop placed majestically atop two large artistically sculpted Lucite bases. The table was set with silver chargers and beautiful china, sterling silver knives and forks, and white linen napkins.

Harold told Dr. Cooper he had to start working on a new novel soon. He wanted to know how long it was going to take before he could start working. "Paul says I need the money! Christ, I always need money, just to pay for you." He directed his last comment to Dr. Cooper. Harold claimed Dr. Cooper's visits were costing over a thousand dollars each day.

During lunch, I sat and listened as Harold and Dr. Cooper talked about the news, Hollywood gossip, and Harold's writing. I absolutely had to pinch myself in amazement! I thought about how life could change in seconds. During my dry Grape-Nuts breakfast this morning, I could never imagine I would be having lunch with the world's bestselling novelist.

After lunch, Harold, Dr. Cooper, and I went upstairs to the study. Harold pulled out a shoe-box-size container stacked with photographs. He handed them to me and asked me to sort them into groups.

He picked up a tape recorder and told Cooper he had a tape to play for him of his speaking exercises. He saw the pack of Lucky Strikes on the desk. He took a cigarette out of the pack, lit it up, and turned to me.

"When I start working, I use these carbon sheets." He pointed to the stack of papers. "I save everything and I like to have copies. I once wrote a whole section of manuscript and the fucking publisher lost it. Assholes!" He took a drag off the cigarette, blew out the smoke, and walked out of the room.

I suppose he was still thinking about the publisher losing his manuscript. Cooper followed him. I sat down at the round glass table in the center of the room, poured all the pictures out of the box, and began to look at them. Some of the pictures had celebrities in them whom I recognized: Buddy Hackett, Tony Martin, Cyd Charisse, Red Buttons, Henry Mancini, Marty Allen, Irving Wallace, Sidney Sheldon, Jackie Collins, and others whom I didn't know by name.

As I was leafing through the pictures, I came across a color photograph, not a "party pic," usually snapped in black-and-white. This was in living color of a beautiful blond woman, stretched out on a velvet sofa in a Marilyn Monroe–esque pose, completely nude and smiling seductively at the camera. I put the picture aside.

Later, I called into Harold's bedroom and told him I was finished sorting the photographs and asked what else he needed me to do. He said Cooper was gone and he would come over to the study.

He walked in and sat down at the table. "Do you want something to drink?" he asked. "I'm going to have a Coke."

"Do you have any Diet Coke?" I asked.

He made a face. "That's shit."

"Okay. I'll have a Coke, too."

He dialed the kitchen and ordered the drinks. He looked at the stacks of pictures I had sorted. He saw the picture I had set aside and picked it up. He smiled as he looked at it, and then glanced at me. "That's my photographer," he said.

"Your photographer? Or did you take that picture?" I asked.

"Yeeeaah," he said, smiling. "She takes all my publicity photos for Europe. Her name is Ini Asman. It used to be 'Assman.' That's what I am, an 'ass man.'" He watched to see my reaction.

I laughed.

Rick came in with our drinks and placed them in front of us and left the room after dumping the cigarette butts from Harold's ever-present ashtray and wiping the ashes away.

"I have a question to ask you, Mr. Robbins."

"Please, call me Harold."

"Okay, Harold," I said. "I need to know my salary."

"How much do you need to be paid?" he asked bluntly.

"It's hard to say, Harold. I don't know exactly what you want me to do."

"I want you to be my assistant; I hate the fucking office and I won't go there. Bobby Weston, my producer, and Lynn Lewin, she's his secretary, work all the movie business from there. You know Lynn, right?" Harold looked down at his Coca-Cola. "I usually like to put a little 'coke' in my Coke," he said, and smiled. "But since my head is fucked up I don't do it. Do you use coke?" he asked.

"No. I don't," I said. "You really put it in your Coca-Cola?"

"Yeah. You know they used to put cocaine in Coca-Cola until the early nineteen hundreds; took all the fun out of it!" He laughed and pointed to his desk drawer. "There's some over there in the desk if you ever want it."

I nodded.

"I'll pay you five hundred dollars cash a week. And you can come to work at eight in the morning and leave at three or four."

"Perfect," I said. "I have another job that starts at five every evening."

"What is it?" Harold asked curiously.

"I work for the *LA Times*."

"At night? What do you do?"

"Sales," I said, not wanting to tell him the only job I could find to keep from starving up to this point was selling *LA Times* newspapers door-to-door and I spent my evenings on foot, knocking on doors. But maybe he figured that out, because he didn't probe any further.

He looked at his watch. It was 3:00 P.M. "Why don't you go now and tomorrow I'll tell you what you need to do here."

I stood up to leave. "Thanks very much, Mr. Robbins," I said, taking his hand. "It's an honor to work with you."

He looked up at me, smiled, and squeezed my hand. "I think you're going to organize me. I'm glad you'll be here with me."

I left. I was floating on clouds and thrilled about the job. I liked him and admired him as a writer. I wasn't sure what was going on with his speech, but I felt he was in the middle of a crisis and he wasn't going to give up. That impressed me.

I couldn't help but think about Harold Robbins and his life that night as I worked at my part-time job selling the *LA Times* door-to-door. From everything I heard from my friends, in the following weeks, along with the gossip reports from the "grapevine," Harold Robbins had an "open" marriage. I was told he had girlfriends and his wife had boyfriends. He was wild and crazy, lived on the edge, did drugs, slept with every woman he met, spent money like there was no tomorrow, and, well, he was just a playboy.

Was that the truth about him?

CHAPTER THREE

THE NEXT DAY

I sat in his study early the next morning, before eight o'clock, and read the black slate plaques on the wall of the study. The first few sentences of Harold Robbins's bestselling novels were etched on each plaque. The words captivated me.

> *Mrs. Cozzolina tasted the soup. It was rich and thick, tomatoey, and with just the right touch of garlic. She smacked her lips—it was good.*
> ### NEVER LOVE A STRANGER 1948

> *I got out of the cab on Rockefeller Plaza. It was a windy day even for March, and my coat flapped around my trouser legs as I paid the hackie. I gave him a dollar and told him to keep the change.*
> ### THE DREAM MERCHANTS 1949

There are many ways to Mount Zion Cemetery. You can go by automobile, through the many beautiful parkways of Long Island, or by subway, bus or trolley.

A STONE FOR DANNY FISHER 1951

It was two thirty when I got back to the office after lunch. My secretary looked up as I came through the door. "Those contracts get here from the lawyer yet?" I asked.

NEVER LEAVE ME 1954

I pulled the car into the parking lot across the street from Criminal Courts. Before I had a chance to cut the engine, the attendant was holding the door for me. I eased out slowly, picking up my briefcase from the seat beside me. I had never rated this kind of service before.

79 PARK AVENUE 1955

It was after ten o'clock and there were only three men at the bar and one man at a table in the rear when the hustler came in. A blast of the cold night air came in with her.

STILETTO 1960

The sun was beginning to fall from the sky into the white Nevada desert as Reno came up beneath me. I banked the Waco slowly and headed due east. I could hear the wind pinging the biplane's struts and I grinned to myself.

THE CARPETBAGGERS 1961

It was a day for losers. In the morning I blew my job. In the afternoon Maris hit the long ball, and as the television cameras followed him around the bases you caught glimpses of the expressions on the Cincinnati Reds and somehow you felt the Series was over even if there were four more games to play.

WHERE LOVE HAS GONE 1962

It was ten years after the violence in which he died. And his time on this earth was over. The lease he held on this last tiny cubicle of refuge had expired. Now the process would be completed. He would return to the ashes and the dust of the earth from which he had come.

THE ADVENTURERS 1966

I was on my third cup of coffee when the telephone began to ring. You wait three years for a phone call, you can wait thirty seconds more.

THE INHERITORS 1969

I was sitting up in bed, sipping hot coffee, when the nurse came into the room. The English girl with the big tits. She got busy right away with the drapes at the window, pulling them back so that more daylight spilled into the room.

THE BETSY 1971

The needlepoint spray of the shower on his scalp drowned out the sound of the four big jet engines. Steam began to fog the walls of the narrow shower stall.

THE PIRATE 1974

She sat at the top of the stairs and cried.

THE LONELY LADY 1976

It was five o'clock in the afternoon when I woke up. The room stank of stale cigarettes and cheap sour red wine. I rolled out of bed and almost fell as I stumbled over the boy sleeping on the floor beside my bed.

DREAMS DIE FIRST 1977

The last time I saw my father, he was lying quietly on his back in his coffin, his eyes closed, and unaccustomed blandness on his strong features, his thick white hair and heavy eyebrows neatly brushed.

MEMORIES OF ANOTHER DAY 1979

He was nervous. She could see that in the way he paced around the room, occasionally going to the window and lifting the lace curtain to look out at the rain-swept Geneva street.

GOODBYE, JANETTE 1981

Harold walked into the study and sat down. His eyes looked tired.

"Good morning, sweetheart," he said warmly.

"Hi, Harold. How are you?"

"Pain in the ass," he said, and pulled out a tiny tape recorder from his pocket. "Tony Martin gave me this before I ever had aphasia and now I have to use it every day to do my speaking exercises, according to Dr. Cooper. I can put it in my pocket!" he said, showing it to me. "Look how small it is. But still a pain in the ass!"

"Why?" I asked.

"I'm bored with my one-sided conversation! I feel like a fucking asshole trying to think of things to say. Christ, it's a fucking bore! It takes me ten minutes to find a word, and by the time I find it I forgot what the fuck I was talking about!"

"I can help with that," I suggested.

"Why should it be a pain in the ass for you, too?" he asked. "One minute everything is fine and the next minute I can't figure out who the woman is in the painting on the wall! That's what happened that night when all this started. Tony Martin Junior pointed to a picture on that wall that some rip-off artist had painted of Grace and I didn't know who the hell it was. I always hated that painting anyway."

"Talk to me, Harold. I'd love to hear about your life," I said.

"Everything changed that night; before I knew it I was in a hospital suite at Cedars wondering what the fuck had happened! Life is shit now and who the hell knows what the fuck is going to happen! Cooper says I can beat this, but what does he know."

I sat silently and let him vent his frustrations.

"Fuck it, I can't do this shit! Like the saying goes, 'Life Sucks . . . and then you die,'" he said, and looked down at his T-shirt and pointed to it.

It had the same saying. "I think life is better than that . . . more than that," I said quietly.

He looked at me and smiled. "Bullshit! Honey, in my life nothing is sacred except pussy."

I smiled back at him. "Well, that's a start."

He sat down next to me and put his hand on my leg.

"Not so fast. What about working on the tapes together?"

"And I thought I was going to get a piece of ass," he said, and looked dejected. "Story of my life. Maybe one day I'll turn these tapes into my autobiography. Anyway, you read and I'll listen; helps my aphasia. I think."

I plugged the electric cord attached to the tape recorder into the outlet.

Harold switched on the RECORD button and began to speak.

"The story of my life by Harold Robbins or Francis Kane or Jonas Cord or who the hell am I??? Once upon a time I grew up in Hell's Kitchen. I was a foundling left on the doorstep of the Paulist Brothers orphanage and grew up with nuns and priests taking care of me. The first part of my life was like living in a factory and I slept in a room with a lot of other boys on cots, ate meals in a big hall; it was shit! We were always in trouble. The nuns and priests liked to use a lot of discipline, but I got used to it; I didn't know any better. I used to wonder what it would be like to have a family, because some of the kids had lived with their family and I heard stories about how other kids lived. We did everything in big groups from taking our clothes off to send them to the laundry; going to mass in age groups. There wasn't any privacy for anyone. You couldn't even 'jerk off' without getting caught." He laughed and looked at me.

"I remember once they sat all of us on a long wooden bench; a doctor

and nurse came down the aisle in front of us. One by one each boy was asked to open his mouth. The nurse swabbed their throat with something and the doctor snipped out each kid's tonsils. I heard the first guy scream in pain and leaned forward to see what was going on. The minute I figured it out, I took off." He started laughing again. *"I ran and hid. They sent some people to look for me and no one could find me. I had run to the library that was in a different building and it was so early in the morning, no one was there, so I crawled into an open window. They didn't find me all day long; I was hiding in the bottom bookshelf reading a book in the back of the library. I think I was about six or seven years old.*

"The next day, the head priest came to my room early in the morning with two nuns and pulled me out of bed. The two nuns took me to the doctor's office a couple of blocks away. They were pissing and complaining to me all the way to the doctor's about how many problems I had caused. They waited for me in the waiting room while the doctor took out my tonsils. On the walk back to the orphanage I talked the two sisters into buying me some ice cream. Chocolate, my favorite."

Harold gave me a sly grin, daring me to believe it or not. He told all stories in such a realistic way it was hard not to believe every word, even if you were sure it wasn't true.

"I don't remember much of anything about the orphanage except how strict the nuns were and the Paulist fathers were tough. When I got a little older I used to sneak out of the orphanage in the afternoons and deliver beer to the whorehouse down the street. The girls paid me a quarter a bucket." He looked into the distance, remembering his past. *"They wore see-through nightgowns and I got to see their tits. It was great because the only tits I had ever felt were the nuns'; but when I saw real ones I was hooked forever on girls. But I got busted when one of the priests caught me buying candy to take to the other kids and he wanted to know where I got the money. The man who owned the candy store ratted me out and told the father that he had seen me over at the whorehouse. He said the girls must have given me money.*

"I told the father that I could've made it from shooting craps with the guys on the corner, but he didn't believe that. He knew they were pretty tough and he knew that I didn't have anything to bet. The father didn't whip me,

but he told me I couldn't leave the orphanage for a month. By the time I got back on the street after that month another boy had taken my job.

"So I traveled a little further and went down to Harlem to the Apollo Theater."

He stopped the tape and turned to me. "Do you know about the Apollo Theater?"

"I know of it but not much about it," I answered.

"It's where the burlesque shows were going on in the afternoon; it's very famous. They had girls walking on the stage in erotic clothes, 'see-through,' and they were naked underneath. It was a big turn on for the old men and I would sneak in and earn twenty-five cents jerkin' off the old men. I made a little money, and I got to see all those beautiful asses."

He gave me another daring look. True or false?

"At Christmastime in the orphanage there were a lot of people who brought gifts for all of us, but there were times there wasn't enough to go around. But on this one Christmas an alderman from the district came by the orphanage and I got to talk to him. He put me on his knee and asked me what I wanted for Christmas and I told him I wanted a bicycle. He said he would make sure that I got a bicycle. So Christmas morning I accidentally overslept. When I woke up I jumped out of bed and ran downstairs. When I got to the Christmas tree all the kids were sitting there around the Christmas tree with gifts and candies. I looked under the tree and there were no presents left. I ran and grabbed one of the sisters asking if there was a bicycle for me from the alderman. She just looked at me and shook her head. I didn't get anything that year for Christmas. But I didn't mind; I got by okay.

"When I got adopted by the Rubin family, it was interesting because I discovered later that Charles was my real father. At least that's what my birth certificate said; my mother was listed as Fanny. I never knew Fanny, and when I asked people later I got a lot of different stories through the years about it. I figured out from all I heard that Fanny died when I was born; I think she was Charles's girlfriend. He may have left her before I was born, who the hell knows, but maybe a midwife or someone else left me

on the steps of the orphanage. Later, Charles married Blanche and they had
other children; then they came and got me.

"*Charles and Blanche lived in Brooklyn. They seemed like nice people*
when I met them, but I always felt like a guest in their house and in their
life. They didn't tell the others in the family I was adopted since they were
still babies when I came to live with them.

"*Overnight, I suddenly had a brother and a sister, cousins, aunts and*
uncles. People don't realize when you've been living on your own with other
kids who are there one day and then gone the next you don't know how it is
when you suddenly join a family."

Harold's birth certificate from the state of New York, #26009,
dated May 21, 1916, listed his mother as Fanny and his father as
Charles Rubin.

Harold's stepsister, Ruth, said of her early life with Harold Rubin, "When we lived in Brooklyn, my mother had to spoon-feed
Harold his supper while he read books. He was old enough to eat on
his own, but he was always reading at the dinner table. Harold loved
books more than he loved food, so my mother would feed him while
he read.

"On Sunday afternoons all the relatives would come over and
Harold would organize the kids in the neighborhood and we would
perform a play. Harold would charge the relatives to see the play. He
did everything. He wrote it, showed us how to act out our parts, and
told us how to wear costumes that we concocted. He once made me
a tiara when I was playing the part of a princess in one of his plays. I
remember he had taken Blanche's [Ruth's mother's] pearls and un-
strung them and used the pearls as decoration on the tiara cut out of
paper. My mother was so upset with him when she saw her pearls
glued on my paper tiara, but she could never stay angry with him.
He felt very badly that Blanche was upset and I asked him about it
and he said he was going to get the pearls fixed.

"I wasn't surprised when the next week he left early on Saturday
morning and later explained to the rest of us he had found a man in

Chinatown to fix the pearls. Or at least, that's what he told us. Harold always made an adventure out of everything he did. All of us kids were fascinated with what we imagined Chinatown would look like. He made us all feel like we were there."

*D*id you ever talk to your father about Fanny?" I asked Harold.

"I always thought Charles was a chickenshit, and I didn't even know about any of this until the sixties when I saw the birth certificate with Fanny's and Charles's names on it. Charles wasn't alive then. Blanche, my stepmother, is still alive, but she'll never talk about it," he said, and went back to his recorder.

"*I worked in Charles's pharmacy when I was about twelve years old. I used to run errands and make deliveries and he taught me how to mix the chemicals and make some of the prescriptions. I learned a lot about drugs watching him mix up tonics and medicines. It wasn't like it is today, where everything is done at a factory. The pharmacist at that time was more like a doctor, and Charles owned three pharmacies.*

"*I dropped out of school in the eighth year, because of the Depression. I didn't like school to begin with, it was a bore and I was always in trouble with the teachers. Spanish was my favorite class. I liked it so well I took it twice.*"

Harold said this last part and looked at me. I was still absorbing the fact that he was a high school dropout who hated school. It was hard to imagine a writer so prolific being a dropout. I had assumed that anyone who had written bestselling novels and sold 750 million copies was a well-educated college graduate. I realized at that moment his talent was a natural genius. I brought myself back to the conversation.

"I didn't flunk Spanish until the final test," he said.

"I thought you liked Spanish," I said.

He grinned his catlike grin. "I knew the answers, but I answered them wrong. I wanted to flunk. When I flunked it got everybody crazy. They called Blanche and told her to come and talk with the school officials."

"Mrs. Lipscomb, the school psychologist [or principal; this fact changed with the telling of the story] of the school called me into her office after I got an F on the Spanish final. She said, 'Harold, you're a very smart boy. I don't understand why you flunked this test.'

" 'Because I like my seat in that class, Mrs. Lipscomb,' I answered her.

" 'Why do you say that?' "

" 'Because my seat is next to the wall and there's a hole in the wall. When I look through the hole I can see the girls' locker room next to the gym.' I smiled at her.

" 'Do you like girls, Harold?' she asked me.

" 'Sure. I like girls and baseball.'

" 'You flunked Spanish because you wanted to watch the girls?'

"I nodded. 'Yes, ma'am.'

"When Blanche came to the school, Mrs. Lipscomb told her there was nothing wrong with me. She said I was simply bored with school.

" 'He took an IQ test for me and he is a genius,' Mrs. Lipscomb told Blanche.

"Blanche was relieved." He smiled and lit a cigarette.

"But I still don't speak Spanish very well," he said after a long silence.

As we went through this exercise, he would have stops and starts. I sat patiently encouraging him with silence as much as anything whenever he would hit a problem word.

Our new system was working. He enjoyed having an audience for his exercises and I enjoyed learning about this extraordinary man and his life.

CHAPTER FOUR

*W̶hen the Depression hit and I left school to make money to help
Blanche and Charles and the kids, it pissed Charles off. Charles
had lost his pharmacies and decided they would move to Florida. I didn't
want to go. Christ, I hate fucking Florida. I ran away about a month before we were supposed to move and joined the Navy. I was only fourteen
years old, but I used some fake papers when I went into the Navy for a few
weeks. They busted me when I had to take a physical and they found out I
had adenoids. Then they found out I was too young.*

*"I came back to New York and started to work a few odd jobs. I lived in
Harlem with a black family, and in the winter I shoveled snow in Harlem
with the city crew during the day and then I'd go across town and shovel
snow with the Manhattan city crew at night.*

*"The rest of the time, I worked at a soda fountain and learned how to
make black and whites and two cents plain and chocolate milk shakes.*

*"When I was about sixteen, I axed to work for the Jamaican, Reggie,
down the street after the soda fountain closed at night."*

Harold hit the OFF button. "I axed," he repeated, and looked pointedly at me. "That's the way they pronounce it in Harlem. I learned it when I lived there with Deana and her family. She was my first black girlfriend. I love black women; they taste so good! I lived there all winter while I was shoveling snow. We all slept in the same room with her parents and brothers and sisters on beds pushed together so we could stay warm at night."

"You like all girls, Harold, in all colors."

"You know I dated Lena Horne in the late forties. We got busted in a hotel room. They burst in through the door and started flashing pictures. We ended up on the front page of the *Confidential Magazine* in New York City; *Confidential* was like the *National Enquirer* today. The press can be nasty and they were especially nasty in that era about mixed-race relationships."

"Was that legal for them to bust into the room?" I said.

"Her husband had us followed. It was a private detective and the magazines."

I laughed. "That's a small detail. I thought it was because of the racial mix."

"It was; her husband couldn't take a joke," Harold said, and laughed at his own joke.

"So, back to the Depression and shoveling snow," I said.

Harold hit the ON button.

"I also delivered beer to the whores at the whorehouse down the street from where I lived with Deana and her family. The same job I did when I was a kid at the orphanage, but now they paid me a dollar for every bucket of beer, and maybe a free fuck every now and then . . . a little pussy . . . that was the best! People had to do things for money and food in the Depression, things they may have never wanted or considered doing before they lost everything. A lot of the girls didn't have any choice; their husbands had left them and they had no way to support themselves. You can't judge a whore, or anyone for that matter.

"I had to always worry about the next day's bread. When I delivered

drugs for the Jamaican, I didn't have time to think about what was right or wrong. I had to eat.

"When people ask me if I always wanted to become a writer, I try to explain I grew up in a time when we didn't have choices or make decisions about what we wanted to do in life like today's kids. We had to work two and three jobs a day to get by.

"I was lucky when I met Deana after my family moved to Florida. The day I met her I didn't have a place to live. I was standing in front of the Jamaican's African Antiquity Store smoking a cigarette. He came walking down the street and asked me what I was doing. I told him I was looking for a job after my shift at the soda fountain. He took me into the store and that's when I met Deana. She helped process the coca rocks in the back room. There was an assembly line to crush it, then cut it and bag it, and I delivered it. He also sold ganch, or marijuana; that's what they call it today. About ten women sat in that back room. They worked ten-hour shifts. The front door to the store was always locked. It was only a front and I never saw anyone buy any of the African statues in the window.

"The Jamaican left the door open at night for people to pick up their orders. Every now and then I'd see Reggie out on the sidewalk talking to the beat cop in the neighborhood. He always had an envelope for him.

"My deliveries started about nine at night after I finished my other jobs. I went up to Cole Porter's apartment to deliver cocaine two or three times a week. He was a nice man, and before I left each night he gave me a fiver for a tip. He was in a wheelchair at the time. He had a lot of pain."

Harold yawned and hit the OFF button. "I need a coffee." He picked up the phone and buzzed Rick. "Two coffees, in the study."

"Were you afraid of getting caught?" I asked.

"Naw, the Jamaican made it look like I was delivering groceries. He put the dope at the bottom of the box in case I was stopped by anyone. He asked me to do the late deliveries of the stuff 'cause he knew that the cops would stop a black man in the area where Cole Porter lived.

"I thought I was pretty great, on my own and making good

money. I had a car that I bought from Reggie, a Cadillac, black with silver chrome. The only problem was it had defective brakes. There were times when I drove it that I had to go slow and drag my feet to finally stop it. I always had two rocks in the seat next to me to put in front of the tires when I parked so it wouldn't roll down the street. I didn't even have a driver's license. But the girls always liked a guy who had a fancy car; they still do. That's why I drive a Rolls."

Rick walked in with our coffees and a plate of fresh-baked chocolate cookies. Harold took a deep whiff of the aroma. "I love chocolate. Almost as much as pussy!"

I never knew what Harold might say or do. But was he kidding about the Cadillac and no brakes? Could you really stop a car by dragging your feet? I was never sure if these stories were true. I was no different from the other 750 million readers who spanned the world and hung on to every word that Harold Robbins wrote and spoke.

True or false, I loved his storytelling. I learned something about Harold and his life in every conversation, and it was fascinating.

After he finished his cookie he returned to his story.

"I left Harlem after the Jamaican shut his business down. I went to work one night after I left the soda fountain and the door was locked and the storefront was empty. I went by to see Deana and she said Reggie had split, so I moved back to Hell's Kitchen and got a job at Rand Tea and Coffee Store on Fifty-sixth Street and Tenth Avenue. I swept the floor and kept the shelves stocked. Rand was more like a grocery store than a tea or coffee shop as we think about it today.

"That's when I got interested in politics. The Socialists used to have meetings upstairs from Rand to organize protests. I went there at first because they served hot dogs for dinner, but then I got interested in what they had to say. I remember in 1934 protesting in Union Square against the formation of the ROTC; and when Mussolini's son described how beautiful the bombs were when they fell on the Ethiopians; Russia's invasion of Finland; the rise of Facism in Europe. I wasn't old enough to vote, but I had already voted many times for the Democrats."

I motioned for him to stop the tape. He pushed the OFF button.

"What do you mean?" I asked, curious to understand.

"When I was a kid on Election Day I went to Tammany Hall and they paid me two dollars for every time I could vote. So I went around the corner to the Republican headquarters and they wouldn't give me a dime. From that time on I voted for every Democrat!"

I laughed at his story. "Did you really get paid to vote?"

"Sure," he answered smoothly. "In those days, they didn't keep all the records they do today. They elected the people that needed to be elected, as long as they were Democrats."

"So how long did you work at Rand?" I asked, leading him back to his story. I pressed the ON button.

"After I had worked there awhile, Rand had me take inventory every week of the coffee beans and cans of corn and peas that Rand carried and I had to put it on a profit and loss sheet for the owner. I took inventory for only one store; Rand had about six stores. I noticed that he made a pretty good profit between how much he paid for things and what he sold them for, so I told my girlfriend Stella about it.

"Stella was a great-looking girl, about six years older than me, with a Hungarian accent. She and her mother had come to New York about eight years earlier and Stella was a showgirl at Billy Rose's Horseshoe. I told her that someday I was going to get enough money to fly around the state and buy crops and sell them to the grocers. She asked me how much money it would cost for me to go into business. I told her enough to buy a plane and I'd be in business.

"I went in business with some of Stella's friends who were showgirls from Billy Rose's Horseshoe. The girls invested money with me and I bought an airplane and flew to the farmers and bought their crops. I made contracts with the distributors and started making big money. This was the first real money I ever made, over a million dollars by the time I was twenty-one years old. In 1941 I made a contract for five hundred thousand dollars' worth of sugar coming in from Puerto Rico. Before it ar-

rived in the states, Franklin D. Roosevelt froze the price of sugar because
of the war and I was busted. I was fucked! I wasn't yet twenty-one years
old and Corn Exchange Bank was suing me for non-payment. I couldn't
even take bankruptcy until I was twenty-one. C'est la vie . . . story of my
life, always fucked."

Harold turned off the tape recorder and fixed me with a serious
stare.

"I joined the Navy after I lost my ass. I had no choice. They put
me on a submarine. It was a small one and there were only about
thirty of us. We were out in the Pacific, floating around. God, it was
a fucking bore!"

I started laughing at Harold's antics. He was swaying back and
forth imitating the motion of the sea.

"Some of the guys got seasick, but I never did. I like that rocking
motion; it reminds me of fucking!"

I laughed as he watched to see my reaction.

"I joined the Navy; this time we were close to being in the war.
I was in the first submarine attacked by the Japanese before Pearl
Harbor.

"A kamikaze plane split the sub in half. The alarm sounded and
everybody ran to their stations except me. I put on my life jacket and
I was the only survivor. I floated in the ocean for a few days until
they picked me up and took me to a hospital in San Diego. I was in
the hospital with back injuries for about six months."

According to recorded history, the first submarine attacked was during the Pearl Harbor raid. But Harold would
repeat this story many times and preface the story with the
fact that he was a self-proclaimed "coward," stating that he
was the only person to survive this attack because while the
others ran to their stations to try to save the ship he put on
his life jacket and survived.

"Were you given a medal?" I asked.

"Hell, no, the Navy never gave me anything. But I got lucky and I met this Chinese girl at the hospital, Muriel. She was visiting her relatives in San Diego and was doing volunteer work at the veterans' hospital.

"We got married after I got out of the hospital and moved to San Francisco. She worked with her father, who owned a Chinese restaurant. We had only been married a month when she died."

"She died," I gasped. I hadn't expected this turn of events. His real life was like his books—unexpected twists and turns!

"She was bitten by the parrot her father had given us as a wedding present. The parrot gave her a virus and she died within twenty-four hours. I went back to New York after she died."

Medically, this can happen. There is a virus that is carried by parrots that if it gets into the bloodstream through a bite can kill a human.

Gene Schwam, Harold's publicist, recalls Harold's marital history quite differently, however:

"We were in New York one night in the seventies; there wasn't much going on. Harold, Ed Gollin, and I were having dinner at 21. We were talking about what publicity story we could feed the columns in the next week. Harold started talking about his 'first wife,' Muriel, and being in a submarine that was hit by a kamikaze. He had married her when he came back from the Navy. As far as I knew at the point Harold had been married only to Lillian and Grace, his second wife."

My head was spinning when I left work that day. How could so many things have happened to this one man? No wonder he could write wonderful stories. His own life was the fabric he used to weave those stories.

I recounted the stories I had heard since I went to work for him: He was an orphan, had no education; made and lost a million dollars before he was old enough to take bankruptcy; almost died in a Navy submarine—the first submarine to be sunk in the war. His first wife, Muriel, was killed by the parrot her father had given her? Wait a minute. . . .

Was any of this true or was it part of the myth? I didn't know, maybe all the facts weren't quite accurate, but Harold had been through difficult times on a personal level and the storytelling that had helped him survive had become, in the end, his novelist's craft, his stock-in-trade.

CHAPTER FIVE

I could hardly wait to arrive at work each morning.

Most of the time, Harold was already having coffee and a fresh cup would be waiting for me. He could hear my diesel-engine Peugeot puttering up the driveway.

As I came up the stairs one morning he was taking his bagel out of the toaster in the upstairs kitchen.

"Can I help you with that?" I asked.

"Only if you want half of it," he answered.

"Sure," I said.

"Do you know that none of my wives have ever known how to cook?"

I shook my head. "How many times have you been married?"

"Too many," he said.

"How did you meet your first wife, Lillian?"

We walked into the study together and he went through his box of taped cassettes. He popped one into the tape player. "Here, we can both listen," he said, and smeared his toasted bagel with cream cheese.

"*I was walking down the street one day and this girl stopped me in my old neighborhood. 'Harold, is that you?' she said. 'We went to school together, up to the eighth year.' That's when I quit. She said her name was Lillian. I didn't remember her, but she seemed like a nice girl.*

"*I was on my ass the day I saw her, but I figured I could spend a few cents and take her to a movie. The only thing I had left after I bankrupted was Reggie's Cadillac. Poor schmuck, he ended up in the 'can.' I asked Lillian if she'd like to go to a movie sometime and she invited me for dinner with her family on Sunday afternoon.*

"*I met Lillian's parents. Dating a nice girl was all very proper at that time. We went to the movie that night, and we started seeing each other every weekend, but only on Sunday since I had to work six days a week at the soda fountain. After we had Sunday dinner, we would always go to the movies. I learned how to light my cigarettes from Gary Cooper!*"

He picked up a pack of matches as the tape played on and in Gary Cooper style lit his cigarette!

"*I married Lillian after I took bankruptcy and . . . after her father caught us in the backseat of my car. We were just playing around a little bit, my pants were down, and he thought I better marry her. He didn't realize Lillian had physical problems and it was almost impossible for her to have sex. She had an impacted hymen.*

"*Fascinating. I married her because her parents thought we had sex, and sex was always a problem with Lillian and me. The doctors told her she could have an operation and correct her problem, but she didn't want to do that.*

"*We lived in Brooklyn after we were married. Her sister was a pain in the ass and never liked me. The family thought they owned me after her father helped me get a job at Universal in the shipping department packing boxes. It was hard work, but I liked the job at Universal and learned how movies were made. The job didn't pay much and I had no money to go out to lunch with the other fellows, so I sat at my boss's desk and read the mail he had thrown away; I wanted to learn everything I could about the business.*

That's why I got promoted! I was eating a Clark bar one day, reading all the advertising material that came through his office that he always tossed into the trash. I picked up a flier in the trash from the U.S. Post Office. In the fine print, there was a notice about a rebate plan for companies that did bulk mailing. I thought since Universal sent out thousands of dollars of mailings a day, I might be able to get some money back.

"I sent in the forms required and pretty soon I got a check back. It was a five-thousand-dollar check! I had asked them to make it out to me. But I've got no luck; they made it out to Universal."

He chuckled as the tape kept rolling.

"When I received the check, I called my father-in-law and told him what I had in my hand and he told me to take it upstairs to Mattie Fox. Mattie Fox was the head of the production department at the time.

"I ran up the stairs to the executive offices—I used the stairs because I was in my work clothes, old jeans and a T-shirt. Only the suits used the private elevator. I had never been on that floor since the first day I came to work and had to fill out some papers. I walked into this big waiting room with a secretary sitting at a large desk. I said, 'I'm Harold Rubin and I'd like to see Mr. Fox, please.'

"She looked at me. 'Do you have an appointment?'

"'No, but I have a check for five grand to give to Mr. Fox.'

"She rang Mr. Fox, and he came outside to the waiting room about two minutes later. He took me to his office, and after I told him how I got the money he asked me if I would like to work in the accounting department next door. 'Sure,' I said.

"After I had worked there about six months Universal decided to buy a book for a movie they wanted to make. Billy Goetz, my boss, who was under Mattie Fox in the production department, sent me a memo and asked me to write a check to buy the book from this author. I had read the book and I sent him back a note: 'That book is a piece of shit. I could write a better book.'

"So he walks into my office the next morning and says, 'Harold, the only thing you can write is checks, so just write me out a check.'

"'How much you want it to be?' I asked.

"'I'll bet you a hundred dollars.'

"We both laid out one hundred dollars and I started to write the book.

"I went home that night and Lillian made me sandwiches and fixed a pot of coffee and I stayed up until dawn writing the first few chapters. After a couple of months I finally finished and took the manuscript, about four hundred and fifty pages, to work with me and laid it on Billy's desk.

"He didn't get in till about ten that morning. So, Billy comes into his office and sees the manuscript. He stood in the doorway of my office without saying anything.

" 'Where's my hundred bucks? The book's finished,' I said, and put out my hand.

"He looks at me. 'So what? It ain't a book until it's published!'

"Shit! I thought to myself. He was right, it wasn't a book yet. 'Who is the best agent in town?' I axed."

Shock value! He was back in Harlem, in character. He looked over at me to see my reaction. He wondered if I had noticed the "axed." I had and smiled.

"Billy told me the best agent in New York was Annie Laurie Williams at McIntosh and Otis. He said she handled John Steinbeck, who was my favorite author, and she also discovered Gone with the Wind. *I put the manuscript in an envelope and mailed it to her. I heard from her about a month later. She called me up at home.*

"Lillian had taken the message and met me at the door she was so excited. I made the call after dinner that night and Annie Laurie told me she had sold the book to Alfred Knopf for twenty-five thousand dollars. I made her crazy and said I wanted thirty-five thousand dollars. She told me all the bullshit about being a first-time writer and Knopf was a very good publisher, the number one publisher at the time, and I told her that I was a very good writer and would be the number one author in the world!"

Annie Laurie Williams in Harold's opinion was the greatest literary agent of her period. Her recollection of first speaking to Harold in 1947 still rings true: "When I hung up the phone that night after speaking to Harold Robbins, I thought, *This is a very arrogant young man.* I almost put his script in an envelope and mailed it back to him. But there was something so special about the way he wrote; it was not an intellectual exercise. It was from the heart. No one in the market had ever written with so much passion. I called Knopf the next day and convinced him to give Harold what he wanted. To my surprise, and the persuasion of his son, Pat, he did."

"I never met Annie Laurie Williams until the day we went to Knopf's office to sign the contract to publish Never Love a Stranger. *Knopf wasn't there when we sat down in his office, and she told me to let her do the talking.*

"Ten minutes later Knopf came through a side door, carrying my manuscript. He did not smile or even speak as he sat down, and I thought he was an asshole. I found out later he was angry. He looked at me and started going through all the bullshit about new writers and how much a publisher has to invest into a writer's first book, and how the editors had to work with you to keep the standard that Alfred Knopf publishing required.

"I nodded and agreed with everything he said, but then he laid it out.

" 'The manuscript has a lot of promise because of the feeling that comes off the page. But we need to tone down some of the four-letter words and take out the explicit sex scenes,' Knopf said as he leafed through the pages.

"Fuck him, I thought. I knew what that meant. He was going to butcher the book. He said he had given a copy to one of his editors who would be working with me on the changes.

" 'Mr. Knopf, I know you're a very successful publisher and I know that you know this business better than I. However, I think the book tells what real people think and feel and do, and what they say. They are not just

cardboard characters on a page—they feel something. I won't change that about the book.'

"Knopf took off his glasses and chewed on the end of his temple piece and kept his eyes on the pages of the manuscript, ignoring me. Annie Laurie jumped in about that time and said I would work with the editor to create the finest book in the market.

"Knopf then turned to me and said that because of marketing reasons and placement of my name on the cover of the book, he wanted to change my last name.

"He suggested I use the last name of Robbins. I wasn't attached to my name since it wasn't my name to begin with, so I said that was fine."

Knopf said that the name Robbins looked better on the book. However, Harold thought it was because Rubin was a recognizable Jewish name. Charles Rubin, Harold's father, saw the book once it was published, and he was very angry and upset when he saw the name Robbins. Harold told him Mr. Knopf had made the decision to change it to Robbins; Charles Rubin said the name change was anti-Semitic. Harold legally changed his name to Robbins in the late sixties.

"Annie Laurie asked some more questions about the time of publication and he was vague. She pushed him to commit the time and he finally agreed that it would be published in ninety days.

"We got ready to leave and he stopped us before we got to the door.

"'Mr. Rubin, when I first read the manuscript I wrote 'REJEC-TION' in red pencil across the title page and put it in a stack with other 'rejected' manuscripts. . . . You know, we get probably ten or twelve manuscripts a week,' Knopf said. 'I didn't want to buy your book, but my son, Pat, took a look at it. He sat on the sofa,' he pointed to the sofa sitting to the left of his desk, 'and he didn't get up until he had read your last page. He's the one that believes in you, Mr. Rubin.' "

Many years later, Pat Knopf would tell the story about Harold's first book. "I can't tell you how I won the battle, my father washed his hands of it and said, 'If you want it, you take care of it.' . . . I ran with it after that; I thought it was a terrific book."

"Did Knopf change things in the manuscript?" I asked.

"The only thing changed in the book was my name and the title of the book. They took out some of the language, but it wasn't important. I did like my title I had originally used, *But One Life*, but I didn't give a shit; all I wanted was the money!" he said, and laughed.

CHAPTER SIX

I used a poem at the beginning of *Never Love a Stranger*, Pat Knopf loved the poem, and that was why he changed the title. It was the feeling before and during the Depression for people in the world."

Harold picked up a copy of the book and read. He almost knew this poem by heart and quoted it:

"'*Call no man foe, but never love a stranger.*
Build up no plan, nor any star pursue.
Go forth with crowds; in loneliness is danger.
Thus nothing God can send, and nothing God can do
shall pierce your peace, my friend . . .'"

"That's a poem from *To the Unborn* by Stella Benson. There were a lot of disappointments especially during the Depression—fuck it—in everyone's life there are disappointments and lost hope. You've had them," he said, and looked at me as though he could read my life like a scanner. "No one escapes. That's why you got to be grateful every day that you get to the next." He smiled and took a long drag from his cigarette.

"I can't imagine not having hope," I said.

He shrugged. "You've never been through a depression. My Depression novels I think are the best books I've written. *Never Love a Stranger*, *A Stone for Danny Fisher*, and *79 Park Avenue*. It was a hard time for people, but it brought out the passions we feel, which sometimes desperation does, and the happiness meant more then; maybe we grew to understand hope through the depression. Maybe that was our legacy to the next generation.

"But not everyone sees my books in the way that I do. *Never Love a Stranger* was banned in Philadelphia when it first came out. They didn't see that I was opening up new worlds to people. I was depicting the world around me; I wasn't trying to win an English prose contest. That's when Alfred Knopf was my publisher and the old man went crazy. He had never published a book that had been banned because of 'blue' language. By today's standards the language used was nothing—back then, *Never Love a Stranger* was 'too dirty'. Fuck 'em, it sold ten million copies. The public saw the truth about the book.

"It shouldn't have been banned. It was based on some of the things that happened to me in my life growing up. It was true; how can you ban the truth? Maybe passion scares Americans, makes them feel out of control. Everything the censors complained about happened to me or in the world around me. I don't think any life should be censored. That's why I knew after I wrote the first one that I would write forever."

Harold said in a 1948 interview: "Why did I want to write? When I was a kid I read all the great comic books, action and adventure with great heroes and villains. . . . I read everything I could get my hands on. When I was growing up in the orphanage I spent a lot of time in the library. I loved the books and I love libraries today. When you read the pages between the covers of a book you discover new worlds . . . worlds you could never imagine in far away countries, and people that you care about or even hate. Reading books brings unconditional freedom to the mind."

When I read Harold's first novel, *Never Love a Stranger,* several weeks later I saw the life he was telling me about, between the lines. I could see his face in Francis Kane, the name given to him in the orphanage and now the main character from *Never Love a Stranger.* I knew his words were not only crafted for the character but also from his own world. It reached a reader because of the truth he spoke.

"I'm sick of it—sick of the school and the orphanage—I'm nothing but a prisoner here. People in jail have as much freedom as me. And I didn't do nothin' to deserve it—nothin' to be put in jail for—nothin' to be locked away at night for. It says in the Bible the truth shall make you free. You teach to love the Lord because he has given us so much. You start my day with prayers of thanks—thanks for being born into a prison without freedom." I was crying. My breath came fast.

—HAROLD ROBBINS,
NEVER LOVE A STRANGER (1948)

Never Love a Stranger became a bestseller. Harold Robbins's first novel sold more than 10 million copies and still counting. It was made into a movie in 1958 starring John Drew Barrymore, Steve McQueen, and Lita Milan.

CHAPTER SEVEN

$\mathcal{T}$ he following week we changed our routine of listening and reading. I read into the phone as Harold watched me from across the room, listening. He lit a cigarette and gazed out the window as I read.

"*The Dream Merchants (1949).*

" '*The air in the musty old courtroom was dull and lifeless as the court clerk intoned in a singsong voice,* "*In the case of John Edge versus Dulcie W. Edge, is the plaintiff in attendance?*"

" ' "*He is.*" *Johnny's lawyer motioned to him to get to his feet.*

" '*Johnny stood up slowly and faced the white-haired judge. The judge's face looked tired and bored. This was nothing but routine for him. He looked down at Johnny.* "*Mr. Edge,*" *he asked in a low monotonous voice, closing his eyes as he spoke.* "*Is it still your desire that this divorce be granted?*"

" '*Johnny hesitated a moment. His voice sounded strange to his ears.* "*It is, your honor.*"

"'The judge opened his eyes and looked at him and then down at the papers before him. He picked up his pen and wearily signed his name to the bottom of them, turning each paper over to the clerk, who stood next to him with a blotter in his hand. Finished, he looked down at Johnny. "Then it is the judgment of this court that this divorce be granted."

"'. . . Suddenly his eyes were wet and he turned and hurried out into the street. What was it the lawyer had said? "You're a free man now." He shook his head. Would he ever be free? He didn't know. There was a heavy sunken feeling inside him.

"'He stopped at a news-stand and bought a paper. Idly he opened it and glanced at the headlines. There was a streaming red banner across the top of the front page.

"'"STOCKS TUMBLE FOR SECOND TIME IN MONTH!"

"'"Millions Lost As Wall Street Panicked!"

"'"New York. October 29 (AP)—The ticker ran more than three hours behind sales today as on the floor of the staid New York Stock Exchange excited ordinarily conservative businessmen screamed and fought their way through milling mobs. Their only concern was to sell, sell, sell! Sell, before their fortunes were gone and the stocks fell any lower in this, the greatest recorded break in stock market history."'

"Was that how you felt when you lost your first million?" I asked Harold. "And when you got your first divorce?"

"I've earned and lost millions many times over. I've owned sixteen Rolls-Royces, and only one of those was given to me by my British publisher, New English Library. I made so many sales on *The Betsy* they gave me my blue Corniche. It has a plaque on the dashboard from the Queen of England. When my publishers gave the car to me they were flying it over with a customs stop in Florida before being shipped to LA.

"The Rolls-Royce people called and asked me if I would permit the Rolls to be shipped to the Bahamas, where the Queen was visiting her subjects. In the Bahamas the only car they had for Her Royal Highness was a jeep and my Rolls was the closest Rolls available. I said it could be used if the Queen would allow a gold plaque signifying the occasion. They agreed and that plaque is on there today. Have you seen it?"

"No, I haven't," I said. "Do you have pictures of the Queen in the Rolls?"

"Yeah, they sent us a videotape of her riding in the car. She's smiling and waving. It's around here somewhere." He looked through a stack of videotapes nearby. "Who knows where it is."

Harold was always casual about important events in his life. Wasn't it important that the Queen had borrowed and ridden in your Rolls that was a gift from your publisher? Some might say it was historical!

"What kind of car do you have?" he asked.

"A Peugeot."

"I hear it every day when you drive up. Why'd you get a piece-of-shit diesel?" he asked.

I shrugged. "It was the only choice I had."

He looked at me quizzically.

"I had an accident in the car I owned after I moved here. I had to buy another car. Car dealers always want to sell you a car and if you let them lead you it will make the financing easier. Since I was new to Los Angeles and didn't have credit established, this was the only way I would end up with the car. I needed transportation and they sold me the Peugeot."

"You're pretty smart. If I'd been there, I would have bought you any car that you wanted."

He made it sound like he actually would have done that, but I had to keep reminding myself these were words, words, words; but it sounded nice. I would find out in the years to come he would and did buy me any car that I wanted, or he wanted.

"What about your first divorce?" I asked.

"Divorces are all the same. A pain in the ass. No one gets a guarantee for a lifetime of happiness."

"But you were still married when you wrote *The Dream*

Merchants," I said, getting him back to his story. I pressed the ON button of the tape recorder.

"The Dream Merchants *was the first book of my movie trilogy. (Later* The Carpetbaggers *[1961] and* The Inheritors *[1969] would complete the movie trilogy.) In the fifties the Depression was still in people's memory. I used to hang around the movie sets when I worked in the shipping department. I had to pick up packages and reels from the directors and I'd spend time watching them shoot scenes.*

"In those days it took only a week or maybe days to shoot a movie. I listened to all the production people and sometimes the old stars talk about the beginning of the movie industry and how it saved a lot of people during the Depression.

"It fascinated me, because I knew I had dreams every time I went to see a movie. It made everyone feel that there was hope for love and romance when you watched Gary Cooper and a leading lady or Jimmy Stewart, Cagney, and Edward G. Robinson made you feel for the guys who were gangsters; they were real people on the screen."

"You don't even remember those actors, do you?" he asked as he turned off the tape recorder.

"I remember some of them, but I haven't seen many of their greatest movies. It was before my time."

He thought for a moment and reached over and turned on the recorder.

"We learned to root for the bad guys and the good guys. I heard hundreds of stories from Lillian's father, who had been with Universal for many years in the production department. He loved filmmaking, but after I began to write novels I didn't particularly like the way they translated into movies.

"I remember when they made the movie out of Never Love a Stranger *I didn't think it was as good as the book, but none of my books make good movies; the directors put what they wanted on the screen, not what I wrote. My characters are an extrapolation of many people I know and they come across on the page, but depending on the actor, it's not the same on film. My books are a guessing game for people. People like to see themselves or others*

as the character. They think they know who I'm writing about, but I write about the passions of men and women. Each person in life has different passions. Those passions sometimes don't come across on the screen.

"The reason people like my characters is because they get to see the world around them, not just their little space in time. They see and feel what the character sees and feels, live what the character lives. Somehow, I want to put what's on the page into their life, and that's one of the reasons why I write."

> Ayn Rand, author of *The Fountainhead* and *Atlas Shrugged*, was quoted concerning Harold's work: "He writes visually. He writes with a cinematic eye and is instantly able to convey that to his reader."

Harold smiled at me when he was talking about passions. By now, I knew that smile. He was getting ready to set me up for a response to something provocative.

"You know I have a passion," he said, looking at me with innocent intensity.

I took the bait, and since he had said it seriously I was all ears. He almost whispered and I leaned closer.

"I have a passion for your ass."

I smiled back at him, going along with his game. "I have a passion for my ass, too. Keeping it safe."

"I'll keep it safe, honey." He laughed good-naturedly.

Harold was always teasing, provoking, probing, and playing with everyone in every conversation or moment in his life. He enjoyed the adventure of seduction. Even though he was very serious in many areas, especially in his work, he kept the daily humdrum of life fun with his lighthearted sense of humor. Or was it?

He looked at me and lit another cigarette. "I never learned how to write by the book, like they teach today. I tell everyone I'm the best writer in plain English. I tell everyone how I *feel* in my books. It's not intellectual; that's a fucking bore. My head is screwy that way. It matters what you feel, not what you think; that's where the truth lies in each of us."

I turned the tape recorder to ON. He turned the tape to OFF. "I'm telling you the best lesson I can give you about writing. I've read all the classics, O. Henry, Dickens, Poe. None of them went to Harvard or Brown or USC film school or Robert McKee's Story Structure. They wrote what they felt and saw. I loved them all. Anybody that writes what they feel, without a lot of bullshit, will be a great writer." He continued, "That's the only lesson you need to become a writer."

I looked at him, trying to comprehend every word. "You don't write outlines and you don't make cards. Every class I've attended teaches a series of steps to develop the story before you ever write a word. Outlines, synopses, or scene cards. You break all the rules, don't you?"

Harold looked at me and shook his head. "Herbert Alexander, my editor, told me if I went to any classes being taught by the assholes that couldn't write it would fuck me up. I don't know all the fancy words for plots and tricks with sentences and arcs and all that shit. In fact, I never know what I'm going to write until I sit down in front of my typewriter. I give my publisher a paragraph of what the next book is about; I send it to Paul and they send me a check; I sit down and I write. That's the way I've done it since 1947."

In 1997, in one of Harold's last public speaking engagements, he talked about the key to writing. A very sophisticated woman, designer dressed for this Sunday afternoon chat with Harold Robbins at the local synagogue, asked, "Mr. Robbins, what is the key to your writing?"

He looked at her with a serious demeanor, squinted his eyes, and answered, "Assglue."

She thought she wasn't hearing his answer. "I'm sorry?" she said.

"Assglue," he repeated. The rabbi standing in the background began to laugh, bringing the house down.

"What do you mean by that?" another lady asked.

"It means you take the glue and you 'schmear' it on the seat . . . you sit your ass down and you write!"

The following day in the local newspaper a lengthy editorial appeared, written by a professor of creative writing at a local university. The headline read "Breaking All the Rules." She talked about the rules of writing and how they should be thrown out to allow genius to appear as in Harold Robbins's case.

"None of it's easy, darling. I do the best I can! What do you want from my life? It's all a fuckin' pain in the ass." Harold was visibly exhausted. Walking in the past and seeing the events of his life again was not easy. There were good times and bad times to remember.

"There's one thing I know about life. It's filled with regrets that you try to make right and with surprises that make it all worthwhile."

"I think you live life every day in a way that takes a lot of courage," I said.

"Are you kidding?" He laughed. "I'm a coward."

Chapter Eight

It was a great cure for Harold's aphasia. I sat before him each day listening intently to every word. I was a great audience and he was a willing performer. He wasn't embarrassed to backtrack and repeat, stop and correct himself. It took humility for a man of his stature and prominence to do this.

When there were days he was discouraged I would find something to distract him. Today was one of those days.

I walked over to the large "boom box" on the shelf in the family room and turned it on. I found the easy-listening radio station.

He looked at me, wondering what I was doing.

"We're taking a break," I said, cranking up the volume. It was a Frank Sinatra tune, one of his sambalike tunes he did with Antonio Carlos Jobim.

Harold's eyes lit up. He got up and walked toward me and began to dance a samba. "C'mon, let's dance."

"I'm a terrible dancer," I said, regretting I had turned on the music. I was never comfortable because of that leg problem.

"Just wiggle your ass and follow me," he said, grabbing me into his arms and gliding me around the room. Somehow, dancing seemed easy with Harold.

"I once had a private plane with Frank Sinatra and Sammy Davis. We were all making great money. Frank made and lost more money than I have and Sammy gives it all away. He lives around the corner with Altovise. We thought it would be great having our own plane for trips. We were going to share the expenses. Jesus, I got the bill the first month for the pilot and gas. I'd taken about fifty of Frank and Sammy's friends to Vegas round-trip every weekend of the month! I lost my ass on that deal! I stayed in the deal about six months and dropped out. I had to write a new book to cover the cost."

"Do you still have a plane?" I asked.

"I gave up planes when I had my pilot's license taken away," he said, and smiled.

"You flew planes?" I asked.

"I learned when I was a kid and flew around to the farmers and bought commodities. I flew all the time in Connecticut, but I flew too low too many times and they jerked my license," he said, running me in circles with his story. "It was a little plane, a two-seater."

I wasn't sure if he really flew planes or not, but I realized when he began weaving his story he had lost his discouragement and was back to being Harold Robbins.

We didn't work on anything that day but having fun. We danced to the tunes on the radio. Gypsy and Kinky (Harold's dogs), Harold, and I piled into the Maserati later that day and drove to Pink's Hot Dogs for lunch, Baskin-Robbins for ice cream, and the Santa Monica Pier for a walk. For a short afternoon Harold escaped the weight of the future.

"Why don't you like to dance?" Harold asked as we were driving from Santa Monica.

"I'm not a very good dancer," I said.

"You're my favorite dancer," he said, and winked at me.

He stole my heart.

*H*arold continued the story of *The Dream Merchants* the next morning.

"The Dream Merchants *was a classic story I wanted to tell about the movie business. The beginning, the old moguls: Cohn who ran Columbia, Jack Warner who started Warner Brothers, Cecil B. DeMille, Mayer, Goldwyn, they were all the 'Dream Merchants' of their time. Those men sold dreams—fantasy. It was crazy, but it is dreams and hopes that get us through the hard times, and it always will be.*"

"What do you dream about?" I asked, caught up in that thought of movies and fantasy and dreams. It was also the perfect setup for Harold.

"Pussy!" he said, and laughed.

I laughed, too. Harold wasn't going to give me a straight answer, ever.

He grinned at me and continued his story. . . .

"The Dream Merchants *was made into two movies and a TV miniseries. Harry Hamlin starred in one; Mark Harmon, he's supposed to be the sexiest actor this year, was in the last miniseries remake.*

"*I was still on the Universal payroll as the comptroller when I was writing* Dream Merchants. *I hired two showgirls from the Copa as secretaries. The problem was they slept during the day and I had to keep the shades drawn, so I had cocktail parties every night after work from five to seven for all the people in the office and on the sets. That's where I began to meet the stars working on the lot, the directors and producers.*

"*I knew about the struggles that Universal had in the years I was there. We'd be doing a picture and run out of money. What's new? It happens all the time, history always repeats itself, only now there are more zeros! Assholes still go over budget, they make promises they can't keep, and that's showbiz, baby. I spent half my time traveling from New York to LA when I worked at Universal picking up money, bringing back money, kiting checks from one coast to the other.*

"I spent time in Palm Springs making deals with Tom Mix for pictures that cost about five thousand dollars for a three-reel picture at his ranch. That's when I started thinking about the character who became Nevada Smith.

"When The Dream Merchants *came out it was on the bestseller list. Everyone thought since I was working at Universal I was talking about the stars and owners of that time and it became a classic.*

"I left work each evening and had book signings. It was kind of amazing to me to see the faces of the people who were reading my books, because when I wrote the books I wrote the story for myself and I didn't think about the people who would be reading them. It's still interesting to see the readers in person. I always like book signings; without them it just seems like a lot of numbers.

"Lillian went with me to some of the signings, but then she stopped. She didn't like all the publicity and being in the public eye. She was a very shy girl."

CHAPTER NINE

I read the entire opening passage of *A Stone for Danny Fisher* to Harold. This work inspired me and I wanted him to hear the words he had penned. I wanted him to understand how much he moved his readers. I had read *Danny Fisher* years earlier and forgotten how good it was and how I was moved by each chapter. After hearing him talk about his life story and writing from the heart I could clearly see that he was on every page.

"I wrote the fucking book; why do I have to hear it again?" he asked irritably when I told him I wanted to read his book to him. "Do you know I never read the books once they're published?" He lit a cigarette.

"You should," I said, teasing. "If you become a reader you'll understand why the world loves your book."

"I read Norman Mailer; I think he's one of the best authors in the world today."

I turned on the tape recorder. "Tell me about *A Stone for Danny Fisher?*"

"You're a pain in the ass." He smiled and began his story.

"*A Stone for Danny Fisher is one of the few books the critics ever praised. It's semiautobiographical, about the Rubin family who adopted me. It was about how it felt to have a home, a family. I still remember what it was like to have my dog die in my arms. You always remember feelings, don't you?*"

I nodded in agreement.

"*When I finished this book and it hit the bestseller list, I tried to get Knopf to make a better arrangement with me so I could make some money. This was when our argument started and I wanted to end the contract with Knopf. I was the one breaking my ass writing them. Knopf didn't want to pay more.*

"*I was still working for Universal at the time. This was around the time I met Yvonne, Caryn's mother. I had just returned from lunch at Universal one day when my secretary handed me a note. It was a call from Walter Kari Davis, who was the assistant to J. Arthur Rank, the number one stockholder of Universal. Mr. Davis told me that Mr. Rank's niece, Yvonne, was coming to town and asked me to extend every courtesy to her, meaning that I needed to make sure that she had a good time.*

"*When I got off the phone I had my secretary call and order me a limo to pick her up at the airport and take her to her hotel. I figured she would be some dowdy, snobbish girl who thought she was better than everybody and I would probably be treated like a lackey, but you know me: I love all girls.*

"*Several ladies came off of the plane. I stood there like an asshole trying to recognize someone I had never met. Two of the ladies who I thought might be her, luckily, had people meeting them before I approached to ask their name. Finally, a very attractive lady came through the gate. Back then, we didn't have ramps. Everybody stood on the tarmac. I remember the wind blowing like a son of a bitch. Yvonne had on a hat and it almost blew off her head and her skirt was blowing. She was a knockout! I didn't care who she was, I went and introduced myself, and it was Yvonne Farrow. She was surprised to see some handsome, young guy meeting her.*"

He smiled at his description of himself and pointed to the comic T-shirt he was wearing that morning. It said *"Stud Service"* and then listed all of what those services included: "wives, girlfriends, nympho-maniacs, lonely women, virility tests, etc., etc."

"See." He grinned mischievously. "I'm always available."

"Yvonne was pretty impressed with me. We hit it off, right away. She said she thought only old men worked for her uncle. I asked her if she would like to go to dinner with me that night at Sardi's and she accepted. I dropped her off at the hotel and stopped at a men's store to buy a fresh shirt and tie.

"When I got back to the office I had my secretary make reservations at Sardi's under her uncle's name, and that gave us the best table in the house. The bill would also go on the company tab. But, I knew I'd have to tip a twenty to the maître d'. After we had dinner that night we went to a few of the nightspots in Manhattan. On Saturday night we went to see a Broadway play."

"Which one?" I asked him.

He looked at me, a little irritated. I had interrupted his story. He snapped off the tape recorder. "How the hell can I remember that? I don't even remember what I had for lunch yesterday!"

"Sorry, I just thought it might be romantic."

He looked at me with a grim expression and shook his head. "Believe me, this is not a romantic story. I ended up wishing I had never met the bitch."

"Love and hate. It's a fine line."

"It was pretty good when we started sleeping together. That started after the Broadway play. I ended up not going home until the next Sunday. Lillian was angry since I hadn't been home all weekend, and I told her that a relative of Rank's was in town and I had to entertain them. I grabbed some fresh clothes and told her I would be gone for a few nights."

He looked at me to see my reaction.

"That wasn't a lie, you know."

I looked at him skeptically. "But you didn't tell her it was Rank's niece who was young and beautiful and you were having an affair with her."

"It wasn't any of Lillian's business who I was entertaining. She knew it was business," he said. He flipped on the tape recorder once again.

"Yvonne had come to New York to find a job. Her uncle had set her up with several interviews. While I was at work, Yvonne went on job interviews. Her interviews were usually with the president of the company, big shots who her uncle had set her up with. They didn't interview her; they asked her where she felt she wanted to work. She had a background in art history and design. She knew all the right manners, the way to set tables, all the society 'bullshit.' She went to work at one of the finest china and silver wholesalers in New York and became head of the department that taught, merchandised, and sold to upscale New York department stores.

"I spent half my time with Yvonne and half my time with Lillian. Then Yvonne and I started living together after she got pregnant with Caryn."

"What'd you tell Lillian then?" I asked.

"The truth. Yvonne was pregnant. Unfortunately, Yvonne and I hated each other by this time and living together was pure hell. She was pissed that I wouldn't leave Lillian and used the baby to get to me. I moved back home and Lillian and I tried to get custody and that's when Yvonne fought me in court."

"You mean Lillian stayed with you even after you had a baby with Yvonne?" I asked.

In 1962, on Harold and Lillian's twenty-fifth wedding anniversary, Harold was quoted in a Connecticut newspaper concerning their marriage as saying, "[Marriage] can only be adjudged successful to its ability to survive all the hazards that two human beings can bring to it. And now, after 25 years, both my wife and I are willing to concede its success."

He nodded. "Lillian couldn't have children. But even if we had gotten custody of Caryn our marriage would have never worked. After our efforts to adopt Caryn failed, I ended up being thrown into jail because I was accused of hiding Caryn from her mother. It was a big fight. At that time, the courts never awarded a child to the father, so I lost the court battle. We had to go back to court several times, and Caryn ended up disliking me at times—and her mother, too."

"Too bad," I said. "But that's all changed now, hasn't it? You just gave her a big wedding."

He looked at me. "Yeah, but back then everything got all fucked up after she was born. And everything got all fucked up the day she was married. That's when this problem with my head happened, the night she married," Harold said, and shook his head. "*Oy vey*, pain in the ass.

"You'll meet her; she's coming by to pick up a check tomorrow. I gave her and Michael a grand a month for the first year of their marriage!"

He looked down at his tape recorder. "Back to this shit." He looked up at me. "Cooper says I'm improving. He says it's because of the Oklahoma kid." He looked at me and smiled.

"I know you are improving, Harold. I want to tell you how much I admire you for sticking with this. And it's because you're doing it, not me. I'm just along for the ride."

A look of satisfaction passed his face. "Yeah? I'd like for you to ride—"

"I knew that was the wrong use of words," I said, and laughed. "But I do admire you."

"Admiration? I'd rather have 'adoration.'" He chuckled at his jokes and began taping again.

"*One afternoon after* Danny Fisher *had been on the best seller list for several months, I was finishing off the cocktail hour and getting ready to leave work and go home and work on a screenplay.*

"*This was when I was still seeing Yvonne, before she was pregnant with Caryn. She walked into my office and I never made it home that night; that's when we started living together in an apartment in Manhattan, at least part of the time. It was crazy; I was trying to be three places at one time. And I was writing every night because I needed money.*

"*I was sinking money into a Broadway play* Go Fight City Hall *that never opened and later a Broadway play of* A Stone for Danny Fisher. *I was working with Leonard Kanter on the play. He was a writer friend of mine in New York. We partnered and wrote the play, but I was footing all the bills. I borrowed money from a lot of people to open the show and was supporting Lillian in Brooklyn, Yvonne in Manhattan, and Constance, a showgirl, one of the girls who served cocktails in the office, but she lived with her husband, so I usually saw her after her performances.*

"*The fucking play caused me a lot of trouble since I took Yvonne to the opening performance rather than Lillian. Lillian saw the pictures in the local newspaper the next morning. At that time the Westport newspaper covered everything I did and they snapped a picture of Yvonne standing behind me. The next morning Lillian called me at work and asked me who she was and I told her it was J. Arthur Rank's niece. Rank was an investor in the play and she attended.*"

Harold looked up at me. "I wasn't lying, was I?"

"Deceiving, I'd say."

Harold laughed at me. "Maybe."

"A Stone for Danny Fisher *after it premiered in New York was successful, but I wasn't making enough money, the profit wasn't good, and I wasn't going to be able to pay back the investors in the amount of time they had given me, so five days after I closed the play I signed an agreement with Hal Wallis to sell the rights for a motion picture. I got a shitload of money considering it was in the fifties, but as usual I had to pay it out to the people who had financed me. I wish I had co-produced the picture. It was called* King Creole; *I knew it would be a hit with Elvis Presley playing the lead.*"

"Did you meet Presley?" I asked.

"Met him on the set one day. He was a nice, polite kid. I sat down and had a beer with him and he was really shy."

"What did he say to you?"

"He called me Mr. Robbins, even though I told him to call me Harold. He said he wished he could just do a dramatic role without having to sing. He wanted to be a good actor, but he said, 'Colonel runs the show. Guess that's why he changed the name of the movie to *King Creole.*' He looked at me sort of sideways. 'I'm grateful to the Colonel; don't get me wrong, Mr. Robbins. I guess I have no right to complain.' He got up really quick and left. I liked him, but he got into a lot of trouble with all the shit that went on around him."

> *A Stone for Danny Fisher* opened on October 21, 1954, at the Downtown National Theatre. It closed on January 10, 1955. On January 15, 1955, the motion-picture rights to the book were sold to Hal Wallis. Harold was paid twenty-five thousand dollars for the rights. That motion picture in 1958 became *King Creole,* starring Elvis Presley, Dean Jagger, and Carolyn Jones.

"Caryn was born in November of 1955. Lillian spent time with her and really loved her; Yvonne just wanted to make Caryn hate me and she did. I spent a lot of time and money trying to make things right. Yvonne was angry and I don't know if I ever made that right; Lillian wanted a child. Who knows? If we had kept Caryn maybe things would have been better for her."

Harold, at times, was shockingly honest with me about his life, his children, his marriages, and his feelings. He never sugarcoated the truth and could be crude and sometimes offensive. But beneath it all he had a heart as big as the world. I saw beyond the crusty exterior into the softness of his heart.

I saw how he cared for his daughter Adréana. I knew he never intended to hurt anyone or anything. His frustration about Caryn had been a part of their relationship since the beginning. It was painful for him. He felt he had made every effort to gain her trust and he had failed. He blamed himself for that failure.

I remember wondering on the first day he hired me what the truth was about Harold Robbins. I was discovering a complex and caring man, one who had vulnerabilities that he would fiercely hide. He rarely allowed anyone into the secret chambers of his heart. I also felt he had opened that door to me and I would never allow anyone to hurt him.

CHAPTER TEN

I left in the middle of the morning to go to the Harold Robbins International office on Sunset to pick up a package of mail and other items for Harold. I was driving Harold's classic 1977 white Cadillac convertible with red leather seats. The top was down and the weather was beautiful. Sunshine and cool breezes. This car was a prized possession in Harold's collection of cars. It had been the last convertible that Cadillac made, and it was as wide as a boat. Gypsy, Harold's gray and white shih tzu, sat on the seat next to me. I took Gypsy into the office with me and picked up the items.

On my way back, going up the hill toward the house, I passed Harold and Linda in the blue Rolls going down the hill.

He waved but didn't smile and Linda was intently driving and didn't even see me. Right away I felt something wasn't right. I didn't know what it was; maybe Adréana, his daughter, had an emergency he needed to take care of. When I left earlier there had been no plans for him to leave. Once I arrived at the house, I asked the guard if everything was okay.

"As far as I know," he answered, and shrugged. "Mr. Robbins and Linda just left a few minutes ago."

I knew that Harold would not say anything to the guard or to Rick if there was a problem. Harold had cautioned me about how gossip was a commodity in Hollywood, a commodity to be sold. Even though there were privacy clauses in contracts with security companies, valet services, and maintenance and gardening services, nothing could really prevent anyone from making a five-minute call to the *National Enquirer* or any ready gossip columnist in the entertainment industry.

Two hours passed. Finally, Harold and Linda returned. I was standing in the kitchen when they came in from the garage. Harold motioned for me to follow him.

He reached out and hugged me when we got upstairs to the top of the landing. We walked into the family room and sat down on the sofa next to each other.

"I had the shit scared out of me." His hands were shaking as he told me the story. "I was fine, sitting in the study watching the news. I heard the phone ring and I looked at the blinking red light on the phone and Linda called up to the study. I couldn't answer. Couldn't get the words out! Scared the hell out of me!"

He reached for my hand and held it tightly. "I went downstairs and found Linda and pointed to Dr. Ablon's name on the speed dial. I pressed the dial and handed her the phone. While she was talking to Dr. Ablon's office, I wrote on a piece of paper: 'Go.' Dr. Ablon told her to go to Emergency at UCLA. That's when we got in the car and went down the hill when I saw you. When I got there a neurologist was waiting, but I still couldn't get the words out. Finally when I was sitting on the gurney in the ER I started to talk." He shook his head, still shocked.

Later in the day, Harold shrugged off the event as an everyday "fuck up" with his head. But I saw how alone he felt and realized he had the same fears and apprehensions as anyone else sitting in an emergency room facing a possible end to a life and a career.

Harold was a man who had always been in control of his life, fearless of the obstacles. He also felt that he couldn't let the people around him down. To some he was a moneymaking machine with all the answers, and to others he was a bigger-than-life character from a Harold Robbins novel. In his books the underdog always won, and that would be the case in this instance.

CHAPTER ELEVEN

WHO'S THE BOSS? . . .

*T*he telephone rang and I picked it up. "Robbins residence," I said.

"Are you the new girl from Oklahoma?" the voice asked.

"I guess I am," I said.

"I'm Paul Gitlin and I'm the one you need to be afraid of. Do you know anything about the man you're working for?"

I assured him that I did: "As far as I know, Mr. Gitlin, he's the world's bestselling novelist." I had heard about Mr. Gitlin, who was almost as legendary as Harold Robbins.

Gitlin and Harold cut a wide swath at Simon & Schuster/Pocket Books. In 1960 Herbert Alexander, who I worked for, brought Harold Robbins over from Knopf to Simon & Schuster/Pocket

Books. At that time, Harold was flat-out the biggest author in the world . . . no question about it. He was the difference between the black and the red.

If we had a Harold Robbins novel on the shelf we could coast . . . we all got bonuses. There were no returns on his books. When Harold and Paul Gitlin would come into the office, it was like God had arrived. Everybody dropped everything and attended to them.

Nor was Gitlin averse to throwing his and Harold's weight around. The first time Gitlin took me to lunch, he said, 'You think you work for Leon Shimkin . . . you think you work for Herbert Alexander . . . But in reality you work for Harold Robbins and you work for me,' he said. 'And by the way, if I don't like you, I'll fire you . . . You don't believe it, I've fired 17 people,' and he reeled off the names.

Herb Alexander confirmed the truth of what Gitlin said.

Luckily, Gitlin and Harold both liked me. When I began acquiring and editing Harold's books at Tor/Forge it was like closing the circle. I thought the world of Harold. I even liked Paul.

—BOB GLEASON, EXECUTIVE EDITOR,
TOR/FORGE

"You're damn right! But remember, he's full of shit! Let me talk to him," Paul said roughly.

"Hold on, Mr. Gitlin," I said.

"He told me I needed to be afraid of him," I said to Harold as I handed him the phone.

"Bullshit," Harold said, and took the phone. "Are you coming out for my birthday party? I've already made reservations for you at the Beverly Hills Hotel."

He listened into the phone. "Okay, I'll have Dav El Limousine pick you up at the airport. . . . No, I'm not sending Jann with the car to pick you up. She doesn't know what a son of a bitch you are. I'll send Patti—Jesus Christ, Paul, you might scare her to death and she would run back to Oklahoma."

Harold had butchered a few sentences while talking to Paul and when he hung up the phone looked exhausted. "What a pain in the ass," Harold said, but chuckled affectionately.

Paul Gitlin was a leading agent/attorney in New York. A leading expert on copyright law. He represented many major twentieth-century authors, including Ayn Rand, Sidney Sheldon, Irving Wallace, the Thomas Wolfe Estate, the Raggedy Ann copyright, Barbara Taylor Bradford, Senator Bill Bradley, Mario Puzo's children's trust fund, David Chandler, and many more famous authors. But Paul was pugnaciously blunt and sometimes lost clients because of his argumentative nature.

Paul, in later years, told me he lost Ayn Rand as a client after having dinner at the Four Seasons restaurant with her. During dinner they became entangled in a bitter political discussion. Ayn Rand stood up and screamed at Paul in the middle of the posh restaurant and hastily stomped out and never again spoke to him.

"If Paul had his way, I'd be sitting in a fucking jail cell with a typewriter. He's a pain in the ass. He always wants me to write, non-stop, and now he's worried about me doing the next book," Harold said after the phone conversation.

Harold and Paul were very close friends as well as business associates.

Harold made no business or personal decision without consulting with Paul. He didn't always follow Paul's advice but always consulted with him.

"I got to be well by my birthday, darling," Harold said to me later. "I want you to come to the party as my guest; you'll meet everybody. All my friends will be here."

"When is your birthday?" I asked.

"It's a week from tomorrow. You know that may not be my birthday, but it's the one the orphanage gave me."

He extended this invitation almost as an aside. Casual. I never expected to be invited to his birthday party, especially as his guest. I had mixed emotions about this invitation. I was shy and still trying to adjust to LA life. Besides, I had nothing to wear and I couldn't possibly enter a room of Hollywood "A"-list people without wearing something new. He really didn't ask for an answer from me, did he? I guess that made the decision for me.

I went through the same anxiety every other girl goes through when she's unprepared for this kind of invitation. Nothing to wear. My roots needed touching up. I needed to lose five pounds. I wasn't prepared for a celebrity LA birthday party. And what present would I possibly give a man who had everything, had done everything, and had been everything for his birthday!?

But the real dilemma was what would I wear?!

Chapter Twelve

Happy Birthday to You!

$\mathcal{L}$ ew Mitchell, the owner of the Orient Express, a gourmet Chinese restaurant in the Beverly Hills area, was scheduled to come by a few days before Harold's birthday. He had been called to cater the small event. Small? Over forty people were attending, a guest list of Harold's closest friends, and no one declined the invitation to his party.

The guest list read like a movie billboard from the forties, fifties, sixties, and seventies. There were MGM actress/dancer of the fifties and sixties Cyd Charisse and her husband, Tony Martin, a famous singer of the forties and fifties. Cyd Charisse starred in the classic film *Silk Stockings, Two Weeks in Another Town,* and other MGM hits. Tony Martin was a well-known singer, crooning songs like "Begin the Beguine" and "Tangerine," which were now classics. Comedian/actor Buddy Hackett and his wife, Sherry, also came. Buddy starred in *The Love Bug* and in 1989 provided the voice of Scuttle in *The Little*

Mermaid. Other guests included legendary comic Phyllis Diller; composer Henry Mancini, famous for "Pink Panther", "Moon River," and many other top-of-the-chart songs, and his wife, Giny; Irving Wallace, author and screenwriter, best known for the *The Fan Club, The Chapman Report,* and *The Prize;* David Chandler, another of Harold's author friends; Prince Nicholas Toumanoff of Russia, well-known in Beverly Hills as one of the remaining Russian princes from the last royal family; Sam Arkoff, a famous producer known for *Beach Blanket Bingo* and *I Was a Teenage Werewolf* and head of the distribution company for *The Betsy,* a Harold Robbins movie starring Tommy Lee Jones, Laurence Olivier, and Robert Duvall; Tony (the original owner of Tony Roma's Ribs) and Eleanor Roma; Jimmy Komack, another Hollywood producer/actor/ singer, who produced *Welcome Back, Kotter* and in earlier years had played the role of the dentist on *The Jackie Cooper Show* and was the original singer in Broadway's *Damn Yankees* of the song "You Gotta Have Heart," and his wife, Kluny.

The list went on and on with names I recognized and knew only through magazines and television.

That question about what to wear had not stopped haunting me since I had been given the invitation. "Harold, what's the dress for your birthday party?" I finally asked.

"Casual," he answered, taking a puff from his cigarette.

"What does that mean?" I asked. I knew in Oklahoma that Levi jeans were casual, but I doubted if he meant jeans, unless they were exquisitely jeweled and chicly designer named.

"Sort of dressy casual . . . how the hell do I know?" he finally said. "Come naked; that's what I would like for my birthday. Show off your ass!"

"You really would like that, wouldn't you?"

"Yeah, you bet, baby!" He raised his eyebrows and smiled lasciviously.

"It might not please everyone, Harold."

"Of course it would," he said. "How could anyone not like it?"

"Your wife might not like it."

"She won't be here; besides, Grace and I have an open marriage and she knows everything about my personal life and I know everything about hers. I have naked girls at all my parties," he said proudly.

"Really? That's okay with her?"

"Honey, she has her life and I have mine. That's the way we live, the way we've always lived. She doesn't give a damn what I do. Shelley Winters floated around nude a couple of years ago in the pool at my New Year's Eve party. When Joe Levine and I had a party at the Four Seasons restaurant in New York I had a naked girl in a trench coat at each table. All the wives nearly shit when dessert was served and each girl got up and took off her trench coat. Jesus, it was hysterical." He was almost rolling in his chair laughing. "I had a few naked girls at the L'Orangerie style show for *Goodbye, Janette*. We did a style show. Joe Cassini choreographed it and Pasqual, the artist, did his sculptured heads. You know I helped Gérard bring L'Orangerie into the U.S.?"

"No, I didn't know," I said. "I hear it's the best restaurant in LA."

"We'll go there," he said, and looked up as a car drove into view of the television security monitor at the gate.

"I think I'll wear clothes to the party," I said.

"I think you're okay, baby," he said, and looked up at the monitor as the gate bell rang. A few minutes later Lew Mitchell was ushered into the family room and sat down with us. Harold ordered his favorite dishes from the restaurant for his birthday. This was not a "casual" Chinese food dinner; it was a culinary extravaganza. Seven courses.

"Harold, you really know your Chinese food . . . ," Lew said, complimenting him after they had gone through the menu.

"Yeah, I was married to a Chinese girl once," he said.

On the day of the party, three cakes arrived by Federal Express in dry-ice containers. They were the famous Chocolate Velvet cakes from the Four Seasons restaurant in Manhattan. They were in perfect condition when the cook unwrapped the package and placed them on the counter. Harold and I were in the kitchen and watched the unveiling. Rick sliced a thin sliver of the cake and placed it in front of Harold. . . . Before he took a bite he sliced a small portion onto his fork and held it out to me. It was pure ambrosia.

Harold loved great food and for his birthday many friends sent him special deliveries from New York delis including rugalach, Nova Scotia lox, bagels, and whitefish and deliveries of caviar, Dom Perignon champagne, and David's chocolate cookies from New York from a girlfriend named Linda. Baskin-Robbins in Beverly Hills sent him a gallon of his favorite ice cream. What else? Dark chocolate.

After work that afternoon I rushed home to change clothes. I kept it simple. Black silk pants and a red silk blouse.

When I returned to the house on Tower Grove a couple of hours later I came in through the side door and walked through the kitchen where Lew Mitchell and his Chinese cooks were preparing fragrant, delicious dishes. I opened the door to the dining room as the finishing touches were being made by the staff of helpers. Softly glowing candlelight from bunched votive holders illuminated the fresh flowers. Each place was set with silver chargers, fine china, sterling silverware, crystal salt- and pepper shakers at the top of each plate, linen napkins decoratively held in a crystal napkin holder etched with an *R*, several Baccarat glasses at each place setting for wine, water, and champagne. The main table was set for twenty.

Presents were placed on a table draped in a white linen and lace tablecloth to the right of the dining room table. I stacked my gift with the others on the table. I had found something called an "itty bitty lite" at The Price of His Toys in Beverly Hills. I thought it was an appropriate gift that could be used for reading.

Other tables for dinner guests had been set up leading out to the foyer, set just as beautifully as the main table. I walked into the living room already filled with guests. The room reverberated with conversations and scintillated with beautiful people as soft jazz music subtly filled the air. Waiters walked through the room carrying silver trays of champagne.

Harold spotted me right away as I entered the room and called me over to the sofa. He took my hand and asked me to sit beside him. As guests approached him, he introduced each of them. Observing the action, he made a few comments about some of the guests to me, pointing out who they were and where they were from. Some people had come from Acapulco and France to attend his party. He did not mix and mingle but held court; people came to him. He had a quiet power that drew others like a magnet. He watched thoughtfully as people milled around the room in conversation. He was absorbing everything, reading every conversation, body language, and posturing in the world around him. It was all an exercise for the next story.

"They're all full of shit, cocksuckers!" he said, leaning back on the sofa and smiling as he observed two people greeting each other as though they were best friends. He sipped his drink. "Those two hate each other." He chuckled. "They produce pictures. They're always trying to undercut the other one."

I smiled, continuing to listen. I was still not certain when Harold was being serious or being funny or just guessing between the lines.

"Yeah, everybody is bullshitting." He started to reach for an ashtray.

I picked it up off the coffee table and handed it to him. Another well-known producer walked over and spoke to Harold. They talked about a business deal they had a couple of years earlier. After he left, Harold told me the story.

"He was supposed to distribute *The Betsy*, but his company took bankruptcy right before the picture was released and it never got to the theaters for release—so none of us ever made any money off that movie. It may end up on the cable, but I won't make a dime. I always take my money up front.

"Christ, the business has really changed," he continued. "Cable movie channels, Betamax, VHS, laser disc. It's the future, anything that can play on our own TV screen. Too bad it got all fucked up with *The Betsy*, because I think it's a great movie. I went on the set while it was being filmed. Laurence Olivier was there, Tommy Lee Jones, Kathryn Beller. I told her she should have her tits reduced."

When he said this, I did a double take envisioning the moment. In my mind I could see Harold probably squinting his eyes and talking seriously to Kathryn Beller. I had seen him say things to his listener that might seem abrupt just to see a reaction. I'm sure it made his day.

"I was there the day they shot the pool scene when she was half-naked. It didn't impress her much when I told her." He turned and grinned at me. "But when she gets older she'll trip over them." He started to laugh at his joke.

I watched as several people ascended the stairway, went into the bedroom, and ten or fifteen minutes later came back downstairs.

"If you want a 'toot' it's upstairs on the family room table. If you want to smoke some dope there's some up there," he said matter-of-factly. "They brought a bunch of shit in from Acapulco."

I shook my head.

"You really don't use any of the stuff, do you?"

"No, I gave it up."

He looked at me. "I can't use it right now, but they're all having a great time."

Suddenly the sound system stopped playing. "Goddammit," Harold said. "I paid two thousand dollars for this fucking system and it's busted! Get Linda over here."

I found Linda and brought her to him.

"Where the fuck is Joe? I want him to start playing now! Marty Yellman's goddamn system stopped playing."

"Joe just got here," Linda said. "I'll check the sound system, too."

Harold settled down again on the sofa. He looked at the Ultrasuede upholstery that was shredding. "Can you believe this sofa is less than a year old and it's falling apart! This is crap! Grace and Phyllis Morris's folly!"

He shook his head and returned to the story he had been telling me.

"When I wrote *The Betsy*, I spent a lot of time in Detroit with the Ford family. The old man running the place had supplied me with Fords . . . a Mustang . . . that station wagon we still have." Harold began to laugh. "After he read the book and I was flying home from New York the day after it was published, he made a phone call to the office on Sunset and asked for all the cars to be returned. I guess he didn't like the book."

"Did you make him a villain?" I asked.

Harold shrugged. "What made him mad was what I said about the Japanese coming in and taking over the market, which is a fact now. All these assholes think a character that I write is them. I wasn't talking about the old man; I was telling a story! It's an extrapolation of many people. Khashoggi thought *The Pirate* was about him and it wasn't. The lead was more about the Saudi finance minister I knew," he said, and lit another cigarette. "Go see if they're ready to serve yet. . . ."

His mind was already on to a different subject, a different girl, or a different book, another story. Harold had a unique way of dismissing a conversation. A veil came down, you could see it in his eyes, and suddenly your time was up . . . he was on to the next adventure. I wasn't sure if I was supposed to start a new conversation or just step away, but I did know one thing: I didn't want to go.

I saw him get up and move around the room toward the bar after I left. He chatted with the bartender. Harold entertained with his stories as people came to him, and he always flirted with the women. He was so confident, with a natural power of knowing how to meet every person's need with a comment, a gesture, or an irreverent joke. But if he didn't like someone Harold could be crude and blunt about it. It was fascinating to watch him moving among the crowd. He didn't play by anyone's rules and yet it seemed to me everyone certainly loved him for simply being Harold Robbins, the character, the writer who broke barriers, the playboy who seduced the girls, the businessman always searching for his next million, the father who loved his daughters, the man who had an answer for everything! It's what made him bigger than life, a trait he cultivated.

I glanced across the room, seeing all of these celebrities, not onstage but just enjoying a party among friends. It made me feel like I had walked into my own fantasy world. And though it was a party of about forty people, the feeling was intimate and being next to Harold made me feel I belonged.

Lew Mitchell was standing in the foyer putting the final touch to each table. The meal was ready to be served.

Joe was seated at the black baby grand piano and he started "Happy Birthday," singing a funky jazz version. Everyone caught the cue and started moving toward the dining room.

Harold suddenly appeared by my side and applauded Joe's song. "Sweetheart, I'm going to have Nicky and Adréana sit next to me at the head of the table. You'll be at the main table."

I nodded in agreement. Prince Nicholas Toumanoff was a good friend, a regal prince at eighty-five years old, and Adréana was Harold's pride and joy. As a newcomer to Hollywood parties I didn't realize how important it was to be at the main table. I would have been content anywhere.

"Mr. Robbins, I'm glad to see you on your feet; the way they're talking down the hill, I thought you were half-dead," Joe said, smiling and nodding at Harold's applause.

"I'll piss on all their graves, Joe," Harold said with a deadpan look.

He and Joe both laughed. Harold turned to Lew Mitchell. "Let's get this fucking show on the road."

"Mr. Robbins, dinner is served," Lew Mitchell said, laughing at Harold's comment.

Paul Gitlin, whom I met earlier in the afternoon, cornered me as the group walked into the dining room. Paul was about the same height as Harold but round in shape, with a gray beard and wisps of gray hair covering his balding head. He actually looked like a writer, and Harold looked more like an attorney. "We're having a meeting in the morning," Paul said.

"I heard," I answered.

"How much is this party costing Robbins?" he said, looking directly at me.

"I don't know, Mr. Gitlin; I don't have the bill yet," I said.

"Call me Paul," he said, and continued to walk near me. "You know, Robbins doesn't have money to throw away," he said, again looking at me to drill his comment into my consciousness. Paul had a voice and a way of saying things that made you think he was the law that you didn't want to cross.

"I understand," I said. "But this is his birthday." I couldn't figure out Paul's concern since Harold was a bestselling author who sold millions of books and appeared to be wealthy enough to throw this kind of birthday party. He had three homes, the one that we were standing in, another in Acapulco, and another in Le Cannet, in the South of France; an apartment in Cannes; an eighty-five-foot yacht in Cannes; and until recently a suite at the Sherry-Netherland in New York. Why worry about a small birthday party? I didn't want to make any waves, so I didn't ask.

Chapter Thirteen

found my place card at the main table in the dining room and sat down. A tall, thin, slightly balding man pulled out his chair and sat down next to me. He smiled warmly and introduced himself: "Hi, I'm Henry Mancini."

I looked across the table and saw David and Rita Chandler, Harold's good friends, whom I had met before. Rita, a former agent, was busy chatting about a few of the former actors she had represented, including Don Johnson, who was supposedly going to begin shooting *Miami Vice* to be aired next year on NBC-TV.

I was trying to stay calm in this Hollywood setting but, at the same time, anxiously wondering what I might possibly say to Henry Mancini. "I love your music" and then what? What would I have of interest to say to this man who had written beautiful movie scores and hit music and lived a life of celebrity? I was quickly put at ease when he asked me where I lived before I moved to Los Angeles. When I answered him it opened the door to a great conversation about his movies with Blake Edwards, who was also from Oklahoma.

Beautiful Asian girls walked elegantly through the dining room, wearing tuxedo shirts, black fishnet hosiery, black tails, and stiletto heels. Each girl was carrying a tray of food and offering items to the guests. The girls knelt gracefully as they served and explained each delicacy and provided individual sauces for each dish. After they served each course, they stood alertly filling any glass that became empty and discreetly offered more servings of food when they saw an empty plate.

I was in awe during the party at the understated elegance and the warm, friendly feeling of the party. I overheard conversations that night about Harold's incredible generosity to his friends. It seemed like each person had been touched in some way by this man's help. He spared no expense when he threw a party for a friend, for himself, or for a charity. He never said no if anyone asked for his help. He was always there for not just friends but also acquaintances who needed a boost if they were down on their luck.

When each person gave a toast honoring Harold he or she would tell a story about him that he or she either had experienced or heard about.

Jimmy Komack started the toasts that then traveled around the table: "I'd like to make a toast to one of the most generous men I have ever met. He has been friends with my wife and me for many years and is one of the best friends I have. I know that he doesn't like to hear people talk about him, but I want to tell you a few things I have known him to do for others.

"Harold knew an artist in the South of France who needed money for an operation. Her name was Giselle Belleud. He bought about twelve of her paintings, so she had enough money for a needed surgery."

"They're all phonies," Harold quipped. "She was a French hooker who I owed money to."

The crowd laughed at Harold's joking.

Jimmy continued, "He provided a home on his yacht for a writer named James Baldwin, in the South of France. As well as a coat, clothing, food, and spending money when Baldwin was broke.

"On many occasions I have sat in his office on Sunset Boulevard. The phone was always ringing, usually from Harold's girlfriends. But he would always take calls from friends, and those friends usually called to ask favors. Some were in financial straits; some needed a phone call made, a connection. He never turned down a request for help and if he gave someone money he never expected to be repaid.

"All of the authors sitting at this table envy his success with his books, but his success is well earned and he makes it all look so easy!"

Everyone toasted to Harold. He shunned the praise and interrupted the applause.

"I'll tell you a story about Jimmy Baldwin. I was sitting on the yacht in the South of France one afternoon and a girl came up the gangplank and she asked me in broken English, 'Are you the famous author?'

"'Yes, I write books.'

"And she stares at me and says, 'Could you please give me your autograph?'

"I signed the paper and she looks at it. Then she looks at me kind of funny. 'You're not the famous writer Jimmee Baldwin?'"

The room exploded in laughter.

"Let's get this show on the road. I may begin to think it's a funeral instead of a birthday party since everyone is being so nice," Harold said.

Joe Lisbona, a filmmaker who had flown in from France, stood up. Even though Joe was Egyptian, he had lived in Paris for many years and spoke with a slight accent. "Harold, you have to let me toast you. I've come a long way to honor your birthday and I don't think you are going to die. You're much too young!"

"Bravo!" one of the guests at the table yelled.

"Harold is the kind of friend who only comes by in life once or twice. Several years ago my family and I were visiting in Cancún, Mexico, and had a very bad car accident. Our injuries were severe and the facilities in Cancún were not good. I called Harold in the middle of the night in Los Angeles asking if he knew anyone who could help us. He called Dr. Villarias in Acapulco and in a matter of hours we were flown to Acapulco and Harold's home there was set up as a hospital. We had round-the-clock nurses and Dr. Villarias would visit us several times a day. Again, my friend, thank you and Happy Birthday."

Harold refused to take any of this seriously. "I'm going to cry. I'm just a regular guy trying to have a birthday and I'm not sure if I'm even going to get laid!"

At the end of the dinner, a birthday cake was brought out and Harold took two big huffs and puffs and blew out all the candles. Photographs were taken by a few friends from the press in attendance and Dom Perignon champagne was poured to celebrate and toast his birthday.

He didn't open his gifts that were piled high on a table in the back of the dining room. But I was told he never opened presents at a party. He told me later it was boring for people to have to watch as he opened packages. I would discover that Harold always felt more comfortable giving rather than receiving the gifts. Even when he was complimented on his work, he would always minimize the work he did, as if it were nothing.

David Chandler told a story at the dinner table about Jacquelyn Susann coming to dinner at Harold's house and passing out copies to everyone of her new book, *Valley of the Dolls*. She placed a centerpiece on the table promoting the book. David said it didn't bother Harold at all. He was always generous in helping, supporting, and giving advice to and encouraging other writers.

Harold ended this story telling how Cornelius Ryan and David gave Susann a hard time, teasing her, asking her throughout the evening who really wrote her books. He said Ryan and Chandler were jealous. David was a great straight man for Harold and went along with Harold's assessment: "They were jealous because she sold millions of books, but she was not an intellect."

David again stood up and toasted Harold. "I probably more than anyone at this table owe Harold a debt of gratitude for the help he so generously gives to others," David said. "He doesn't like to talk about his genius in writing, and as a writer I only wish I had the genius that touches the public's pulse the way he does."

Tony Roma interrupted David. "Are you sure that it's the pulse or another word that starts with *p* he wants to touch?"

Everyone at the table laughed.

"Harold, we all owe you, every writer in the world owes you, for the doors you've opened for each of us."

David knew Harold as well as almost anyone in the room and David knew in his heart Harold loved to write, spin stories, bring entertainment to the world around him, shock people, wake them up, and push the envelope Why else be alive?

Harold stayed quiet and nodded his appreciation. He wasn't ready to stand up and speak that night, and no one forced the issue.

By ten o'clock that evening I saw he was getting tired. I told him good night and he kissed me on the cheek and thanked me for being there. I made my exit and floated on a cloud back to my apartment happily and looking forward to tomorrow. I had entered a world tonight that in my wildest dreams I could not have imagined, the world of Harold Robbins.

Chapter Fourteen

A Little Scotch in My Coffee . . .

*T*he next morning I arrived early and sat down at the bar in the living room. Paul Gitlin came downstairs and greeted me. He was wearing Rockport walking shoes, baggy jeans, and a T-shirt emblazoned with the words "Justice for All." He walked behind the bar, took out a new bottle of J&B Scotch, twisted the cap to break the seal, and took a big swig.

I had never seen anyone start their day out with a drink from the bottle. Not a splash of water on ice, not in a glass! I thought, *This is a character out of one of Harold's books.* Harold claimed he always wrote about the world around him, and Paul Gitlin was definitely a character in the world of Harold Robbins. In fact, I realized, all the characters from the party last night and today were the makings of a Harold Robbins novel. And now *I* was a character in that world.

Paul turned around and looked at me after he had replaced the bottle cap. "I hear you don't drink?"

"No, I don't," I said.

"Good," he said gruffly. "Drugs?"

"No," I said.

As Paul grilled me Harold came into the bar. His face lit up when I turned to him. "Good morning, sweetheart," he said.

"Good morning, Harold." I smiled.

"Are you sleeping with him?" Paul asked abruptly, and pointed toward Harold.

Harold yelled back at him good-naturedly, "Gitlin, that's a personal question!"

I looked at Paul. "No, I'm not sleeping with him."

"I'm asking the questions; why don't you go work, Robbins?" Paul said, looking at Harold.

The houseman came out with mugs and a pot of coffee. I jumped up, glad to have a distraction, and poured coffee into the cups. I put two cubes of sugar into Harold's coffee and handed it to him. I handed a cup to Paul. He opened the J&B bottle again and poured a shot into his coffee.

Harold wandered out of the room.

"You know what happened to him, don't you?" Paul said, talking to me again.

"He said he slipped in the shower."

"Well, that's for the public. He had a stroke and it caused something called aphasia. It interrupted the mechanism that gives us the ability to speak what we are trying to say." He thought a moment. "At least, that's how I understand it. Who knows with these crazy doctors in LA. I wanted him to come to New York. They have real doctors there. I don't trust these assholes out here."

"He told me he had aphasia. And he seems to be getting better. He's determined to get completely well, and I'm right there with him."

"He has to." Paul looked at me directly. "He needs the money and when Grace gets back I'll tell her to quit spending so goddamn much money! And I expect you to keep a tight rein on expenses. He wants you to tell him how much he's spending. None of us know. Money is pissed out every day. The Mexicans in Acapulco steal from him. He buys groceries for the family who live and work in the house and probably ten other families who they know in Acapulco. They gouge him in Le Cannet, and the staff on the yacht." Paul rolled his eyes. "We've got to have some breathing space. Robbins just writes a check, whatever they ask for, and sends it.

"Lynn at the office tries to keep everything paid up here in this house, but she can't keep tabs on everything."

"I'll do whatever I can, but I'm not an accountant. I came to LA to write, Mr. Gitlin," I said.

"I told you, call me Paul," he barked at me.

"Okay, Paul."

Harold walked back into the room. "Paul thinks everybody steals from me. Is that what he's telling you?"

"She says she's no accountant," Paul said, ignoring Harold's question and my answer. Paul sometimes spoke of others as though they weren't in the room. Harold was the opposite; he included everyone, and he was onstage every time he spoke.

"Leave her alone, Paul. She's smarter than both of us. I'll hire an accountant to set up a simple system of keeping track of the bills. She can do it." He turned to me. "You can do that, can't you?"

I felt I could do anything as long as he needed it done. "I'm sure I can." I had never felt more confident. I wanted to live up to his expectations and mine.

"We've got accountants in New York; we pay them thousands. She doesn't have to be an accountant!" Harold said.

"You know, you'll be responsible for over one hundred thousand dollars a month in expenses for all the houses. That's one-point-two million dollars a year. You ever managed that kind of money?" Paul asked.

"I managed advertising budgets as an account executive for my clients. That is the only experience I've had with budgets of that size," I answered.

"Paul, for Chrissakes, her job is not to manage money; that's yours and mine!" Harold said. "Somehow we managed to get this shit done!" Harold gestured at the house.

"Yeah, and none of it's paid for!" Paul retorted.

"That's not fair, Paul. It will be. *Spellbinder* will be out soon and we'll get a big payment from S and S." Harold shot back.

"Well, I'll be watching over everything," Paul said, and shrugged.

. I had seemed to satisfy his concern. He and Harold began to talk about deadlines for his next book, as yet untitled, and other publishing business while I listened.

"Linda went to Switzerland to the spa; she's getting a lot of information about the health treatments they offer. She's trying to get the information about heads of state who have been there in the past. A few Russians have gotten treatment with lambs' placenta. The idea for the next book is starting to come together."

Paul made no comment.

"By the way, Paul," Harold said as he sipped the last of his coffee. "We need to write a check for fifty thousand dollars today and pay for the Bayliner."

Paul nodded in agreement.

*T*he remaining visitors from out of town who were staying at the Westwood Marquis began arriving at the house by 11:00 A.M. They were all dressed for a day at the beach. They were going out to the slip in Marina del Rey and over to Catalina to christen the new Bayliner named *Spellbinder*, a fifty-foot cabin cruiser Harold had acquired several weeks earlier.

"Did you bring a swimsuit?" Harold asked me.

"No, I'm sorry, I didn't. I really have made other plans for the afternoon."

"We'll get you a suit over at Catalina; that's no problem," he said.

"No, I really appreciate the invitation, but I've made other plans."

He looked at me a little warily. I wasn't sure if he believed me or if he just thought it was strange I was passing up an opportunity to go to Catalina with an elite group. I didn't think he was happy about it, but he accepted my answer.

I was trying to keep my job on a business level and stay out of the fantasy of Harold Robbins's world. I wondered to myself if I was making a mistake. I had been told by everyone who knew him how notorious his reputation was for sleeping with every girl he met—loved them and left them. And it was undeniable. He was sexy even at the age of sixty-six—he seemed ageless, dangerous, and lovable.

I needed my job more than I needed a one-night stand, regardless of how much fun it might be. And I was sure that it would be fun, because that was the way he was.

CHAPTER FIFTEEN

ou passed inspection," he said, and chuckled, a few days later. "Paul liked you. He thinks you'll organize me."

"What if I hadn't passed inspection?" I asked.

"I would have kept you anyway." He moved in closer to me.

I hugged him. "Thanks, I appreciate that."

"I'm having a CPA come over this afternoon and set up a system to organize the house," he said. He noticed my expression. "What's the matter?"

"Harold, I came to Los Angeles to write. I'm not sure I want to become a bookkeeper. I love working for you, but it's not what I want to do."

He reached out and patted my hand. "Don't be a fuckin' pain in the ass. I told you already, you're going to help me when I start writing. I don't know if you'll learn anything, I'm a schmuck that got lucky with the books I've written, but you'll be involved when I go to work. I told you that you were my assistant and that's what you are: organize the houses, take care of my manuscript, edit with my approval, make my appointments, go on interviews with me, drive the Rolls and the Maserati. Why don't you get rid of that diesel Peugeot?" He smiled. "And you'll rub my ass a little bit. What's not to like about this job?"

I shook my head and laughed. "Are you ever serious?"

"I am serious," he said as his eyes danced.

His private line rang. I left the room as he picked it up.

"Hi, Linda," I heard him say into the phone as I was leaving.

Who was Linda? I knew it wasn't the Linda working in the house.

"Hey, come back here!" I heard him yell.

I turned around and went back into the study. When he hung up the phone, he handed me some papers to mail.

"That was my girlfriend; she's in Switzerland," he said. "She does research for me. I have to send her a check."

He was full of surprises. I wondered how many girlfriends he had.

Chapter Sixteen

We began our routine of reading again after all the guests had returned home over a week later. Harold held the phone to his ear, making faces and clowning around as he listened to me reading a passage from *Never Leave Me* (1954).

" 'The cold air came rushing into the room and the nausea went away. For a long time I stood there looking over the city. You're a dope, I told myself. You're acting like a teenage kid. You got everything you ever wanted in this world. Dough. Position. Respect. A Cadillac. What more do you want? No dame is that important.

" 'That was it. No dame was that important. I knew that all the time. That's what I always said. I closed the window and walked back through the office. I sat down on the couch and opened another bottle of Scotch. I poured myself a big one.

" 'This time I could feel the liquor hit my stomach and bounce through me. I fished a cigarette from my pocket and lit it. The smoke went tingling through my nose and I leaned back against the cushions. I was tired and beat so I closed my eyes—and she jumped back into the room.*

"'*I could feel the softness of her hair, see the gentle curve of her smile, hear the sweetness in her voice. I rolled over and buried my face in the cushions until I could hardly breathe. But it was no good.*

"'*I punched my hand into the cushions to drive her face away. No dame is that important. I opened my eyes but she was still in the room, just out of sight.*

"'*I got to my feet defiantly. I was shouting now.* "*Go away! Don't bother me!*" *I shut up guilty as my voice bounced back in the empty room.*

"'*What am I acting like a fool for? I asked myself. I can get any dame I want. Any size, shape or color. She wasn't the only broad in the world.*'"

Harold had switched to a more serious demeanor and leaned back in the chair, spoke into the phone, and closed his eyes. "That was a bitch!" He lit a cigarette and opened *Never Leave Me* to the copyright page. The copy I had been reading from was a paperback.

"I've written two books in seven days, *Stiletto* and *Never Leave Me*. *Never Leave Me* I wrote when I was trying to support Lillian, Yvonne, and go into rehearsals for a Broadway play that I co-wrote with Sam Dann and Ethel Rosenberg. It was called *Go Fight City Hall*, a musical. Noel Herron wrote the music. It was a great play, but I lost my ass, financially.

"My agent had gone to Knopf and asked him for an advance on future royalties to fund the play and other debts. Knopf wouldn't hear of it even though the books were bestsellers. He also wouldn't increase the royalties, so I had no other choice but to write something outside of my contract with him.

"I sat down on a Sunday evening to write. Lil was pissed at me because I hadn't been home all weekend. I had missed Sunday brunch. When I saw her look of anger as I sat down the idea came to me. I wrote from my own life about the three women I was involved with. The sophisticate like Yvonne, classy and big in society; my wife, Lil; and Connie, another girl I was seeing. She was one of the girls from the Copa who served drinks during cocktail hour in my office at Universal. She was crazy, wild."

He grinned and raised his eyebrows.

"I got booted out of Universal not long after I finished this book. Yvonne got pregnant in January or February of '55 and Rank was her uncle and chief stockholder at Universal. Christ! That changed everything."

He turned and looked at me. "You want an omelet?"

"Sure," I said.

"I'm going to fix you one of my specials." He picked up the phone and dialed the kitchen. "Rick, put the omelet pan, some butter, onions, and lox and eggs on the dumbwaiter.

"You're going to have some Jewish heaven!"

We walked to the small upstairs kitchen. I heard the dumbwaiter trundling up on a rope system lifting a tray from the first floor to the second.

"I'll make some coffee," I said, and pulled out his favorite coffee. Yuban.

"I learned to cook when I worked as a short-order cook, behind a counter. I learned to make old-fashioned black and whites and served two-cents-plain sodas. Do you know what those are?" he asked me as he finished preparing lox, onions, and eggs. "This will be the best lox, onion, and egg omelet you've ever had."

"No, I don't know what two cents plain and black and whites are," I answered.

"You missed a lot growing up in Oklahoma." He chuckled and carried the plates into the family room.

I didn't dare tell him I had never had a lox, onion, and egg omelet before. I knew it was sacred fare in his world.

"How did you ever write a book in seven days?" I said.

"Cocaine!" he said, and laughed. "Necessity! I always had to hustle for money—story of my life. I've pissed out millions on women. That's what happened with Lillian, Yvonne, Grace, Linda, Lisa, Caroline, Dominique." He paused.

Was he putting me on? Who was Lisa? Caroline? Dominque? Were those more wives?

"Maybe you should have stuck with one wife at a time," I kidded him.

He looked at me, his eyebrows furrowed. "Do you know the three most boring things in the world?"

I shook my head.

"Home cooking, home fucking, and Dallas, Texas!" He laughed at his joke. I was becoming his greatest "straight man" for comedy!

We ate the omelet together and he told me the story of *Stiletto*, the only other book he wrote in seven days.

CHAPTER SEVENTEEN

Stiletto is one of my favorite books. This one I wrote in late 1959. I had returned from Japan after writing *The Carpetbaggers* and was staying at the Hotel Elysee. I had left some money here in the States with a friend of mine while I was gone. I tried to contact him when I returned to New York and discovered he had left the country. Gone to Brazil, along with my money. I didn't have a fucking dime to survive while I waited for Paul to straighten out the IRS, so he made a deal with Dell Publishing for a paperback novel, not hardcover. Seven days later I sent in the manuscript. Again, it had to be less than one hundred thousand words so I didn't violate the contract with Knopf. It's a book I really loved.

"A story about the Mafia. The original Italian Mafia when there was a code of honor among the men in power. How they came to America and began businesses legal and illegal. Count Cesare Cardinali, the main character, was part of New York society, an intriguing, handsome playboy, but he liked to kill people. It was in his blood, a taste for violence. You know some people have that; he couldn't help it. Then his godfather asks him to kill four witnesses that were going to testify in a trial against his mentor."

Stiletto was originally published in 1960 by Dell. Publishing executive Donald Fine made the original softcover contract. It was distributed mostly in Europe. In 1997 it was again published in its original form for the first time in hardcover by Penguin Books, Donald I. Fine Imprint. *Stiletto* had come full circle and the book was as riveting in 1997 as it was in 1960. The book came out after Harold's passing, and I walked into a bookstore and saw the book on the shelf. He opened the book to the dedication page. It was a surprise that Harold had kept from me. The inscription read: "This novel is one of my loves, but the greatest love of my life is my beautiful wife, Jann." His eloquent words of dedication brought me to tears.

Harold also wrote a foreword in 1997 for the hardcover edition, called "Harold Robbins Memories":

I began working in a grocery store on 125th Street near the corner of Convent Avenue in Harlem when I was seventeen years old. My job was a combination of delivering orders, cleaning the floor with a rag mop, dusting the shelves that held the cans and packages, and refilling the stock on the shelves when empty. Fortunately, it wasn't a very busy job because there were three other clerks who worked at the grocery store and helped the customers with their purchases. I had enough time to hide out in the back room and read the magazines that the clerks always seemed to leave open on the cases in the storeroom. They were exciting reading. I would take them home with me to my room at Mrs. Green's boarding house. In a short time I had my room covered wall to wall with these magazines. I

remember these names: Amazing Stories, Ace Magazines, *and* Detective Stories. *As I grew older, I was
surprised that everyone knew and loved these stories. By
this time I had been introduced by a friend who worked for
the library to reading hardcover novels. It was in the thir-
ties that I first read a novel by Donald Henderson Clark
called* Louis Beretti. *I loved it and found a new world. It
was the story of an Italian boy growing up on the Lower
East Side of New York, smoking opium with his Chinese
friends, and learning about love and sex with his girl on
the rooftops of the tenements. He grew up and became a
killer. As soon as I finished reading this novel, I went back
to the library to check out another book by the same author.
This book was* Millie, *all about a Lower East Side girl
who worked her way up in society and married a very rich
Fifth Avenue man who was president of a Wall Street
bank. The two books were fantastic, and I soon learned
that they had been made into movies.*

*Two years later, to my surprise, my first novel was
published. As part of the publicity for the book,* Never
Love A Stranger, *I was invited on an important radio
program called* Books On Trial, *hosted by one of New
York's most important critics. Sterling Lord. It was a
half-hour program broadcast during evening prime time.
As I sat in the witness chair, my knees were already shaking. The cast included myself, as the author on trial for*
Never Love A Stranger; *the prosecuting attorney, who
was supposed to destroy the book; and the defense attorney
on the side of the book, who was a well-known newspaper
columnist who would appraise the novel and me as the author. I was sweating near the end of the program because
the prosecuting attorney said it was stupid to think that*

readers would believe there was a crime syndicate in existence. It was then I had the best idea of my life. I told him that he was stupid to believe that there was not such a thing as a crime syndicate. He evidently had not read the newspapers, about the Kefauver Commission in Congress. The Mafia was all over the newspapers and if they were not a syndicate, what were they? I began to develop an idea for a novel about the Mafia. In the back of my head I already had thought of an extraordinary character, but it would be many years and four novels later before I would write Stiletto. *I read and learned a great deal about the Mafia, such as how its members came from Sicily to America and found their way into many businesses, illegal and legal. Count Cesare Cardinali was ordered to go to the United States by his Sicilian Mafia don. To the outside world he drove dangerous, high-speed automobiles and owned a foreign car dealership on Park Avenue in New York. The world also knew that he was one of the most romantic playboys in New York society, one the newspapers wrote about every day. What the world did not know about him was that he was a deadly assassin who belonged to the Mafia.* Stiletto *is one of my favorite novels. I feel even today, after many great novels have been written about the Mafia, that* Stiletto *was one of the most important forerunners.*

Stiletto sold 1 million copies in 1960. It has been translated into more than forty foreign languages. It was the first publication in Harold Robbins's career to include his photograph. Harold's American novels rarely included his picture, yet he was a recognizable icon.

Stiletto became a movie in 1969, starring Alex Cord and Britt Ekland.

CHAPTER EIGHTEEN

I was too big to cry, but the tears hovered beneath my eyes. Mom knew it the moment I came in the door. She moved quickly toward me. I turned away to go to my room, but her hand caught mine and held me.

" ' "She's not for you, Mike," she said, softly.

" 'I didn't answer, just stared at her.

" ' "I'm not telling you who to like, son," she added. "It's just that she's not for you. She's been brought up without love and has no understanding of it."

" 'I had pulled my hand away and went to my room, but what she had said stayed in my mind. Without love.' " (Harold Robbins, 79 Park Avenue *[1955].)*

"This is getting to be a fucking bore," Harold said into the phone raspily one morning after I finished reading the page.

"I love it," I said, and smiled. "You are such a good writer and I always enjoy reading these passages."

Harold was not always willing to go through the exercises for Dr. Cooper and certainly didn't like to do things over and over again in the same way. "You read it now and I'll listen," I said, teasing him out of his grumpy mood.

He lit a cigarette. "What do you want to know about *79 Park Avenue?*"

"Everything," I answered.

He chuckled. "You're a good girl!

"*79 Park Avenue* became a bestseller within the first week it was published. It appeared on the *New York Times* list the same week Caryn was born. That was also the beginning of a big battle between Yvonne and me and Lillian. The women in this book were an extrapolation of the women I had known in my life. Yvonne accused me of using her as a woman without love in the book. She threatened to sue me, but instead she wouldn't let me visit Caryn, but she wanted me to send money." He looked at me and smiled. "Cunt! It's gotten me in trouble all of my life."

I smiled and shook my head.

"Well, *c'est la vie*, what can you do?" He paused. "I love women."

"Why do you call women cunts and pussies?"

"That's the way we talked when I was a kid growing up. Street talk, and that's the way I write. I've heard it all of my life. But you're too young to say things like that. You don't think women use words about men? I've had a lot of women call me 'cocksucker' and 'bastard'!"

We both started laughing. "And you probably earned those names."

"Street names change with the times, but there's been prostitution since the world began. That was what *79 Park Avenue* was about, and prostitution will always be here. I don't know what cavemen called it; maybe they drew pictures. That's called pornography now. People make their own choices every day about what they are willing to do. We don't have the right to judge them or label them. At least walk in their shoes before you do. *79 Park Avenue* did one thing for the public; it made people think about these girls being real, not just hustlers. The book was about walking in their shoes and understanding. Maybe it was a book about forgiveness. I never know; the reader is the only one who can decide.

"It opened a lot of doors for my other books. After *79 Park Avenue* we got the first book made into a movie, *Never Love a Stranger.* It starred John Barrymore, who was drunk all the time, and Steve McQueen. McQueen was just a kid. We got along great; we both loved cars."

Harold walked over to his black credenza in the study and pulled out a photograph of McQueen and him standing by an Avanti automobile. McQueen was sitting in the driver's seat and Harold was handing him the car keys. "This was a publicity shot after he did *Nevada Smith* and I had brought in an Avanti to LA from Europe. He went crazy over the car." Harold sighed. "Poor guy, he really fought his cancer, but it didn't do him any good." He looked over at me. "You know we offered him the role of Jonas Cord in *The Carpetbaggers* and he turned it down. He kicked himself after George Peppard became a star from it. When we offered him *Nevada Smith*, he jumped at it. It's still my favorite movie of all of them."

"Do you still make money on those movies?" I asked.

"Hell, no. I take my money up front. I'm the one who set up the accounting practices used by all the studios and I never want to be involved in back-end deals."

Harold boasted during many dinner parties that he had helped to devise the formula that allowed the studio huge profits in spite of the expenses that were shown on the balance sheets. He claimed Cary Grant was still angry with him for a deal he had constructed for Universal many years ago concerning his films. Universal had made the largest percentage off of his movies; and Cary Grant, only a small percentage.

"Somebody always gets screwed with the studios. Remember, whoever signs the checks wins."

Park Avenue sold over 4.5 million copies. In 1968 the book was adapted into a television miniseries starring Leslie Ann Warren. It was the most highly rated television show ever at that time.

Chapter Nineteen

arold continued his story the next day about life in the late fifties: "I was really in the shithouse after *79 Park Avenue.* I was busted, broke, and had quit my job at Universal.

"I was walking down Fifth Avenue one day and ran into Jack Warner. I asked him if he had some work I could do. He said to come to his office the next Monday and he'd have a desk waiting for me. I asked Lillian if I could spend the weekend in Connecticut and work on some ideas that I could give to Warner. On Monday morning I had my briefcase filled with all these ideas for screenplays when I showed up at Warner's office.

"The secretary said Jack was busy and showed me to my office in the writers' building. She said Mr. Warner would call me later. I waited for him to call and then a few days went by and then a few weeks. Every time I called his office and asked what he wanted me to do, the secretary gave me the same answer: 'Mr. Warner will contact you when he's ready.'

"For several months I received a paycheck every week, but I sat doing nothing. Finally, I said fuck it. I left my office and went to Lillian's and packed my bags.

"Lil saw me packing and wanted to know what I was doing, and I told her I was buying a small house in Japan, not far from a Shinto monastery, and I was going to write a book. She had something else in mind. She thought we were probably going to settle down and live a normal life, but I had to write.

"When I write, I have to do it without distractions. Something that none of my wives understand. I can't have Grace's asshole friends around when I'm trying to write. I have an apartment in Cannes, away from the house in Le Cannet. She has never understood what it takes to write; she only understands how to spend the money!"

Harold stopped for a moment and laughed at his own joke. "Anyway, I knew that this book would have to be done with no distractions, no women or alimony to worry about, no kids, all the bullshit that comes across a day in a life. I was in Japan for nine months, with two geisha girls." He flashed his grin.

"What about no distractions?" I asked.

"They were just taking care of me," he said, feigning innocence. "All I remember is hitting my head on the ceiling every time I got out of bed."

I smiled and wondered, *What is true and what is false?* I never knew, but he was completely adorable and completely mesmerizing telling his stories. I was hearing the story behind the story.

"It took me some time to write *The Carpetbaggers;* when I finished the book and came back to the United States I moved into the Hotel Elysee and tried to reconcile with Lillian. I was friends with Leon Quain and his sister, who owned the Elysee, and they gave me a suite on credit. I was living below Tennessee Williams and above Marlon Brando. Tennessee had boys sneaking up the back elevator and Brando had girls sneaking in the side door to see him. It was a wild place. Lillian didn't let me come back to Connecticut for about a year. Leon didn't make me pay until I got a royalty check.

"I was eating on credit at 21, the Copa. Ed Gollin, my publicist,

brought me food to eat while I tried to get the *Carpetbaggers* manuscript to the best agent in town at the time. Annie Laurie Williams
couldn't represent me because I was breaking the contract with Knopf.
I had to avoid any contact with anyone associated with Alfred Knopf
since he was trying to stop me from publishing. She didn't even know
I was in town."

"What ever happened to the job at Warner's? Did you tell them
you were leaving?"

Harold started to laugh. "Jack Warner is still pissed off about
that! He paid me for six months after I left. He called me up in my
office one day and couldn't reach me. Finally a telegram got to me in
Japan saying he was looking for me and I arranged to call him back.
He told me he wanted me to come to his office in an hour; he had a
project for me. I said that would be pretty hard since I was in Japan.
He asked me what the hell I was doing in Japan. I said, 'Writing a
book.' He hung up on me and I didn't get any more paychecks. Then
he was really pissed when he didn't even get first right of refusal on
The Carpetbaggers!"

Harold laughed even harder as he finished his story. I couldn't
help but laugh with him. "I found Paul Gitlin to get me out of all the
financial problems. At that time he was a well-known agent with
Ernst, Cane, Berner and Gitlin. His partner Mel Cane was a legend
in the publishing business and he lived to be over one hundred years
old. He came to the office every day! Paul was the best agent in New
York. But if it hadn't been for Zelda, his wife, *The Carpetbaggers*
would never have been published."

CHAPTER TWENTY

I read from the pages of *The Carpetbaggers* the next day:

"'"I'm pregnant," she said. "I'm going to have a baby."

"'Laddie felt a dull ache spread over him. Somehow, this was the way he'd always known it would turn out. Ever since that first summer two years ago. He looked up at her, squinting his eyes against the sun. "How do you know?"

"'She spoke quietly, as if she were just talking about the weather. "I'm late," she said simply. "I've never been late before."

"'He looked down at his hands. They were sun-darkened against the white sand. "What are you going to do," she answered. Her white-blond hair glittered in the sunlight as she turned and looked out at the ocean. "If nothing happens by tomorrow, I guess I'll have to tell Mother."

"'"Will you—tell her about us?"

"'"No," she said swiftly, in a low voice. She picked the next question from his lips. "I'll tell her it was Tommy, or Bill, or Joe."

"Page two thirty-five:

"'She reached a hand out to his. "I shouldn't have let you do it," she whispered.

" ' "*You couldn't have stopped me,*" he said. "*I must have been crazy.*"
He looked at her. "*If we were anybody else, we could run away and get*
married."

" ' "*I know.*"

" ' *His voice turned bitter.* "*It isn't as if we were really brother and sis-*
ter. If only they hadn't adopted—"

" ' "*But, they did,*" *Rina said quickly.* . . . ' "

L ater, at lunch, Harold continued the story of *The Carpetbag-*
gers. "It was probably the best book I ever wrote according to
the sales figures. Paul almost turned me down when I asked him to
represent the book," Harold said and recounted Paul's reaction:

" 'Jesus Christ, you can't talk about incest like this. The publishers will never accept it. This author, Robbins, he's got a book that
reads great, but it's a ball breaker for publishing,' Paul said to his
wife, Zelda. He had been reading the *Carpetbaggers* manuscript after
he came home from the office in 1960.

" 'He's also in big trouble with the IRS, he's got wives, girlfriends, kids, and everybody wants money.'

"After Zelda read the manuscript, she told Paul he had to get the
book published. She was certain it would be a bestseller. If it hadn't
been for Zelda I might have still been beating the streets in New
York with my manuscript."

"Did you expect it would sell millions of copies?" I asked.

Harold looked at me with certainty. "Of course I did! I'm the
best writer in the world in plain English! I already knew that and
I wanted to make big money on this one."

"You may be a great writer in plain English, but you're published
in forty-two foreign languages, Harold."

He shrugged. "Crazy."

The aroma of corned beef and pastrami was in the air as the
waiter placed two plates with mile-high-piled pastrami sandwiches
on the table. We were sitting at The Bagel Restaurant in a Jewish

neighborhood in West LA, a favorite haunt of Harold's. We watched out the window as several Hassidic Jews with long beards walked to synagogue.

"Reminds me of New York. The Diamond District on Forty-fifth Street. They're always 'hondling' on the diamonds." He looked at me. "Do you know what 'hondling' means?"

I shook my head.

"It's a Jew word, means making deals. The more lox, bagel, and cream cheese you eat, the more you'll understand Yiddish," he said, laughing, as he bit into his sandwich.

Ed Gollin, a publicist and longtime friend of Harold's from New York, would send him a couple of pounds of pastrami and bagels, along with rugalah, every month from Zabar's, the Carnegie, and other New York delis.

Harold also worked in delis in his early years. He learned to make matzo brie using heavy cream, eggs, and cinammon and French toast using heavy cream, butter, eggs, and thick challah bread to make them rich and delicious. He and Joe Levine, who produced many of Harold's movies, once had a "matzo brie cook-off" at the Four Seasons restaurant in New York. Both boasted of winning that contest.

"I once had a seder in this restaurant," Harold said between bites. "Adréana was about ten years old and she was curious about the ritual, so I arranged for about fifty people to come to the event. I had the rabbi from Beverly Hills come and officiate. But no one stayed very serious. George Burns and Hackett were sitting across from one another. George was puffing on his cigar, and Buddy hates smoke. Every time George took a puff Buddy had a comment and George had a comeback. I wish I had recorded it."

"Tell me about Zelda and the book," I said.

"After Zelda read the manuscript of *The Carpetbaggers* and told Paul that it would become a bestselling novel, he agreed to talk to a publisher about a contract. He went to Leon Shimkin, who was head of Simon and Schuster at the time, and gave him the manuscript. After Shimkin read it, he wanted it.

"On the day we went to sign the papers in Shimkin's office an IRS agent in charge of my case went with us. I owed the government a lot of money." Harold started laughing. "When Shimkin made the original offer for the book he talked about the amount that would go to Paul for his commission and to the other debts I had, including the tax money, and how much I would receive. The agent got up suddenly and stood over Leon's desk.

"He put up his hand and stopped the negotiations. 'Mr. Robbins has to have more money for this book. He can't afford to live on what you've offered him after we take our portion.'" Harold started to laugh hysterically. When Harold laughed, really laughed, he didn't laugh loudly; he laughed with his whole body. Anyone watching couldn't help but laugh with him, it was contagious. "Shimkin raised the advance! If it wasn't for the IRS we might have never changed the way of doing business at S and S."

"It seems like all the authors in the world should give you a copyright percentage. Like a franchise!" I said.

"It was the three of us that came up with the idea; Paul, Herbert Alexander, and me. We were at a cocktail party before the meeting with Shimkin and Paul said, 'Let's go over and talk to Herb Alexander; he's just crazy enough to see the value of the paperback split.'"

Herbert Alexander, Paul, and Harold created a company called Trident to publish *The Carpetbaggers*. Traditionally, the author only received half of that paperback advance, the other half going to his or her hardback publisher. In fact, if the author's hardback advance did not earn out from the hardback sale, the author's share of the paperback money would be applied to the unearned hardback advance. The author also had to split royalties. Harold and Gitlin sold Herbert the hardback and paperback rights simultaneously, with the author getting 100 percent of his hardback *and* paperback money—advance and royalties both. The author didn't have to split it with the house. It's now called hard/soft buy. Now it's all done that way.

Harold, Gitlin, and Herbert Alexander revolutionized book publishing and liberated writers financially when they created Trident Press and published *The Carpetbaggers.*
—BOB GLEASON, EXECUTIVE EDITOR, TOR/FORGE

It was hard to believe *The Carpetbaggers*, a book that had been wildly successful, selling over 20 million copies in forty-two languages, later made into a movie that at the time was the most expensive movie ever produced, had nearly ended up in the rejection pile of unpublished manuscripts.

I thought about it later that night. What if Paul Gitlin had decided not to sell the book? What if Zelda had not been persuasive and convinced him to talk to the publishers? What if Harold Robbins had not had the courage to write the book or change the way publishing was done in the world? I wondered if he ever faced the dilemma that most writers face, and that is, *Can I really do this? Who do I think I am to write a book worthy of success?* Harold Robbins had not only a dream but also the imagination and courage to turn his world into reality.

Harold would say many times in interviews and conversations with me that he wanted literature to reach the masses, and that is why he, Paul Gitlin, and Herbert Alexander made it possible for literature to be in both hardcover and softcover.

I guess there are a thousand what-ifs and maybes in everyone's life, but I couldn't help but wonder how it would have affected Harold's life or, for that matter, the world itself if the what-ifs had been accepted. Maybe Harold would have gone back to being an accountant. No, that would never happen. Harold was too sure of his writing by this time in his life. Harold Robbins believed in his work and he always had a purpose.

CHAPTER TWENTY-ONE

The Carpetbaggers was the first big money I made. Money gave me a lot of freedom, but no matter how much you make, there's always somebody chasing your ass for more."

"Do you think you'll ever run out of ideas to write about?" I asked.

"I've always got six books in my head all the time," he said. "I won't live long enough to write all of them. Every day the world changes and there's a new idea waiting to be seen."

I would discover later that as he wrote each new book Harold had something to say that he felt was important. This was his true motivation, not only money. But saying that he only wrote for money was always the mask to keep people away from his real feelings. Many times even the people closest to him didn't realize this fact.

"I choose the subjects I write about because I want to know more," Harold said one afternoon. "I'm always curious about how each person's life finds its way, or how the world of movies came to be, or television, how moguls live day to day, their idiosyncrasies.

John Kluge, who is one of the world's richest men, has been to my house for dinner many times, and he once stood on his head on the coffee table after dinner. I don't know why the hell he did it. But it's an inside look that everyone is curious about. I've met Donald Trump; he's a kid who got lucky with his father's money, and someday he'll be last year's mogul. Kirk Kerkorian, Merv Griffin, all moguls, they are today's rock stars. And people will always want an inside look."

When I read Harold's books during the year I realized he was usually ahead of his time, a visionary.

- In *The Betsy*, long before Japanese automobiles became mainstream cars in America Harold wrote about it.
- In *The Pirate*, long before America realized the many conflicts the Mideast would bring to the United States, and the rise of terrorism and zealots Harold wrote about it.
- In *Spellbinder*, before the scandals of Jim Bakker and Jimmy Swaggart were brought to light, Harold wrote about the corruption within their faltering dynasties.
- In *Memories of Another Day* people recognized the horrors and struggles in the coal mines of Appalachia. Harold showed how the unions became strong enough to protect the voiceless workers in those mines.
- Many years ago Harold began writing about moguls as rock stars of the business world in *The Carpetbaggers*, *The Inheritors*, *Dreams Die First*, and *Descent from Xanadu*. Today moguls have hit television shows and movies and memoirs portray their lives. Harold made us look at them beyond the suits.
- *Descent from Xanadu*, written in the early eighties, depicted the obsession with physical youth and stopping the progression of age. Today it has become a multi-billion-dollar industry.

Harold Robbins gave his reader a familiarity with the world of the rich and famous. His goal was to erase the page and talk with his readers and tell them of the people he had known, met, and dealt with in his life. He had an intensity in his writing that helped the reader experience between the lines.

CHAPTER TWENTY-TWO

e have to go to the doctor this afternoon. Dr. Ablon wants to get a picture taken of my head. Tell Rick to take out the Corniche and put the top down."

When we arrived at Dr. Ablon's office, we went past his usual entrance and halfway down the hall to an unmarked door and knocked. A girl with a white jacket answered.

"Harold, it's so good to see you!" She smiled, hugging him.

He patted her ass and looked at her and grinned. "You've got a great smile, Rocio!" he said, and continued to pat her ass.

"Harold, you've got great hands," she kidded, and extended her derriere for another pat.

Other men would sometimes watch Harold patting a woman's derriere or talking about her tits or other body parts and be amazed that he could get by with it without being slapped. What they failed to realize was that Harold loved women not only for those voluptuous body parts but for the total female, inside and out. He loved all women from society jet-setters to working girls, short, tall, skinny, fat, or in between.

> An unidentified employee of Madame Claud's stable of escorts in France commented in an interview once about Harold Robbins: "Monseiur Robbins' was always our favorite yacht to visit. He always served the finest champagne and caviar. During the Cannes Film Festival, several of us would be invited by a guest attending a party on his boat the *Gracara* and he was always very adorable and sex-ee. He once hired three of Claud's girls to entertain the author Irving Wallace while having lunch on the yacht. However, Mme. Wallace became very angry when we greeted them as they came onto the yacht topless. Unfortunately, they did not stay for lunch."

It became evident that Harold was a popular patient when the other nurses and receptionist fluttered around him. It was the first time I had been in a doctor's office when it seemed more like a party than a dreaded appointment.

Dr. Ablon, a tall, slender, bald-headed man who resembled Fred Astaire, came out of his office and into the hallway wearing his white doctor's coat. He and Harold exchanged greetings and they invited me to come back to the examining room with them.

I wondered if it would be safe.

"Want me to take my shirt off?" Harold asked.

Ablon nodded while looking at his clipboard notes.

"Why don't you ask her to take her shirt off? Check out her heart?" Harold said, looking at me and laughing.

"I don't know her as well as you, Harold," Dr. Ablon answered, and winked at me.

"Lucky doctors, all they have to do is make a simple request and women take their clothes off!" Harold continued talking as Dr. Ablon tried to listen to his heartbeat.

The doctor looked up at Harold and smiled. He pulled the stethoscope out of his ears. "You're going to have to stop talking and let me listen."

Harold then held his breath.

Dr. Ablon laughed and shook his head. He gave up trying to listen to the heartbeat. "No heartbeat, Harold."

"I must be dead!" Harold said, laughing.

"I haven't seen you in this good of a mood since we were in France last summer," Dr. Ablon said.

"That's because I'm doing good. Feeling good."

Dr. Ablon shook his head and patted Harold's knee. "I know you are going to be able to write. We need those bestsellers to keep coming."

"I love all of you doctors. 'I know you can do it!'" Harold imitated him. "That's why I think you're all full of shit!" He laughed.

Dr. Ablon laughed with him. "I guess we are."

The two men were very good friends. They chatted about the medications Harold was taking; a nurse came in and took blood tests. All the time, Harold was mugging for my benefit.

"I got some steaks from Peter Luger's yesterday; you want to come over for dinner tonight?" Harold asked Dr. Ablon after the blood tests were taken.

"They sent you steaks from New York?"

"Federal Express. Four beautiful porterhouses!"

"Of course I'll be over," Dr. Ablon said enthusiastically. "I wouldn't pass up that invitation."

"C'mon, Ed, you never pass up any invitation when it comes to food!" Harold said, kidding him.

Peter Luger's was a famous steak house in New York where Harold had been a patron for many years. It was located in Brooklyn and is, to this day, one of the best steak houses in the world.

Harold carried Peter Luger Steak House cards in his wallet,

with his account number scribbled on each card. He gave these to friends that were traveling to New York and told them to give the card to whoever waited on them. This card signaled the waiter that the meal was to be charged to Mr. Robbins's account.

Dr. Ablon also was very excited about the fact that Harold was going to cook. Harold had a great reputation for grilling steaks.

"Universal Catscan on Beverly is waiting for you. They'll do a quick scan and I'll tell you the results tonight."

Harold paused to light a cigarette as we were leaving.

"Would you stop that smoking?" Dr. Ablon asked.

"I know. I should," Harold said, walking down the hallway toward the elevator.

Chapter Twenty-Three

𝒜 lot of people can't handle CAT scans," Harold said as we were driving to our next stop. "They get crazy, some kind of anxiety. It doesn't bother me. Goddamn, this head thing is crazy! I was once on an airplane with my publicist, Gene; we're going across the country doing a publicity junket for *The Adventurers*, the movie. Gene had an anxiety attack and we had to turn the plane around and go back to LAX, let him off, and then take off again."

Harold laughed hysterically remembering that moment. I laughed with him. He was very fond of Gene Schwam, his publicist, who had engineered many of the tremendous successes that Harold had experienced.

"I think your CAT scan is going to be good. A picture of the inside of your head. All those ideas flying around," I said, laughing. "There's nothing wrong with your head, Harold." I knew that to be true. All I could see was how smart he was, and wise.

"You think so?" he said. "I can't tell—it pisses me off that the words come out wrong." In frustration, he popped the cigarette lighter in, waited for a few seconds until it popped out, and lit his cigarette.

"Ablon wants you to stop smoking."

"Fuck him," he said, and puffed away.

I sat in the waiting room reading a magazine while Harold was inserted into the CAT scan tube for his brain scan. He never seemed to mind all the medical procedures that he had to go through. In fact, he was fascinated by them. He asked questions of the technicians and was learning during each procedure. By now, I knew everything Harold experienced would end up in a book.

I opened up one of the local Beverly Hills newspapers. There was a comment in one of the gossip columns about Harold writing his next bestseller, "*Descent from Xanadu* . . . about a man who wants to live forever . . . Harold Robbins is the man to do it," claimed the columnist. "He's proven it in his own life!"

I showed Harold the column when he came out to the waiting room.

"Bullshit," he said, and we left.

"*Y*ou want to go to lunch?" he asked as we drove back toward the house.

"Sure," I said. "Tell me where?"

He turned on the portable phone that was in a briefcase in the backseat of the Rolls-Royce. "I'll use this asshole phone. They just installed it about a month ago and I haven't even used it." He dialed the number. "Hi, this is Mr. Robbins. Is this Riff?" He waited a few seconds. "Riff, I'm coming over for lunch; you got a place for two of us?" He waited. "I can barely hear you; these fuckin' car phones aren't worth shit!" He laughed. "We're on our way." He turned to me. "The Polo."

The valets at the entrance of the Beverly Hills Hotel started positioning themselves as usual when we turned into the long winding driveway. They all recognized the car and were happy to see him, like an old friend. They knew me now since we came here for lunch often.

Everyone spoke to Harold and me as we walked through the lobby of the hotel. Hotel employees recognized and greeted him. Jack Valenti and Red Buttons passed us. They both stopped and chatted. When we reached the Polo Lounge, the maître d', Riff, seated us at Booth 1. Booths 1, 2, and 3 were prestigious spots in the Polo Lounge, positioned across from the entrance.

"I used to live here in Bungalow Number Three. Then Grace wanted a house. Jesus, it's breakin' my fucking back." He looked off into the distance. "I wish I still lived here; I hate that fuckin' house."

"It's a beautiful home, really magnificent."

"It's a fuckin' museum; no one can live in a museum!" He looked down. "I was in France while it was being built. Paul kept calling me every few hours screaming that I was going to be bankrupt by the time it was finished and he was right!"

A short, middle-aged waiter with graying hair walked up to the table. It was the same waiter every day. He had been waiting on Harold for years and knew his likes and dislikes. Service was and still is what makes the Polo Lounge famous.

"The usual, Mr. Robbins? Aquavit," the waiter said, and turned to me.

"And a 'Virgin' Mary for the lady; she's not a drinker!"

The drinks arrived and Harold ordered his all-time favorite. "Lox and onion omelet, and the McCarthy for her."

After the waiter left the table there was a long silence as Harold looked around the room and lit another cigarette. At these moments it could appear that he was angry. He squinted and became aloof. I would learn that at such times he was composing what he was going to say and how to say it. Harold used words carefully, a trait that I respected, but I was surprised at his request.

"I want you to move into the apartment above the garage. You can live there rent free," he said as he stirred his drink.

"That's a tempting offer. It's expensive in LA. I was unemployed for six months and I'm still playing catch-up."

"That's all we ever do." He smiled.

Now I was the one who needed to compose my answer. I had been warned by those who knew him that if I was asked to move in I should say no. "Well, I have two cats and that might not work out with your dogs," I said. I didn't want to offend him and tell him that I didn't want to risk a move into his house. I liked working for him and I wanted to stay independent if I could.

"Bring the kitties with you." He smiled, cocked his head, and got that mischievous look in his eyes. "I'll have three new pussies in the house!"

I laughed, knowing his meaning, and shook my head. "You'd like a harem, wouldn't you?"

"My favorite subject—pussy," he said, smiling.

"You're a married man. Why don't you talk about that with your wife?" I said, teasing him.

"I've already told you the three most boring things in the world, home cooking, home fucking, and Dallas, Texas." He grinned cockily.

"Have you ever been to Dallas, Texas?" I asked, trying to deflect the conversation.

"How do you think I know it's so boring?"

Harold was an exercise of implications, propositions, and innuendos. He always kept me on my toes.

He looked at me innocently. "When I start writing, I will need you there," he said. "I never know if I will work during the day or night."

That was another issue—I had been told if I moved in I would be accessible twenty-four hours a day. Did I want that? I wasn't sure.

I knew I would love being around Harold anytime and anywhere, but what about Grace?

And if I moved in would that just take me one step closer to having an affair with Harold? He was very hard to resist, especially since he was part of an open marriage. This fact had been stated in many interviews by both him and Grace. I already knew Harold was interested in me beyond being his assistant. And then I heard myself saying, "Okay, when you start writing, maybe then. . . ." I couldn't say a definite no and I couldn't commit to yes and all of the implications.

"There's even a kitchen in that apartment," he said. "The pussies won't bother the dogs; they can stay upstairs in the apartment."

I laughed. "I am not a cook. I could only use the kitchen to make coffee; that's about the extent of my cooking," I said.

"That's why I have a cook; I don't know any woman who cooks anymore," he said. "But I'm a great cook. You'll see tonight."

We left my moving in a possibility.

The waiter came to the table with our orders. He tossed the McCarthy salad with great flair and moved everything, again artistically, on the table, water glasses, silverware, bread baskets, and made a beautiful presentation. Harold's meal was brought immediately, as the salad was being placed in front of me. It was symmetry, as though he were acting out a scene in a movie. But at the Beverly Hills Hotel everyone working there was professional and expert at what they did.

"How'd you stay out of drinking and smoking?" Harold asked after we had finished our lunch.

I nodded my head. "I used to, but I had a party one night that lasted until four or five in the morning and I didn't even know the people sitting in my living room at the party. They were complete strangers, my cat had been thrown into the Jacuzzi and survived but was hiding out after that, the ashtrays were filled with cigarette butts, my mirrored coffee table had lines of cocaine still on it, and it scared me. I didn't want to live like that, so I threw everyone out,

poured all the alcohol down the drain, tossed out a carton of cigarettes, and made a decision to change my life."

"What about the cocaine?"

I laughed. "There was none left."

"You're tough," he said, looking at me with a glint of admiration
in his eyes. "I've got no character, no discipline." He smiled as he lit
a cigarette after finishing his meal. "I've tried to quit smoking, but
I can't."

"It's not easy," I said.

He nodded at some people standing at the door of the Polo
Lounge. Martin Landau walked over to our table and sat down
with us.

CHAPTER TWENTY-FOUR

On our way out of the Polo Lounge, Harold handed Riff, the maître d', two twenty-dollar bills. "I need fives and tens," Harold said as he signed the check to his charge account at the hotel and noted a 20 percent tip on the bill.

Riff returned the change. Harold handed him a ten and stopped by the concierge desk and left a ten with Nick. As we reached the car, there were four valets. Harold passed out a five-dollar bill to each of them.

When we arrived home, a messenger had hand-delivered another bill from Dr. Cooper. For his forty days of working with Harold his bill was forty thousand dollars. I handed it to Harold after looking at the bill. He glanced at it.

"We'll pay for it out of the Special 'A' account," he said, and handed the bill back to me. "Come upstairs and I'll write the check." He glanced over his shoulder on the way up the stairs to the family room. "I hope I can still write a book; otherwise, I'll ask for a refund!" He laughed at his joke.

Why didn't he blink at the cost? How could he make a joke about a forty-thousand-dollar doctor bill? This must be the difference between being rich and poor; the numbers don't make you sweat. In later years I would watch Harold write out much larger check amounts and he was always fearless, even if he knew he would not have any money left after writing a big check. Money was a different commodity to him, a tool used to have fun and get things done. He had a great view of life because he rarely took it seriously. He loved to live his "bigger than life lifestyle." You can't worry and be bigger than life at the same time.

This was a very different world that I was living in and it was very seductive. Every day was a new adventure and every night was spent thinking about Harold. There were times when he would call me at midnight.

"What are you doing?" he said on the first night he called.

"I'm sleeping," I said groggily. "What are you doing?"

"Watching television."

"You can't sleep?"

"I never sleep all night. I always wake up and watch television."

"'S that why you take a nap after lunch?"

"Probably. How are your pussies?"

I started laughing. "I knew that's why you called!"

He laughed. "I'll have to meet them sometime," he said.

We chatted for a few more minutes.

When I hung up the phone I thought about how much I loved this world of Harold Robbins that I was living in. I could see the pictures he had shown me of Times Square in New York with the caption on a huge billboard "The World of Harold Robbins" and the book covers below the caption. Was this world I had entered into real? I fell asleep asking why he was making me a part of his world. What role would I play in his life?

CHAPTER TWENTY-FIVE

*H*arold was holding the cover for his upcoming novel, *Spell-binder*, as he held the phone to his ear and listened, casually fanning the cover back and forth. "Cocksuckers!" he grumbled after hanging up the phone. "That was Paul. He called to tell me they banned *Spellbinder* in the South at some of the bookstores." He shook his head. "That's not right." He stopped and lit a cigarette and looked over at me. "This is the book I finished two weeks before Caryn's wedding." He thought for a moment. "The day my head blew up. Paul said some of the sellers in Georgia and Louisiana canceled delivery. It's being shipped in a couple of weeks. He said not to worry; it's still on the *Times* list."

"Why did they cancel?" I asked.

"They think the pay TV preachers are sacred ground! Bullshit! It's big business and they feed off poor people."

"Is that what the book is about?"

He walked over and picked up the manuscript. "I'll read you the first page."

"'"Preacher!" The hoarsely whispered shout hung heavily in the shadowed humid jungle air. There was a rustle in the underbrush that sent the birds abruptly shrieking into the trees, then silence. Preacher's voice was low and calm. "Where are you?"

"'"Over here. In the hole. Hurry, Preacher. I'm hurt real bad."

"'A moment later, Preacher's head and shoulders appeared over the edge of the small crater. He peered down at the wounded black soldier and nodded silently. He elbowed himself forward and rumbled clumsily into the crater, rolled over and sat up, the white band with the red cross on his arm barely visible for the mud covering it. He slipped the medical pack from his shoulders and placed it on the ground beside him. "Where are you hit, Washington?" he asked without looking up from the pack he was opening.

"'The soldier grabbed at his arm. "I'm gonna die, Preacher," he said in a frightened voice. "Will you hear my confession?"

"'"You crazy, Joe?" Preacher looked at him. "You're not Catholic, I'm no priest."'"

Harold laid down the page and looked up at me.

"Congratulations," I said.

He looked at me a little quizzically. "Yeah, about the book?"

"No, you read the page almost perfectly without talking into the phone," I answered.

He looked at me and smiled. "Well, what the hell, I'm fed up with that taping shit."

"It's a big moment, Harold."

"Spellbinder is about this guy who went to Vietnam and decides he wants to be a preacher. After he gets out of Vietnam he starts his own religion and he starts out really wanting to help people, but he also wants to make a lot of money, and he wants to get a lot of pussy." He smiled at me. "My kind of man, honey."

I smiled back and he continued telling his story.

"He preaches about God and love and peace and later gets involved with a big oil 'asshole' from Texas and Preacher realizes that all his motives to help others are being corrupted by the profit and loss sheet under the control of this mogul. The oil guy wants nothing but money and they've all lost sight of the man he preaches about, Jesus Christ. Preacher tries to change things, but the money is too powerful."

I nodded. "You know Oklahoma has a very wealthy TV preacher, Oral Roberts. He's considered off-the-wall by some and a healer by others. He has a university and seems to be very prosperous. I met his son one day when I was visiting a friend at one of the stores here in Beverly Hills. He was dripping with diamonds."

"I know; some of these TV preachers fleece the public and use it for themselves. They think they are the chosen ones; they ought to know the Jews have that title. Everybody wants to claim their superiority; no one wants to practice what Christ taught. Makes them all hypocrites.

"I was in Tulsa and I was at Bakker's and Falwell's. Read the book; you'll like it," he said. "If you want to read the manuscript it's here in the office," he said, opening the door to the credenza and pointing it out.

I couldn't wait to read the manuscript. I had never read an original manuscript from a novelist, and this would be a bestseller. All of Harold Robbins's novels were bestsellers. "I will," I answered. "Thanks."

"The cancellation bullshit, it's good publicity," Harold said, referring back to the current crisis. "This is what happens to a lot of my books. When I won the case in Philadelphia after my first book, *Never Love a Stranger*, was banned, Alfred Knopf thought it would kill the sales, but it didn't. You know what the judge said when they lifted the ban?"

I shook my head.

" 'I would rather my daughter learn about sex from the pages of a Harold Robbins novel than behind a barn door.' I've always felt the First Amendment, Freedom of Speech, has to be protected at all costs. It's what the country is built on."

"Did you think any of the preachers you researched were sincere?" I asked. I had seen my father give money to the very people

Harold was talking about. I was stunned the first time I saw my father donate to the PTL Club on television. I asked him once why he sent Jim Bakker money. He said it made him feel good. At the time, I wondered if any of that money went to "good causes." In light of what happened several years after this conversation I questioned any validity of television preachers.

"The only one that's real is Billy Graham. He's honest, always has been," Harold answered. "I don't agree with him, but his heart is in it."

*H*arold always looked at life in a unique and honest way. He searched below the surface, tearing off the shroud of secrecy that bound many professions, and he wrote about it and exposed the hypocrisy without judgment.

Spellbinder gave us his observation: "When I create any character I'm saying 'look, these people are real. They are no different from you and me.' Don't hold people up to be gods, they make the same choices that real flesh and blood people make. I show the things they do behind closed doors and sometimes it's greed, power, anger, but sometimes it's sacrifice and love. The point is see them as human, don't hold them in idolatry. Jesus was human and supposedly he had a divine mission. Did he make mistakes? He ended up on a cross."

When I listened to Harold I always felt I was peeking behind the curtains of world situations when he discussed the power people he had known, the events he had seen. His observations were always unique. Now I was hearing the story behind the story and talking to the source of those books. He spoke with an intimate knowledge of his characters. He knew them well and each of them was a part of him.

He continued his discussion of *Spellbinder:* "I went to listen to Jerry Falwell, the biggest hypocrite of them all. I had been told that he was going to speak about the horrible, nasty fiction books published in today's society. I went and sat in the audience and he bad-mouthed what was being published about sex, immorality, or what he judged to be immoral. He mentioned a couple of my titles and after his sermon I went up and introduced myself to him. He didn't make the connection of me being the one who wrote the books that he had just bad-mouthed! He doesn't know what he's really talking about; he's just putting out bullshit and trying to collect money. They make millions from people who don't have money to give and those people think they're buying a ticket to heaven and all they're doing is lining these preachers' pockets with money.

"The Catholics have done it for years. You know the Vatican has more money than any of them. But none of them really follow the teachings of Jesus Christ. He was all about love and truth. The churches have all failed in following him."

Harold could quote passages from the Torah, the Koran, and the Bible. He had studied all of the holy books to research *Spellbinder.*

"I don't believe in God, but I think Jesus Christ was a great man," he said.

"You have really changed the way people think about the world, haven't you? You started the sexual revolution."

"I really didn't change anything; sex, drugs, power have always been a part of our world. I told you about delivering cocaine to Cole Porter when I was a kid. People have taken drugs throughout time, opium, heroin, cocaine. When I was a kid on the streets of Hell's Kitchen I used to go to the opium dens and lay down on one of the beds and dream dreams." He smiled wistfully, remembering his past. "You know, there used to be opium dens right on the street.

"Things that I talk about in my books are nothing new. Men have had mistresses throughout time; women have had gigolos. People have had rough sex, good sex, gay sex. Fucking is a part of life." He looked at me with a twinkle in his eye. "I could use a little sex. What kind of sex would you like?"

I shook my head. I wasn't going to go there with him. I always kept his reputation in mind, but this rascal image also made him lovable. One minute he was a scholar, wise and powerful; the next minute he was propositioning me. He was always waiting to see what he could get you to do or think or feel. He already knew my feelings.

I laughed and shook my head. "You are a man of many faces, Harold. And you've always got a great line to deliver."

He slipped back into a more serious note. "I'm not the first one to write about all these things. People were writing sexy books thousands of years before I came around. What about the Holy Bible, Song of Solomon? Ovid wrote about sex in his time, Plato in some of his discourses. Chaucer, Boccaccio, Henry Miller, all down the list they were writing about sex because sex is an important part of people. In the Victorian era they were sweeping it under the rug; books were being written at that time and hidden. They are being revived today. When I started writing books, everyone said you can't use words like 'cunt,' 'cock,' 'pussy.' I wasn't trying to change the world or even shock people when I used these words. These words were used in everyday life in the world around me. It was honest. People in the 1930s and '40s didn't talk about sex; it was hidden, suppressed, and screwed up a lot of people. It didn't mean they weren't fucking like crazy!" He laughed and watched again to see my reaction.

I listened to what he said without shock, because what he was saying was true. It was honest. He wasn't afraid to break the rules, go against the status quo of the times.

"Why did you get interested in the pay-TV preachers?"

"I saw all the fuckin' money they were taking in. We don't realize how desperately people are searching for answers. The preachers play on their fears and people send money to pacify their fears.

"When I wake up in the middle of the night I always turn on the television, so with the cable now I started flipping through all of the channels and watching these guys Falwell, Swaggart, Bakker, Graham. They were saving 'souls' by telephone and cash donations and I started doing research and it turned out to be millions of dollars and it became big business. Bakker is building a resort on his PTL donations. It is all crazy. It is big business. Remember that movie with Burt Lancaster *Elmer Gantry.* It was true then as well as now. Great movie."

"I saw some photos in your office that had Jim Bakker on a stage speaking; did you go there?"

"Yeah, I went with my girlfriend, Linda." He laughed again. "She took those pictures."

"Is she your photographer, too?" I asked, since I had already met his photographer in a photograph on the first day of my employment.

"No, that was Ini. This one is Linda. She lives in New York; she does research for me."

I grinned at him. "You're very busy with all of your girlfriends."

He grinned back at me and rolled his eyes playfully. "Yeah, I love girls!"

Harold wasn't like other men I had known who wanted to "play around" outside their marriage. Those men were willing to cheat as long as they didn't get caught. But Harold wasn't concerned with getting caught; he was open.

The telephone intercom interrupted our conversation: "Dr. Cooper is on the way upstairs," Rick said.

A moment later, Dr. Cooper walked into the study. "How you doing, Robbins?" he said, sitting down on the queen-size bed. "I'll tell you something, you are working hard and you're making progress. I listened to those tapes yesterday that you gave me and I think the only thing I have to correct now is her Oklahoma accent!" he said, pointing at me and laughing.

"It's simple, Cooper. I'm fighting for my life. It limits my choices," Harold said, looking at him seriously. "And it's costing me plenty."

Dr. Cooper shrugged. "I'm the best in the business, Robbins."

"Yeah, and I do all the work! And wait till you hear how I was reading today." He looked over at me proudly. "Tell him."

After I told Dr. Cooper how Harold had read the page perfectly with no phone and no tape recorder, the doctor smiled and shook his head.

"Well, I guess I am no longer needed." He looked up and I could see he was very proud of Harold's hard work. "Give me one more hour on tape, Robbins, and you're finished."

Chapter Twenty-Six

*D*uring the rest of the week Harold made his final tape. He read from *The Pirate*.

To me, his speech pattern had returned to normal. I had heard many of the interviews he had done on tape before his aphasia, and there was a slight pause at times in his normal speech pattern. When he read that day you could almost put the before and after tapes side by side and there wouldn't be any noticeable differences.

Harold read eloquently and passionately on this final tape, remembering the original moment when those words were put on the page.

"'A thoughtful expression came into the old man's eyes. He seemed lost for a moment in memory, then his eyes cleared. "It may sound strange to you but in an old man's bones there is a feeling that we may find the answer in Al Fay. The winds that blow across the desert no longer originate in the East—they come from the West. The Arab sheiks have awakened to the power of their wealth. That will be the real end of Russian influence. Communism has no answer for them. And control of the Middle East is only the *beginning. If they invest their wealth wisely they may be able to soon control the world without ever firing a shot."*

" 'He looked around the silent table. "I hate to disillusion you, gentlemen, but the fact is that we are no longer important to Islam except to their pride. They must achieve some victory no matter how minor just to regain face. The big thrust will come after the battle is over."

" 'He turned to the Americans. "We will need your help. For now. Later, you will need ours."

" 'Harris was polite but disdainful. "What makes you think that?"

" ' "Because we, more than anyone in the world, understand them," the old man said, his face settling into grim hawklike lines. "And because you, not we, are the real target." ' "

As he read, I considered what he was saying. The sheiks had no importance to Islam; the money, the wealth, the power of their day was passing by and another power was emerging. I had not realized this the first time I read his book or the second. I had a feeling that he had read this passage for a reason. Could this scene be his reason for writing the book? The Arab world was changing. America thought the sheiks were in control, but they were not. The power structure was changing. At that time, saying this was as radical as saying to the Vatican that the Pope no longer needed Christianity for his power.

"I wrote this book because all they do is fight over there. The Jews and the Arabs will never accept one another, but they are all one people. My Arab friend that I took as the character of Badyr was the finance minister under the King in Saudi Arabia. He was introduced to me by Adnan Khashoggi.

"He was only about thirty years old and came to Los Angeles to have a complete physical done by American doctors at UCLA Medical Center. He found out he had stomach cancer. He was staying here at my house." Harold shook his head sadly. "He only lived about a year after they diagnosed him.

"*The Pirate* was banned in the Arab countries. There was a lawsuit from Khashoggi's wife, trying to stop the publication in England. She thought she was the female character." He laughed. "Egos; they've all got 'em.

"Paul told them I used my own wife as the female character! She's probably fucked more Arabs than Johanna in the book. Anyway, they went to court in London. It created a lot of publicity in all the newspapers.

"*The Pirate* was big news around Cannes during the film festival. That's when Joe Lisbona wanted to produce the movie. We had gone to see *They Shoot Horses, Don't They?* It was a big winner that year. Have you ever seen that film?" he turned and asked me.

"It's the one with Jane Fonda?" I asked.

"Yeah. Gig Young won an Oscar for his performance. Hell of a movie. Joe lined up Alain Delon for *The Pirate*. Delon wanted to co-produce the picture at a fifty-fifty split and on a fifteen-million-dollar budget. Delon was bringing most of the money to produce the film from Japan. I was staying at the George V Hotel, and Delon and Joe came over to have breakfast and we worked out this deal. But then it got all fucked up and never happened."

Harold motioned for me to come downstairs with him. He walked over to the closet in the foyer and opened the door. He pulled out a sword with tassels hanging from the handle. He took the sword out of the sheath. "See that printing?" he asked, pointing at the Arabic script across the dull side of the sword.

I looked at the Arabic letters on the blade of the sword. "Yes."

"It says: 'Kill all the Jews.' It was a gift from Badyr," he said, replacing the sword and laughing. "They'll end up killing themselves off. That's what I was trying to say in the book. They are all the same. Badyr, in the book, was a Jew raised as an Arab. They learn to hate one another; it's taught. No matter how much we hate, it will never change the fact that we're all human beings. It even says it in your 'shiksa' Bible, 'neither Jew, nor Greek . . . nor rich, nor poor . . .' But nobody gets it; we all just keep fighting and killing one another.

One day the sheiks will be like prehistoric dinosaurs, extinct, but that's what happens in societies. Someday we will all be dinosaurs."

"Do you think they'll ever stop fighting in the Middle East?" I asked.

"What would they do if they couldn't fight?" He smiled. "It's a way of life."

After we finished working that evening we went to Lawry's for dinner. As we were taken to our table, a man at one of the nearby tables motioned to Harold. I looked up and I saw the most beautiful blue eyes I had ever seen. Immediately I recognized Rock Hudson, a screen idol from the fifties, sixties, and seventies. Starring in over twenty blockbuster films, including my favorite, *Giant* with Elizabeth Taylor and James Dean, *Pillow Talk, Come September, Magnificent Obsession*, along with a leading role in the television series *Dynasty*.

I felt like a teenage groupie when Harold introduced me to this screen star idol. He was absolutely the most handsome man I had ever seen. When he extended his hand to me he radiated warmth. Harold chatted with the group of men sitting at the table and soon we moved on to our table.

"I met Rock and Tony Curtis when they first came to town. They both changed their names at the studio," Harold said once we had sat down and ordered our cuts of prime beef.

"It's hard to believe he's even more handsome in person," I said, still thinking about those dazzling blue eyes. "When I was about ten years old, my first boyfriend took me to see *Pillow Talk*. It was very romantic."

I could see that Harold was hardly listening to my conversation. He was thinking about something else. I was devastated when he told me.

"I'm going to France next week," he said.

"Why?" I asked. I could hear the disappointment in my voice and so could he.

"I can't live with the bullshit that goes on at the house. I need to rest and Grace wants to have her singing soirees. I have to start working again after the summer is over. I wanted to stay here and have her go over to France, but she won't leave until later."

Thoughts were racing through my mind. My job was over and I felt my stomach turning. "Well, I really appreciate the time I've been with you, Harold. I'll miss our morning coffee together." I was trying to be gracious, but I felt I was just babbling. I was sure he could hear my disappointment.

"What are you talking about?" He looked at me irritably. "You're still with me. Grace and Adréana will come over to France in a couple of months and I'll need you when I come back in the fall," he said. His expression had changed and now he was looking at me like the cat that swallowed the canary! He knew I would think that my job was over.

"You really thought I'd just leave you out in the cold?" he said.

"Well, that's what it sounded like," I said.

"Honey, that's not going to happen," he said. "But I do think you should move into the apartment."

"What will I do, once you're gone?"

"Pay the bills, do whatever the fuck you want. You'll have to answer the phone for Grace for a month and she'll probably ask you to RSVP her parties. She's a pain in the ass. But other than that you can lay by the pool all summer."

"Harold, I really appreciate the offer, but I'm not a social secretary."

He looked at me. "You won't be working for Grace; you're working for me and answering the phone for me. Just try to keep the fucking house from falling apart." He looked at me with pleading eyes! "I'll talk to you every day. If you don't like something, just tell me and I'll straighten it out."

"But why would you want to pay me just to be at your house?"

"Honey, I once paid a secretary for nine months before she ever did a bit of work for me. She lived in London and when the time was right I brought her over to Los Angeles; she was with me for a long time." He laughed. "It's only money."

I would be moving into the apartment above the garage.

CHAPTER TWENTY-SEVEN

hen are you moving in?" Harold asked the morning before he left for France.

"After Grace and Adréana leave," I answered.

"Give me an expense report and I'll pay for whatever it costs to move."

"I brought all of my furniture out to LA when I moved," I said. "It was the biggest mistake I made. This will be the third time I've moved in six months. I'm selling all of my furniture that isn't worth sending back to Oklahoma."

"You're a genius!" He smiled with pride. "You don't need all that shit! I'll make sure you have everything you need. Look at the furniture upstairs and if you want anything go out and buy it. I'll pay for it."

"Promises, promises," I said, kidding him. "I'll just bring me and my babies, Caio and Judge."

"Kinky will love those pussies!" Harold said. "Gypsy will be calm about it."

Kinky was Harold's white Pekingese . . . with huge black eyes and black nose. Gypsy was his gray and white shih tzu that he adored. Kinky and Gypsy flew the Concorde to Paris twelve times. They dined on their own Lawry's Prime Rib English Cut order (takeout) and celebrated Harold and my first New Year's Eve together in a private room at Verita's La Cantina, sitting between us, Kinky wearing a black bow tie and Gypsy donning a dazzling tiara. They were the hit of the party.

I was sitting in Harold's clothes closet cross-legged writing out checks as he gave me instructions. He was leaving the next morning to fly to New York, where he would meet his girlfriend, Linda, and the next day he and Linda would leave for France and arrive in Nice and his staff in Le Cannet would meet them and drive them to Le Cannet, above Cannes.

"Call Viviana up here," he said.

Viviana was the housekeeper. I went to the family room and called for Viviana on the telephone intercom.

Harold handed her items that he wanted to pack. He had taught her how to pack his clothing. It was a very meticulously neat process and she was the only one he allowed to pack for him. He wrote down the things he wanted from the kitchen.

1. Taster's Choice Instant Coffee (Red label) Yuban coffee (3 cans)
2. Pepto-Bismol (2 bottles)
3. Toilet Paper (Charmin)

He looked up at me after he wrote "Toilet Paper." "The French toilet paper scratches my ass!" He laughed.

Harold looked at each one of the checks I had written to pay the bills in between picking out items to take to France. He signed the bottom of each check.

"I like the way you sign your name," I said as I watched him.

He took a piece of paper and wrote out "Frankie Kane," then "Harold Rubin" and "Harold Robbins." Each with equal importance.

"Are those your aliases?" I asked, making a joke.

"Sort of; all of those were my names. I was born in 1916, they're not sure of the day, but I think it was May 21, and I've had three names."

"What's your favorite?" I said, playing along with him.

"Harold heir to the Tsar of Russia!"

I shrugged and laughed. "It won't fit on the cover of your next book."

We both laughed.

"Honey, always remember the name is nothing. It's what you have to say that's important."

As Viviana went through his luggage she found an old audiotape stuck in the side pocket. He popped it into a portable audiotape player and pressed the button.

"The name is Robbins. Harold Robbins. I write books, today kind of books, books about the world in which I live. I write 'dirty books' and 'clean books' and books about good people and bad people. Most of all I write about the things I see, the things I hear, the things I feel. A writer can't avoid putting himself into his books; there are many things in some of the books that I've written that are peculiarly about me.

"Harold Robbins is almost a trade name to me. It was a name that was given to me. When I walk through the airports and see my books on the rack, the name sometimes feels far away, like a trade name, so I detach from that book because it's last year's book and I'm already on to next year's book. In *Never Love a Stranger* I wrote about the beginning of my life. In *A Stone for Danny Fisher* part of it was about the family that adopted me, but mostly in my books are the way I feel and the way I see. If you want to know me, read my books."

The interviewer asked about how Harold came up with his ideas.

"I have this editor in my head. I just listen and write. They say that's 'genius,' but I don't know how to write! I can only write about the world around me. I look at the television, the news, read other books, read the newspapers. Listen to the world around me, and I see it differently and that comes out on the page."

The tape ended, "I hope to hell that Harold Robbins can still write a book."

There was a certain ritual once Harold arrived in New York that always took place. Paul paid for the limo to meet him at JFK and Harold took great delight in this. He and Paul always played games about who paid for what and whether Paul would bill the publisher for an expense.

Once Harold was in the limo, they went directly to the Four Seasons restaurant. Paul Gitlin represented the Four Seasons Restaurant Cookbooks and had lunch there every day. It was one of the most prestigious restaurants in New York at the time, frequented by publishing moguls, authors, and celebrities from all walks of life.

Paul and Harold were seated at Paul's regular table in the Pool Room lined up next to the marble fountain the length of a lap pool in the center of the room. Each room in the restaurant had an individual pecking order.

When the staff noticed their arrival at the restaurant they would bring the Harold Robbins caviar salad. This salad had been named for Harold in April of 1966 when the *Adventurers* book party of over one hundred guests was held at the Four Seasons. When a reporter from the *New York Post* asked him about the salad, Harold said it was his own concoction, with the main ingredient being green—money. The ingredients were fresh green butter lettuce, four ounces of beluga caviar, olive oil, and lemon (freshly squeezed over the salad). If the item was on the menu, it would be priced at over five hundred dollars. Two chilled glasses were filled with ice-cold Stolichnaya.

Later, the main course was ordered. A traditional cheeseburger rare, *pommes frites*, and Chocolate Velvet cake for dessert, topped with whipped cream and a scoop of chocolate ice cream.

Paul's main course would consist of crab cakes and more Scotch or vodka on the rocks.

Harold would smoke a pack of Lucky Strikes between courses while he and Paul chatted about business, finances, and the world of Harold Robbins.

As the afternoon wore on, there were orders of Glenmorangie on the rocks. Harold had discovered this Scotch while doing research for *The Inheritors*. His main character was a Scotch drinker who always requested eighteen-year-old Glenmorangie. Once the book was published and the product became a well-known choice of Scotch the owner of the distillery sent Harold a case of the single-malt Scotch whiskey and gave him and Paul an invitation to visit Glenmorangie House and tour the distillery. From that time for the following twenty years a case of Glenmorangie arrived at Christmas.

Harold called me from the limousine that next day on their way to the Four Seasons. "Call Marty Yellman and tell him I want a better car phone for the Rolls. I can hear you on this phone and you're halfway across the fucking world." Then he quickly changed the subject. "The trip was good and we're on our way to the Four Seasons. I'll think of you when I have the Chocolate Velvet cake." He chuckled. "I'll call you later."

CHAPTER TWENTY-EIGHT

*A*re you having a good time?" Harold asked on the first morning he called from France after his arrival.

"Sure, I'm having a good time. I'm in California lying by the pool in Beverly Hills and on clear days I can see the ocean," I said, teasing him with my answer.

"Bullshit, it's nothing but smog soup out there. It's only clear enough to see the ocean two days out of the year." He laughed.

"How are the doggies, my little Gypsy and Kinky?" he asked.

"The doggies miss you; we all do," I said. "I'm reading one of your books today, me and forty thousand other people."

"What a bore," he said in his deadpan voice. "Why don't you write the next one for me?"

"Only if you tell me all the words. You're the genius," I said. "Did you hear what I said about forty thousand people every day throughout the world read your books?"

"What are you talking about?" he said.

"It's in *The Wall Street Journal* this morning. Paul called me and

I went out and got some copies of the paper. The headline in bold says: 'Forty Thousand People a Day Read a Harold Robbins Novel.'"

There was a silence on the phone. I heard a shrill female voice in the background. "Hold on; I'm talking to Jann," he said away from the telephone receiver. "Send me that article. Tell Grace I'll call her later; Linda is getting me crazy here."

"I'll let you tell her," I said, and put him on hold and buzzed Grace.

Six weeks later, Grace and Adréana left for France. I moved into the upstairs apartment with my kitties, Caio and Judge. Rick, the majordomo, had planned on having a wild summer at the Robbins estate and was very upset about me being in the house. Now I understood why Harold wanted me to live in the house.

Rick made every attempt to intimidate me. Each morning he would gossip that Grace had told him she hated me and was going to fire me after she spoke to Harold in France. Rick urged me to look for another job.

I explained to him I didn't work for Grace, I worked for Harold, and I would talk to Harold and would ask him to let me know when I was going to be fired. Of course, that ended Rick's threats about me losing my job.

I spent the rest of the summer studying all of Harold's books. I recognized in *Never Love a Stranger*, *The Dream Merchants*, *A Stone for Danny Fisher*, and *79 Park Avenue* Harold's beginnings in a tough world, one with little love and care, only hard times and hard lessons. I recognized some of the stories he had told me of his real life in the lives of his characters.

In the later books of the sixties and seventies, as the world of Harold Robbins evolved, he depicted the world of the rich and famous jet-setters, the lust, greed, and power of the elite. His books were dubbed "roman à clef" novels. *Where Love Has Gone* was supposedly about Lana Turner when her daughter was accused of killing Lana's boyfriend, Johnny Stompanato. The sixties books depicted the world of power, money, sex, and drugs. In *The Carpetbaggers* Harold used the models of Howard Hughes, whom he had met on several occassions; and Tom Mix, whom he had signed contracts with and listened to his stories of the Old West for hours, as Nevada Smith, a prominent character. Jenny Denton, another character in *The Carpetbaggers*, was based on a real-life prostitute Harold knew in Hell's Kitchen growing up. A girl shared by the gangsters who had the money and power in the world he knew as a young man.

The Adventurers in the seventies escalated power, corruption, money, drugs, and sex to a new level. His books throughout the sixties and seventies were titillating, with searing honesty about the rich, powerful, famous, and infamous. It was the world around him, he walked in the paths of the men he wrote about within these pages, and through this I glimpsed the Harold Robbins of that time. His views were constantly changing, but each book embodied how he felt about things, how he saw the world around him, and how he lived within that world.

Eight weeks after his departure Harold returned from France earlier than I had anticipated. We had lunch together the day after he returned. He was still a little punchy from jet lag but happy to be home.

"We're going to work on Monday," he said.

"I spent the summer reading your novels."

"Why?" he asked.

"You said in that interview we found, if anyone wanted to know you read the books." I smiled at him. "Now I know you, cover to cover."

"You're going to help on this one," he said. "I'm going to give you notes on what I want to do, and you keep everything I say. I may need to refer to the notes. Who knows if I can remember anything!"

It was no surprise; he was under the gun financially and I learned each crisis was what pushed him to start a new book. The big question still hung in the air. Could he write? No one knew for sure. His speech was fine and his energy had returned, but could he get the words on the page? That was still a looming question.

The phone rang on his private line during lunch. I usually left the room when the call was private, but he motioned for me to stay.

"Linda, I'm having lunch with Jann. I'll call you back." He hung up the phone. I could hear Linda's voice still talking as the receiver hit the cradle.

CHAPTER TWENTY-NINE

he new book was titled *Descent from Xanadu*. Harold called
me into his office to take notes.

"Judd Crane is a man who wants to explore the possibility of
living forever. Some call it life extension. He is an heir to billions
of dollars from a company that his father started and that gives
him the power to find the answers he is searching for," Harold
said. "I always wished I could inherit billions; that's how Judd
Crane does it."

"Another J.C. character?" I asked. "Is that on purpose?"

"Who else has initials *J.C.*?"

"Jonas Cord and a few of your characters. Is this a sequel?"

"Could be." He pondered for a moment. "Only this book is
about immortality."

"What do you think immortality is?" I asked him.

He lit a cigarette. "Love, the love we have in our own hearts for
life, for others, but not the love from others, but the love we give;
love we receive comes and goes."

"Will Judd Crane find that answer?"

"Maybe, if he finds what he loves! Every story searches for its own answers. And love is something we have to continue to find; otherwise, we're dead."

"I think it'll be a great book."

He looked at me. "I don't even know if I can write."

Today he would face the doubt haunting him since that night in April, almost seven months earlier. No one knew the answer to his dilemma. I walked over to the other side of the table where he sat and hugged him. "Better get to work. I know that nothing can stop you from writing."

He smiled, dropped his seriousness, and his eyes twinkled with mischief. "I'd like it better if you'd work on this a little bit," he said, motioning toward his crotch.

"Time to work, Harold," I said, smiling.

"Cold ass," he complained, and got up to go to his study.

I had prepared the study earlier that morning, and I followed him to his desk and turned on the light. It was "showtime." He sat down facing the black wall and checked to see that the drapes were lowered to allow no distractions. Cigarettes, lighter, clean ashtray, pen, yellow pad of paper, typing paper, and four carbons behind each page of white typing paper. All of the items were near the type-writer, with the phone close enough for him to reach. It was turned off so he did not hear the rings.

I sat his freshly brewed coffee to the left of the ashtray and dropped two sugars into his cup. "Wish me luck," he said.

"You can do it," I said, and left. As the minutes ticked by, I tried to keep myself busy, all the time anxious to know the outcome.

Chapter Thirty

Two hours later . . .

*H*is voice was ecstatic and triumphant as it boomed through the intercom, "Get Paul on the phone for me, and get up here."

I quickly hit the speed-dial button connecting me to Paul's office and got him on the phone, buzzed Harold, and ran upstairs. When I walked into the study it was a celebration. He was laughing and talking to Paul. I could tell by the conversation that Paul was as happy as Harold. He kept repeating over and over again, "I can do it; I can still do it."

I felt tears come to my eyes. The world had lifted off of Harold's shoulders. I don't think even he knew the underlying anxiety he had been facing since the day of the accident. Harold was a very private man, a shy man in reality, and did not make his innermost feelings known. He blanketed his emotions with a "tough guy" act, but he was vulnerable and I had felt his unspoken doubt and now I felt his happiness.

He handed me the pages after hanging up the phone. I started to read: " *'Chapter One.*

" *'The tiny doctor, hidden by tinted European eyeglasses, rose from her desk to face the windows. She gestured to him.*

" *'He towered above her, then followed her hand to a giant fountain in the expanse of green-blue grass.*

" *' "Do you know what that fountain is, Mr. Crane?" she asked, in her mid-European accent.*

" *'He nodded. "Of course, Dr. Zabiski. The fountain of Ponce De Leon."*

" *'She looked up at him. "It's a legend, Mr. Crane. An allegory. It's not a reality. There has never been a reality like that."*

" *'He was silent for a moment. "I know that too, Dr. Zabiski," he said.*

" *'She went to her desk and sat in her chair and waited until he was seated opposite her. She held her tinted eyeglasses in her right hand, then placed them in front of her. "You have dark cobalt blue eyes," she said.*

" *'A faint smile crossed his lips. "And yours are tawny yellow-brown, almost like a cat's."*

" *'She met his gaze directly. "If it's immortality you seek here, Mr. Crane," she said in a soft voice, "you've wasted your time."*

" *'His gaze did not change. "That's not what I heard."*

" *' "Then you've heard incorrectly," she said.*

" *'His expression did not change. "Twenty million dollars incorrectly?"*

" *'Her tinted glasses covered her eyes again. "I guess what I've heard is true," she said. "You are one of the richest men in the world."*

" *' "Now you have heard incorrectly," he said softly. "I am the richest man in the world."*

" *'She tilted her head. "More than the Saudi King, Getty, Ludwig, Hughes?"*

" *' "They're all like children playing games," he said. "With a snap of my fingers I can take away their marbles."*

"'"*Then there is only one game left to play,*" she said. "*Immortality.*"'"

In these first pages he grabbed me as a reader. I could see, feel, and almost touch the character, the scenes, and the tone. I was there with him on that page. With only two pages I wanted to know more! Harold had accomplished his desire that he had spoken about in a taped interview many years earlier. "I want to always do it better next time, for the page to disappear and allow the words to be me talking to the reader."

CHAPTER THIRTY-ONE

*H*arold put the phone on hold after talking to Paul one morning. He rang Grace on the intercom. "Paul wants to talk to you," he said, and glumly hung up the receiver.

"I have to finish the first part of the book before the IRS grabs my ass," Harold said. "He's been screaming at me for an hour; now he's going to scream at Grace about her spending."

"Harold, I don't know how you write with all the pressures you have," I said sympathetically.

He had completed almost one hundred pages of the first section of *Descent from Xanadu*. He was averaging about three to five pages a day, an aggravation to him since he normally did at least ten to twenty pages a day.

"I've told Grace to cool it with the parties. My head can't take it right now and I sure as hell can't afford the bills she's running up. She wants to sing and she fuckin' hits flat notes all night! Expenses run about twenty-five thousand dollars a month for this house, and the rest of the houses (Acapulco, Le Cannet, the yacht) run another twenty-five thousand. Then there's the credit cards. It's a lot of money per month."

"The only way to keep it under control is to work within a budget," I said.

Harold started to laugh. "You're tellin' me."

I smiled at him.

It still amazed me that Harold Robbins had financial problems. How could that be possible with forty thousand people a day reading his books and over 750 million in sales from the time his career began? I was beginning to realize the more money you make, the more mouths you have to feed, the more hands are waiting to be paid. Everyone had to be paid before Harold ever saw what he earned. The IRS, the lawyers who make the deals, the accountants who manage you, the employees to keep track of all your money, the staffs that maintain your homes, the property taxes, the crew that maintains the yacht, and the escalating debt of $2 million plus interest that had built the house in Beverly Hills and paid off a staggering amount to the decorator.

"I'm busted right now, but when the paperback comes out for *Spellbinder* that's where I make my royalties."

"I'll help you any way that I can," I said.

"I know you will, sweetheart," he answered, and took my hand.

"If you need to pay my salary after the money comes in," I said.

I watched the people around him every day asking for more from him, demanding more from him, and blaming him if there was a problem. I wondered at the time if anyone ever paused to think about what he was going through.

Adréana, his daughter, was the only one who gave him unconditional love, and that was the only thing he wanted.

He looked at me sullenly. "It's my fault. I should have never gotten sick."

"Well, that really wasn't your fault. You didn't plan it."

"Jewish guilt," he said, and sighed.

Harold discussed "Jewish guilt" frequently. "Paul uses it; Grace uses it; Bobby Weston uses it; Lillian used it; Caryn uses it; Linda uses it. It's been going on in the world for years—every Jewish boy has Jewish guilt. I guess we never outgrow it. It's as natural as being circumcised." He grabbed his crotch. "You wanna see?" he asked, smiling his most endearing, impish smile.

"Harold, should I use Jewish guilt to make you stop that?" I kidded him.

"Shiksa, you're too good to use 'Jewish guilt' on anyone."

"Harold, why do you have Jewish guilt? You've said that you don't believe in religion—so why have guilt?"

"I believe in me."

CHAPTER THIRTY-TWO

Ten days later, Harold completed the first part of *Descent from Xanadu* and it was sent to Paul Gitlin's office. The next day a check was cut at Simon & Schuster for five hundred thousand dollars.

"Paul, we need money here and they need money in France." He listened to Paul for a few moments. "Won't the IRS take less than two hundred and fifty thousand dollars? I know one hundred thousand dollars goes to you." He listened for a moment. "Yeah, I know twenty-five thousand dollars has to be paid to the accountants. How much can you send the staff in Acapulco?" There was another pause as he listened to Paul's answer. "Fuck it; call Wells Fargo and tell them to roll the two million over."

He slammed down the phone and turned to me. "Have someone get the Maserati out; we're going down to the Polo Lounge for an interview. I think it's with *USA Today*."

*H*arold sipped on his aquavit after we arrived and answered questions. "They say *A Stone for Danny Fisher* is the best book I've ever written. That's when the critics liked me." Harold laughed.

"Yeah, and you laugh all the way to the bank," the reporter said.

Harold smiled. "Yeah, the only problem I have today is my banker keeps the money!"

The reporter didn't take issue with that statement, assuming like everyone else that Harold had millions in the bank and he probably didn't need to work if he didn't want to work.

"Harold, you're always on the top of the bestseller list, and yet the critics pan your books. What's the secret?"

"It seems like the more they say they don't like my books the more the public buys. It's crazy," Harold answered.

"I have a quote from Mario Puzo." The reporter read from his notes, " 'Puzo says you sold out and started writing for money after you wrote your first three books.' "

"I helped Mario contact some people in Italy for his research for *The Godfather*. He's a great writer." Harold deflected the answer or comment to that question. Mario was a friend.

"What's your favorite Harold Robbins book?" the reporter went on to ask.

"They're all my favorites; they're like children and I love them all. I guess it's always the next one that you love the most. It's like you always look for the 'next' wife and she's the one you love the best." He looked at the reporter.

I had become accustomed to these interviews with Harold. I had been on every press interview since I came to work for him. They usually took place at the Polo Lounge and he would do them only if he had a new book coming out. Today's interview was about *Spellbinder* coming out in paperback. He was promoting. He wanted to stir up the interview, which was, so far, predictable. His last comment was him seeing how much the reporter would allow him to get by with. The reporter took the bait.

Harold watched the reporter for a moment.

"Are you looking for a 'next' wife?"

"I never look for one, I'm like little Jack Horner, putting my finger in the pie." He laughed and looked over at me. "She may be next."

"Harold, how many times have you been married?" the reporter asked.

"So many, I can't remember." He looked off into the distance. "Too many times. But I'm like my character Preacher in *Spellbinder*. He loved pussy and I love pussy." He shrugged and looked for the waiter.

"Let's have some more Bloody Marys," Harold said once the waiter arrived. "Aquavit for me, a Virgin Mary for her," motioning to me. "Bloody Mary for him," nodding to the reporter.

Harold then became very serious. "You know Jann," he said, again motioning to me. "She went to college," he said with a wistful look in his eyes.

The reporter, spellbound, was waiting for the punch line. He knew Harold and had interviewed him before.

"It makes me sad," Harold continued wistfully. "I never went to college. I didn't have the opportunities available today." He flashed a grin. "Think of all the girls I could have chased. I was born at the wrong time!"

The reporter winked at me. "You would have chased Jann?"

"I could have been her teacher! You betcha," Harold said, and grabbed for me. "Teach me tonight, honey." He laughed. "I chase her around the desk every day!"

He wasn't lying. He was after me and I was still trying to resist his charms.

"Harold, it's been reported that you've sold seven hundred and fifty million books. How much money do you have?"

"How would I know? My agent says I always need more! I have three or four households to keep running, a yacht in the South of France. A few ex-wives, ancient stud fees." He laughed. "Harold

Robbins International on Sunset Boulevard and more accountants and lawyers and agents. I don't see most of my money. No matter how much I earn, I always spend more. I'm selfish."

"What do you mean, 'selfish'?" the reporter laughed.

" 'Give and live,' it's my motto. Money is to be used, shared, and lived. They say it's selfish because I don't save anything."

"You've made a movie out of *Lonely Lady*. I heard you were paid a million dollars for the rights," the reporter said. "Did you write the script?"

"I got fired the last time I wrote a script!"

The reporter peered at him.

"Paramount Pictures with Bob Evans at the helm had bought the rights to *The Adventurers*. I was hired to write the screenplay. They were going to pay three hundred thousand dollars to me, so it took me about ten weeks, in my office in Cannes, to dictate the pages. Christ, it was almost three hundred and thirty-five pages by the time I finished," he said. "Too long, but I thought the director would cut it down.

"I remember when I gave my secretary the final line of the movie script. I was sitting on the fucking sofa, exhausted. It was a good line, the way it came to me: 'Hold my hand, child, and I will lead you safely across the mountains,' and I stopped. I opened my eyes and saw my secretary crying.

" 'But everyone knew that Dax was going to die,' I said to her, laughing. I thought if it got to her it must be pretty good! So, I sent the screenplay off to Lewis Gilbert, the director. And I went to the Monte Carlo casino and dropped one hundred and fifty thousand dollars at chemin de Fer.

"Several days later, the phone rang at my house in the middle of the night in Le Cannet. It was Gilbert.

" 'Robbins, you're fired!'

" 'What the hell are you talking about?'

" 'It's too dirty, too violent, and too much like the book!'

" 'Send me the fucking check and chop the screenplay up any way you want!' I said, and slammed down the phone.

"That was the end of my screenwriting career! I don't like writing by committee and that's what you have to do when you write screenplays or television shows! Drives me crazy! I didn't write the *Survivors* television series; I put David Chandler in charge."

"*The Adventurers* was about Rubirosa, right?" the reporter asked.

Harold nodded. "I met Rubi in the South of France. He had a reputation of being a great fucker, playboy, whatever you want to call it. One of his famous girlfriends said he fucked like a 'jackhammer.'"

The reporter laughed. "Which celebrity was that?"

Harold shrugged off the question. "I was living in the Beverly Hills Hotel when I finished *The Adventurers*. I had been up all night writing the last pages and the phone rang. It was a friend of mine who lived in Cannes; he said Rubi had been killed in a car accident." Harold looked off into the distance sadly. "I think it was suicide. He was finished. His looks were going; he couldn't live the life. The women were going to younger men. He was fucked!"

The reporter jotted notes as Harold weaved his story about screenwriting, sex, and power and the sad ending of Rubirosa.

CHAPTER THIRTY-THREE

*I*t was 10:00 A.M. and the bell at the gate rang. The limousine had arrived a little early. I dialed the intercom to the bedroom since I hadn't heard from Harold during the morning. He had invited me earlier in the week to attend a screening of the *The Lonely Lady*, starring Pia Zadora. A rough cut at a screening room of Universal Studios. I had reminded him of his appointment the night before.

"Harold, the limousine is here to go to Universal," I said into the intercom.

I heard some movement. "Holy shit, I overslept! Tell Andrew to bring me some coffee and I'll be down in a few minutes."

Thirty minutes later we were in the limo on our way to Universal Studios. "I thought Grace was coming."

Harold looked at me through bleary eyes. "No way, she saw this piece of shit in Cannes," he said. "Besides, we were up till dawn. A friend of ours, Rhodelle, who we had dinner with, spent the night. Grace finally told me what happened in Cannes with *Lonely Lady*. It was a disaster. I got pissed off because she waited until last night to tell me and then she got pissed because she thought I was fucking Rhodelle." He spat these words out angrily.

Was that story for real? I didn't ask any questions. The driver stopped and bought coffee for us even though we were already late. I dropped in two sugars and stirred the coffee and handed it to Harold. His face was still grim. There was silence as we drove into the lot toward the screening room.

When we got out of the car, Harold smiled and greeted several Universal executives and Bob Weston, the president of Harold Robbins International. They all shook hands and began to talk about *The Lonely Lady* being a big success for everyone, but there was still a lot of work to be done, they cautioned.

We all sat down in the VIP Screening Room, with about twenty-five movie seats. Harold was making jokes and chatting with the men when the lights went dim. There was enough tension among the group to fill a war room.

I had never seen a "rough cut" of a movie, and it left a lot to be desired. With no music and bad acting, the film version of *The Lonely Lady*, a book that I loved, was a disappointment. I sat next to Harold during the showing. I glanced toward him several times. He was slouched in his seat, wearing his dark sunglasses, and several times I thought he was sleeping. I saw his eyes were closed behind his heavy dark shades.

When the movie was completed and the lights came up, he stood up, never removing his sunglasses, thanked the executives, and told Bob Weston, who was the producer of the project, that he did a great job.

As we were driving home, Harold asked me what I thought of the screening.

I tried to answer this diplomatically. "It's the first 'rough cut' I've ever seen, but I like the book better than the movie."

"It's crap!" he said, taking off his sunglasses and looking at me. "I don't know what the hell happened in Italy, but it turned into shit!" He was silent for a moment. "This is why I stay away from writing movies. They can never do my books. Bobby told me Riklis [Pia's husband] wanted Pia in every frame of the movie. Jesus! She is not an actress. She can't carry a picture. I don't know how the hell she got a Golden Globe for *Butterfly*."

"Were you sleeping while it was playing?" I asked.

He chuckled for the first time that day. "Hell, yes! It was boring as shit. The last time I fell asleep in a presentation I ended up on the front page of *Le Monde* in Paris. I was researching *Goodbye, Janette* during the YSL showing. I was sitting on the front row, next to the catwalk. I'd been out all night with the models."

*P*aul Gitlin was on the phone the morning after the movie opened several months later. *The Lonely Lady* was awful. Reviewers were vicious about the performance by Pia Zadora and trashed every element of the production.

Harold had Paul on the speakerphone. "This is a fucking disaster. I haven't heard one thing good about the picture. We're screwed, Robbins," Paul barked. "It's time to close up Harold Robbins International. There won't be any more pictures."

I could imagine Paul pacing around his office, holding his back with one arm and looking into the future with anger. Whenever Paul was standing he held his back, trying to cope with the pain of deteriorating disks.

"Hell, Paul, if we close HRI it'll be a disaster. We've done some good business since we've had it," Harold insisted, gazing at the flame lighting his cigarette.

Paul grumbled for a few more minutes.

"Paul, let's see where this goes; we have bad reviews all the time. What's the difference? We've been paid."

"I have another call!" Paul bellowed, and was gone.

"Paul hates everybody!" Harold said after hanging up the phone that morning. "He can't stand Bobby, or Gene Schwam, or Dr. Ablon. Christ, he thinks Bob Mayer, a lawyer he found out here, and

California law is fucked up and he always wants to fight." Harold looked disgusted. "And I'm in the fucking middle! What does he want from my life? I don't worry about the movie; I got my money up front."

The phone rang again.

"Is he there?" the person on the phone said. I recognized the voice; it was Bob Weston, president of Harold Robbins International.

"Hold a minute, Bob," I said, and handed the phone to Harold. "It's Bob Weston."

Harold took the receiver. "What the fuck happened?"

Harold listened as Bob talked. "Whose idea was it to put Pia in every fucking frame of the movie? Bob, she's not an actress that can carry a movie."

He listened as Bob spoke, probably trying to defend himself.

"Yeah, I know." Harold hung up the phone. "Get Gene Schwam on the phone. Universal will do nothing to help this picture."

CHAPTER THIRTY-FOUR

*T*he guard called from the gate while Harold and I were in the family room having coffee. Harold pressed the speakerphone and looked over at the television monitor showing the gate area.

"Mr. Robbins, there's two gentlemen from the FBI here to see you. They showed me their ID badges."

Harold's expression never changed. "Send 'em up."

I looked at him questioningly. "I'll go downstairs."

"No, you stay right here," he said.

When the two men were brought upstairs they introduced themselves and again flashed their badges.

"Would you like some coffee?" Harold asked.

"Thank you, but we've already had our morning coffee," one of the men said politely.

"What's on your mind, boys?" Harold asked, and lit a cigarette. They looked at me.

"This is my assistant, Jann Stapp. Go ahead," Harold said.

"We've acquired a list from our southeastern Georgia office.

A 'hit' list. It's been identified as coming from a 'skinhead' group. Radicals and political misfits."

The other agent spoke. "This group has a history of violence, but mostly in the South. The list includes about ten other people and you're on that list."

"What do I need to do?" Harold asked.

"Keep an eye out and if anyone is hanging around outside the property call the police; take note when you leave the property if any car follows you. Actually, you've got your own security and I don't think you'll have any problems, but we wanted to let you know."

"My book *Spellbinder* came out a few months ago and it was banned in some of the Southern towns."

"Well, Mr. Robbins, you're in the public eye and that makes you a target and their preachers are 'patriots and saints' as far as they are concerned."

Harold wrote down a name on a piece of paper. "Here's my attorney in New York. Would you keep him posted, along with me, if anything comes up?"

The agent handed him several cards.

"Give one to Jann. She is the person you can contact here in case I'm out of town."

The men chatted for a while about some of Harold's books. "Honey." He turned to me. "Get me a couple of the *Spellbinder* hardcovers."

I went to the study and picked up two books.

Harold signed the books to the men and their wives. They shook hands with both of us and left.

"Call Charlie at the security office and tell him I want extra security. I want someone to follow Adréana to school and home.

"This is why I don't have my pictures on the books in America. It's too dangerous. Too many assholes," he said. "I don't worry about it in Europe. They are different when it comes to celebrities."

"You ought to write a book about 'celebrity.' You've lived it," I said.

"Irving Wallace already did. *The Fan*, it was a good book. I've got it if you want to read it."

CHAPTER THIRTY-FIVE

*T*hey must think I'm about to croak," Harold said as he sat at the Selectric typewriter taking a break. He had just received a call from Simon & Schuster.

"What do you mean?" I said, laughing. Normally when a person would say this I would take it seriously, but this was Harold Robbins. He joked about everything. He always joked and laughed talking about when he "croaked," when he was going to "croak," or when someone else "croaked."

"S and S and Pocket Books are giving a big presentation to me for *A Stone for Danny Fisher*. It's the twenty-year anniversary since they published the book and it's still on the shelves. They want me to come to the sales convention. Jesus, I'd better find a new publisher; this is the kiss of death!"

"Why would you say that? It's a great honor."

"You better believe it! They've sold about twenty million copies and made a shitload of money! I wish I knew where the hell it went.

"Someone said to me the other day, 'Mr. Robbins, if you had

only a dollar for every book that you sold, you'd be worth seven hundred and fifty million dollars.' I wish it were that easy." He grinned happily and mimicked Groucho Marx with his eyebrows. "Think of all the girls that would be chasing me."

"I think you're doing pretty good with the ones you have," I said.

"Yeah, but you're the one I want," he said, and reached for me.

"Umm . . . hmmmmm . . . and then you'd want another and another and another, right?"

"Never!" He feigned loyalty and sincerity in his voice.

"When is the presentation?" I asked.

"Two weeks, in some resort in Florida. They're sending Paul the tickets and I'll meet him in New York and we'll go down to Florida together." He looked at me.

"That's really exciting. I hope they take pictures."

"Why don't you go with me?"

"I'd love to go with you." I looked at him.

"I'll get you a ticket." His expression and demeanor had changed. He was serious.

I knew he didn't mean for me to travel as his business assistant but as his companion. I could feel the heat inside at that thought. It took my breath away, but still there were Linda and a few other girls who called him on the phone, along with his wife. "I don't think that would be a good idea," I finally said.

He laughed and kept his eyes on me. "You know it would be good. You can go if you want."

"I think it will be a great evening for you. Won't Grace be with you?"

"No, she has a busy social life here, and she doesn't give a shit about these things."

*H*arold called me from Florida after the event.

"They're all kissing my ass tonight," Harold said, chuckling and telling me about the presentation. "They put one of the original copies that Pocket Books did of *Danny Fisher* into a Plexiglas rectangle-shape container with a gold plaque on the bottom."

I could hear the pride in his voice.

"They made speeches about how important I was to the company. That I had been a driving force of Simon and Schuster's success in their earlier days."

After I hung up the phone that night I remembered hearing the legendary tales of Paul Gitlin and Harold Robbins's power at Simon & Schuster. Paul had once told an S & S employee whom he really worked for and who made it possible for him to have a paycheck. "You know who you really work for," he said to the young man. "You work for Harold and me—I don't give a shit who signs your check. Harold is who you work for."

Harold was very proud of his accomplishments for Simon & Schuster and he was a very loyal author to them.

CHAPTER THIRTY-SIX

*A*fter he returned from Florida he had a new determination to write many more novels. We sat together and talked about ideas in the world ahead of us. He had great characters already developed and he was excited about the future.

But the next several months were spent working night and day with another IRS crisis looming. Harold spent each day going to his IBM Selectric typewriter, banging out pages, running a race to beat the deadlines imposed by payments to the government.

I would work late into the night filling in "blown" words and correcting sentences. Harold asked author David Chandler to also look at the pages and make corrections if needed on story content.

David would come over in the morning, take the pages I had completed overnight, and make his corrections. I saw a problem right away when David returned the pages. They would be corrected to reflect David's style of writing rather than Harold's. I pointed this out to Harold.

"Fuck it. I have been reading his work. He can't help it; he writes his own shit. I'll straighten it out when I get to New York. He needs the money we're paying him and I need the money to finish as soon as possible. We'll work it out. This is one of Gitlin's ideas; maybe he doesn't think I can write anymore."

"If he thinks that he's a fool. You've already made history in the publishing business and I think someday you'll be known as the Charles Dickens of your time." I grinned at him. "I'm not an important critic, but that's what I think."

He started to laugh. "You're so prejudiced," he said, then looked at me seriously. "But I agree with you."

On Christmas Eve morning, Harold became Santa Claus. He wanted to have breakfast at The Bagel Restaurant and let the cook have the day to prepare a huge feast for later that evening. Harold and I then went shopping at his favorite stores in Beverly Hills. The money machine was flowing again. We had completed a good portion of the book and sent it to New York a few days earlier. The contract amount had been paid; the IRS was satisfied. Now it was time to party.

There were about twenty people invited for dinner that evening. A huge turkey with Polish-style dressing was being prepared, along with goose and leg of lamb, with mashed potatoes, several choices of vegetables, and fresh bread prepared by our Polish cook and his wife. And, of course, chocolate cake. Five layers with chocolate ice cream, hot fudge sauce, and whipped cream as a topping. It wouldn't be a Harold Robbins dinner without chocolate.

When the party began it was a madhouse. More than forty people showed up. Harold would turn no one away on Christmas Eve. Some of the people he didn't even know. They were a friend of a friend of a friend. After dinner champagne was served and guests continued to arrive. By the time the party ended about midnight there were more than eighty people who had dropped by during the evening, including Rod Stewart, Bette Midler, Lily Tomlin, Barbara Eden, Joan Collins, Diana Ross, Billy Davis and Marilyn McCoo,

Quincy Jones, Buddy Hackett, and Reuben and Linda Cannon. Harold was enjoying himself and was feeling good.

"Hello," I said as Buddy Hackett sat down next to me on the piano bench in the foyer.

He kept his eyes on me and didn't answer. "Who are you?" he asked. Then he made a comment about my ass in the black leather pants I was wearing.

I laughed.

"What the hell are you laughing about? I just made a sex-uuu-al comment to you."

And I started laughing again. "I know, Buddy, but all I have to do is hear your voice and look at your angelic face and you make me laugh. I'm Jann Stapp, Harold's assistant."

He smiled back at me. "I've heard all about you; he's told me! But he never told me about those black leather pants," he said, mugging Buddy Hackett style.

I left early the next morning to go to a party in Marina del Rey on a sailboat. When I returned to the house that night, it was quiet. After a few minutes the intercom on my phone beeped into the room and the red light flashed.

"What's happening?" Harold's voice filled the room.

"I just got home. Did you have a nice day?" I asked.

"Adréana and I are sitting in the study. Why don't you come up?"

Harold was propped in his chair in front of his typewriter, twirling in circles like a bored teenager. He was smoking a cigarette and blowing smoke rings.

"Where did you go?" Harold asked.

"To Marina del Rey, a great Christmas party on a sailboat. They had fake snow on the deck about a foot deep and Christmas lights on the sails plus a huge Christmas tree at the front of the boat."

"What kind of sailboat?" Harold asked.

"I have no idea, but it was a big one."

"Somebody stole some silver last night," he said. "And the gold ashtrays in the bathroom."

"You're kidding? Are you sure?"

"They've looked all over for them and they're nowhere. About three knives and forks are missing."

"Who would have taken them?" I asked.

"Euro-trash. The last group that came in. I don't know who the hell they were. They wanted souvenirs," he said.

Harold left for New York the next day.

CHAPTER THIRTY-SEVEN

e pulled up in front of Gatsby's, a beautiful restaurant owned by Harold's friends Bill and Helen Rosen. We were coming to celebrate the completion of *Descent from Xanadu*. The maître d' led us to our table and we sat down. Before I knew it Harold had his hand up my leg under my dress before I hit the seat. I looked at him and smiled. "Harold, you're fast. Really fast," I said, grabbing his hand and placing it on the table.

He smiled.

"You just want to see what you can get by with, don't you?"

"I've told you Grace and I have an open marriage. She does her thing and I do mine," he said. "You know her boyfriends."

Even though he was being casual with this comment, I saw a sadness in his eyes that I had seen from the first day I met him. I wondered if it was for the marriage that was no longer working or the marriage that could have been. I didn't know.

I tried to change the subject, but it didn't work.

"You know both of us have friends," he said.

"I know, Harold, but I can't be casual. I'm from Oklahoma, not Hollywood. I fall in love, and when I love somebody I can't just flip a switch and say, 'Well, that's over,'" I tried to explain.

He looked at me. "I love you already—I'd only love you more."

"You always know the right thing to say, but you have too many girls. I'd be one of many," I said. I didn't believe his devotion for a second, but in another way I wanted it to be real.

"Are those other girls here with me tonight?" he said as he buttered a piece of warm bread that had been brought to the table.

"What about Linda? What about Grace? What about Ini [his German photographer, who had recently moved to Los Angeles]?" I tried to remember some of the other names of girls who called Harold. "Judy? Wendy? Dominique? And the girl that kept calling in the middle of the night from Rio?"

He smiled. "Ye-a-a-a-ah," he said with sort of a growl mixing with his voice.

"Too many girlfriends," I said, teasing him. "I can't even remember all of their names."

He looked at me. "Not the one I want."

Bill Rosen came over to say hello. He sat down with us. "Tony and Cyd are coming over in a little while," he said. "Do you want to have dinner with us?"

"No, I'm trying to talk her into a little sex," Harold answered casually.

Bill smiled and winked at me. "How are you doing?"

"She's tough, you know. Cold ass."

About that time Helen joined the table. Bill told her Harold was trying to talk me into having a little sex. "I don't think he's doing too good."

"Good for you, Jann, keep him guessing," Helen said.

I laughed. It all seemed very normal to them. They had seen Harold and Grace with many companions, and nothing surprised them.

Chapter Thirty-Eight

The phone rang early one morning, around seven o'clock. It was unusual for anyone to call this early. There had been a terrible rainstorm with strong winds the night before and the electricity had gone off and on several times. Harold and I traipsed outside with flashlights to a small room that housed a generator that would light certain areas of the house when the electricity failed. The generator had failed to work and we spent hours trying to get someone to come and fix it. Finally at 2:00 A.M. our electricity was restored and we went to bed. As the phone rang and echoed through the house I started to let the answering service catch it, but something stirred me to answer. "Robbins residence."

"Jann, let me speak to my father?" Caryn, his daughter, said into the phone. Her tone was very serious.

"Hold on," I said. My mind was racing. I felt this was urgent.

I buzzed the family room; there was no answer. I buzzed the study. No answer.

I buzzed the bedroom. The intercom was turned off and I got a busy signal.

"Caryn, he's still sleeping. Can I have him call you?" I asked.

"It's an emergency and I've got to talk to him," Caryn said tearfully. "There's been an emergency."

"Hold on," I said quickly. "I'll go upstairs and wake him up."

I ran up the back stairway and knocked on the door of the bedroom. Harold answered the door in his robe, barely awake. "What's going on?"

"Harold, it's Caryn and it's an emergency."

He took a deep breath and walked toward the family room. I started back down the stairs.

"Come into the family room," he said. "Have Rick get me some coffee."

I followed Harold to the family room—stopping at the nearest phone to call Rick for coffee. When I walked into the family room, Harold was asking Caryn questions and trying to comfort her.

Michael, her husband, had been killed in an auto accident in the early-morning hours on his way to an appointment. The violent storm and high winds had blown out the traffic lights in West LA. A truck rushing through an intersection hit Michael's car.

Caryn needed her father to go with her to identify the body at the morgue. She and Michael had been married only a short time. It was a tragedy.

I need to call Caryn's mother," Harold said grimly, once he had accompanied her to the morgue and returned to the house with Caryn.

He handed me a slip of paper with a phone number.

"You stay here while I talk to her and then I need to give you a list of people to call."

I dialed the number and handed Harold the phone when it started to ring.

"Yvonne, this is Harold."

Harold told Yvonne the story of Michael's death, and to his surprise, Yvonne was unaware Caryn and Michael had gotten married.

After Harold hung up the phone, he looked at me. "Goddammit, she told me Yvonne couldn't come to the wedding! What's wrong with this girl! Yvonne doesn't understand; they've talked on the phone every week and she never told her she was married." Harold took a deep sigh. "I'll never understand her."

Harold sighed and looked at the ceiling. "Caryn will move into the study for a few days. Tell Andrew to move my typewriter and papers into the family room."

Harold spent many hours with Caryn during those several days, helping to sort out the remnants of her life.

"Caryn's had a rough life," Harold said a few days later. "I told her she had to keep living and doing the best she can."

He looked off into space with sadness in his eyes, almost defeat. He knew that he could love her for the rest of his life and there would always be a scar in their relationship. On occasion Harold was asked for advice by friends going through divorces and trying to get custody of their children. He would always recommend not fighting, letting the children come to their parents by their own choice.

"I don't know what I can do to help her."

My heart went out to him. He had shown me letters he had written to her over the years, and he always made it clear that he was her father and he would always take care of her. I hoped that she would lean on him now.

Chapter Thirty-Nine

I'm going to go to Paris in August and appear on France's most popular talk show. It's a very important literary program in France. They're giving me an hour. I have to speak French for the interview!" Harold was leaving again for France in June. "I'll be sending you some pages, rewrites for *Xanadu* to fix up and then send them to Paul. Adréana and Grace will come to the South of France, Le Cannet, in July."

The phone rang and I picked it up. A woman with a heavy European accent spoke: "arold, is he available?"

"May I say who's calling?"

"Oui . . . Dominique."

I put the phone on hold and turned to him. "Dominique," I said.

His expression was unchanged as he picked up the phone after he had lit a cigarette. "Dominique, ça va?" He listened for a few minutes. "Yes, darling, everything is fine. I feel much better. I hope all is well with you, too."

He listened again and then answered in his pidgin French, "*Oui*, I know Ken gave the interview to that rag newspaper in France. I hope they paid him well. *C'est la vie*, what can you do? He needed the money. His wife is very sick."

They spoke for a few more minutes and he hung up.

"She just read some rag sheet in Paris, about orgies I supposedly had on the yacht. Her name was in the article. Ken, the captain of the *Gracara*, sold a whole load of shit to the press. They're dirty; they even had some pictures. Gary, my captain now, is going to send me a copy of the paper from Cannes."

"Who is Dominique?" I asked. "Do you have orgies on the yacht?"

He laughed. "You're just a gossip at heart. Dominique's the main character for *Goodbye, Janette*. I met her in Saint-Tro, on the boat. We were together for a while. . . ."

A WEEK IN THE PORT OF ST. TROPEZ*

It was eight o'clock in the morning and Margo, my cook, had just put breakfast on the table in front of me. Ham and eggs on half a baguette fresh from the bakery and a full pot of Taster's Choice coffee. I never had a taste for French coffee at breakfast, even if it was served au lait. But, the breakfast, sandwich style, was delicious even though Margo thought I was stupid not to eat a proper meal.

The telephone rang and Margo answered it in the kitchen. I could hear her voice clearly. Oui, Monsieur, . . . Oui, Monsieur, Monsieur Robbins is awake. . . ." She couldn't speak English well, but enough to be understood. She came back in the dining room. "Monsieur Bobby is calling you from California."

---

* A story by Harold Robbins excerpted from the unpublished autobiography *After the Tropic of Cancer* and originally published by *Playboy* magazine in short-story form under the title "The Stallion."

I left my breakfast and walked over to the phone in the entrance hall. "Good morning," I said as I picked up the receiver.

"Having your lox, bagel, and cream cheese this morning for breakfast?" He laughed.

"Don't make me crazy. I would love to be at my favorite deli," I said. "But, I've been on a ham and eggs diet out here in the uncivilized world." I reached for a cigarette. "What are you doing up so late? It has to be midnight in LA."

"I've got good news. Universal Studios picked up the television mini-series sequel to 79 Park Avenue and they agreed to pay you two hundred fifty thousand to write the story," he said. "But, Sid Sheinberg has one stipulation. They want it in a hurry. They want Lesley Ann Warren to star in it and they don't want to give her time to sign onto another project."

I thought for a moment. "How much of a hurry are they in?" I asked.

"Two weeks. Sid said they had to have it in their hands in two weeks," he said.

Bobby's voice sounded tinny over the intercontinental telephone wires.

"That s why they're willing to pay you that much money," he continued.

"Two weeks!" I said, incredulously. "Nobody can write that fast."

"C'mon, Harold," he said. "You wrote Stiletto in a week."

"But, that was another time. Less distractions. Right now we have my in-laws visiting here from the States. There are a half a dozen people arriving tomorrow to celebrate Adréana's birthday in two weeks." I took a drag off of my cigarette. "I can't even get into my office near the port because Grace gave it to her gay friends until the birthday party."

"But, if you had a place to work, you could finish the script?" he asked.

"Sure, I could do it."

"You've got the yacht. Get on it, take it someplace where no one can bother you, write the 'bible' and you'll be back in time for Adréana's birthday. You have a crew of four on that yacht, and I know Cathy is a super cook." He was silent for a moment and then spoke again. "Besides, we need the money. You're late on your taxes and we have to keep the company running."

"Okay," I said. "Just start praying." I put down the phone and went back to my breakfast. After I finished with breakfast, I walked back over to the telephone and called the boat. Ken answered. "Good morning."

"Good morning," I said. "Everything okay there?"

"Fine, sir," he said.

"Ken, do you still have the keys to my office with you?" I asked.

"Yes, sir, right here with the boat keys. I always keep them together," he answered.

"Okay," I said. "Take Anton with you and go to the office. Bring my typewriter and about three packages of paper. Also get some BIC pens and two little bottles of Wite-Out liquid for type-writers. Bring it all back to the boat and get ready to set for St. Tropez. Call the port captain and tell him we want a good place on the quay. We'll need it for about a week. Also tie into the port telephone lines."

"Yes, sir," Ken said. "But, aren't Mrs. Robbins' friends still staying in the apartment? She'll get upset if I wake them up too early, and also, she planned to take them to Monte Carlo this afternoon on the boat."

"Fuck all of them," I said. "I don't care if you have to wake them up. If I'm lucky, they'll get pissed off and go to a hotel and I won't have to pay their booze bill. Just bring what I asked for and I will be down in about an hour. Be ready to take off as soon as I get there."

"*Yes, sir,*" *Ken answered.*

"*Thank you,*" *I said and hung up the phone.*

Grace was standing behind me in the hallway. I turned and looked at her. She was wearing her morning robe which had been ripped off from the Carlton Hotel.

I went to the breakfast table and she followed me into the dining room. She sat down on a chair and reached for a cup of coffee. She stared at me. Not angry, but possibly. "*Why are you taking the boat to St. Tropez for a week by yourself?*"

I smiled at her. "*A quarter of a million dollars.*"

"*You're lying,*" *she said, her voice rising.* "*You knew that I had Cliff and Victor here and I promised to take them to Monte Carlo.*"

I turned away from her. "*You can get Jacques to drive you there. The new Seville has enough room for everyone,*" *I said.*

"*What about my mother and father?*" *she asked.* "*I thought I would take Adréana with us.*"

I looked at her. "*You know damned well that your mother won't get on the boat. She was sick as a dog the first time she ever got on it. She said she would never get on it again. It's been three years and she's kept her word.*"

"*What the hell are you really going to do in St. Tropez?*" *she asked suspiciously.* "*You're probably going to pick up your eighteen-year-old windsurfer and screw your brains out.*"

"*Leslie isn't my idea of a good piece of ass,*" *I said.* "*She's still in kindergarten. It's your friend Tony Roma that has the hots for her, not me.*"

"*Tony hasn't even been here for a year. I know that you were giving her money.*"

"*So what?*" *I asked.* "*Poor thing doesn't make enough money teaching windsurfing and her family in Australia doesn't seem to give a damn for her. I don't give her half the money that you spend keeping your friends around here to entertain you.*"

"You're really selfish," she said. "I guess you won't even show up for Adréana's birthday."

"It's two weeks away," I said flatly. "I'll be there."

It took a little more than two hours to make the trip from Cannes and get into the port at St. Tropez. The port captain moved us into a good location, in front of L'Escale, which was one of the best restaurants on the port, and next to John Von Neumann's Baglietto that was painted like a grey Navy Corvette and was probably one of the speediest yachts on all of the Cote D'Azur.

I sat on the bench on the deck of the Gracara, the name I had given the yacht. Cathy got me a fresh coffee while Ken went down the gangplank to give the port captain his daily payoff.

Fifty francs. That was not for the port fees, parking, electricity, telephone service or water which was billed at the end of each week. It was a token to make sure I always got a good spot at the port, even on short notice. It had paid off today.

It was not too crowded in the port today. It was too early for the lunch crowd. Most of the tourists were just arriving at the beaches. I lit a cigarette and went downstairs to the dining room where I began to set up my work place. There was a serving table that pulled out from the wall. I placed my typewriter mat and typewriter on that table. I pulled up a dining room chair that fit comfortably under the typewriter table. Cathy had already set up the paper, eraser liquid and carbons on the office table Ken had put in the dining room. The last thing to do was plug in the electric typewriter into the wall socket. Luckily, I had the yacht wired for 110 volts as well as 220 volts. Now all I had to do was work.

I looked at my watch. By now it was one o'clock and I was hungry. The last thing I wanted to do was work. Cathy came up from the galley while I was standing at the rear deck. She smiled at me. "Would you like Salad Niciose?" I looked at her. She knew that I *didn't care for salad or for any vegetables for that matter. "What else do we have in the galley?"*

"Actually, nothing, Mr. Robbins," she said. "I was going to prepare omelettes for the crew. We left so quickly this morning, I didn't have time to do the marketing."

I knew the timetable. I also knew the rules. The crew eats before the passengers. Owner or not. "You have your lunch," I said. "Then you can go off to the market and get the things we need. I'll grab a bite at L'Escale."

"We're not upsetting your schedule?" she asked.

I smiled at her. "It's okay, Cathy. I'll be alright."

"Thank you, Mr. Robbins," she answered. "I'll give you a super dinner tonight, I'll even bake you a chocolate cake."

"You're wonderful, baby," I said as I walked down the gangplank.

The crowd was beginning to thicken now. It was early July and not until August would all the French workers be vacationing in St. Tropez. Now, all the hustlers of every sort from all the other countries were here.

Fritz, the owner and maitre d', saw me as I stood on the sidewalk in front of the restaurant. He held up his hand and waved me inside. He placed me in a small banquette that leaned against the entrance aisle wall. "You're alone?" he asked.

I nodded. "I've come down here to work."

He laughed.

Somehow coming to St. Tropez to work seemed funny.

"Okay, Harold, what would you like for lunch?"

"Entrecote blue, pommes frites and a Heineken," I said.

He laughed again. "An American working man's lunch," he said as he quickly moved to greet his other clientele lining up to come into his restaurant.

Soon, a little waiter placed a beer and a chilled glass in front of me and a small baguette and several pats of butter individually placed on aluminum squares. "Bon appétit," he said.

"Merci," I said and poured my beer into the glass.

A voice boomed in front of me. "Harold! What are you doing here? And alone!"

I looked up. It was Wally, a pleasantly round faced man, with a smile and a body weight to match. He lived in the apartment above the restaurant and I had known him for several years.

"I came here to work," I said. "There's too much going on at the villa in Le Cannet. I have to be alone."

Wally nodded and smiled. "It's because of Adréana's birthday party, no? People are coming in. I know. I received my invitation yesterday."

"Are you coming?" I asked.

"Are you?" he laughed.

"I'll be there," I said. "It's my daughter."

"I will be there. My wife is coming from Moscow with my daughter. I thought it would be fun for them," Wally answered.

Wally was an interesting man. From what I had heard he was in the C.I.A. when he met his wife. After he was married he resigned from the C.I.A. immediately and moved to St. Tropez with his new wife. They then went to Paris and had a baby. His wife and baby moved back to Russia because his wife did not like France.

She would visit him on holidays and vacations so that he could stay in touch with his daughter. Of course, she might have been a communist, but she also knew that he was a very rich man and she wanted to make sure that their daughter received her inheritance.

"That should be good," I said. "How old is your daughter now?"

"Six," he answered.

"She'll have fun," I said.

A very attractive lady joined him in the small aisle. She smiled at me. I smiled back. Wally noticed and introduced us.

"Dominique," he said. "I'd like you to meet the American novelist, Harold Robbins." He then turned to me. "Harold," he said. "I would like for you to meet Baronne de Guilame of Paris."

I tried to stand up. But there was no way sitting on the back side of a banquette. "Madame la Baronne, my pleasure."

She smiled. "Please, be seated, Mr. Robbins. And the name is Dominique, to friends. And I hope we will be friends. I have read several of your novels and enjoyed them."

"Thank you," I said.

Fritz gestured to Wally. Wally turned to her. "Our table is ready, Dominique." Then to me. "We'll meet soon."

"I'm looking forward to it," I said. Then I watched them as they went up the aisle. She had a great ass and long legs. Too tall to be French I thought. I wondered where she was manufactured. Then the little waiter brought my food and I ate quickly. Once while I was having my coffee, I looked across at Wally's table, his back was towards me. But, her eyes were watching me. It was hell. She was with Wally and I had to work. Damn.

I began working as soon as I finished lunch. It was a comfortable setup. Avis, my stewardess, knew my working habits.

While I was at lunch, she set up a box of papers for me. One white sheet and four onion-skin carbons behind. When I finished, I would send the original and two sets of the story to the States. I would retain two sets for my files.

The story began moving immediately. I had thought a long time about a sequel to the television mini-series of 79 Park Avenue. So it was easy to write. The sequel would begin when Marja, the main character, would come out of prison. Her conflict would be how to keep her old life from destroying her new life that she vowed would be better. But it was not that simple. She could not get away from the society where she had been. No matter how hard she tried. It was going to become impossible for her to make a life for her and Michelle, her daughter, who she loved so much.

By seven that evening, I had finished with almost all of the opening act. I stretched and went up onto the deck. Twilight was just beginning to fall. Avis had already brought a Glenmorangie on the rocks before I had a chance to sit down. She placed it on the table in front of the bench. I sat down and looked out onto the street.

The crowd was just beginning to return from the beach. The tourists were walking around, looking into the storefront windows, checking the restaurants. Those with children were buying ice cream or candy. As they moved along the street they usually did not look up at the boats along the quay. Not unless they had heard that there was a celebrity, singer or football player on one of the boats. That interested them, otherwise, they would pay no attention.

"Harold," a young voice called from the bottom of the gangplank.

I squinted to see who it was. "Leslie," I answered.

She had proper manners. If you want to board a ship, you had to ask permission. "May I come aboard?"

I laughed. "Of course, Leslie."

She came up the gangplank and stood next to me and leaned down to kiss my cheek. "How are you, Harold?" she asked. "I haven't seen you down here for quite a while."

"I've been jammed up," I said. "Come, sit down beside me. What would you like to drink?"

"Vodka tonic," she smiled, as I pressed the button to call Avis.

Avis came up. She knew Leslie and smiled. "I know," she said. "Vodka tonic."

"Thank you, Avis," Leslie nodded. She turned back to me.

"Are Grace and Adréana here with you?"

"No," I answered. "They are in Le Cannet. I came over here to work for a week."

Leslie looked puzzled. "I never heard of anyone coming to St. Tro. to work."

I waited until Avis put down the vodka tonic in front of Leslie.

"There are just too many people at the villa. People are staying in the office. I had no place to work."

Leslie smiled and took a sip of her drink. "Anyway, I am

happy that you are here. I've been wondering what you have been doing."

"Nothing important," I answered, looking at her. She was small, maybe five three, with long, long blonde hair, blue eyes, and her skin was almost black from the sun. That was natural, she spent the days windsurfing in the nude. She only wore her bikini when she gave windsurfing lessons. She had come from Australia a year ago with her boyfriend. She was eighteen. Her boyfriend left her broke on the beach soon after. I met her early that same summer as we backed into St. Tropez to dock. Tony Roma, one of our guests, saw her sitting on top of a post next to the dock. She caught one of the ropes from Anton and tied it onto the stanchion. Tony called out to her. And she was here every time we came in to dock.

"Want to have dinner?" I asked.

"I'm not dressed," she answered.

"You're bikini-ed," I laughed. "We're eating on the boat. You don't have to change."

"That's lovely," she said. "I was just going to have a baguette and cheese. There haven't been many windsurfing pupils in the last few days."

"The season is just beginning to start," I said. "You'll be okay."

Cathy served a simple dinner. Caesar salad, roast chicken with pan roasted potatoes and a lovely chocolate cake that she had promised. Leslie ate as if food was going out of style.

I knew that she had not really eaten for a while. She had a second serving of chocolate cake with her coffee. Then she smiled at me shyly. "I've pigged out, but I really needed it."

"I know," I said. "But, it's okay. I'm glad you came to dinner. I don't like eating alone."

"You're very sweet, Harold," she said. "May I have another vodka tonic?"

"No problem," I answered and gave the order to Avis as she

cleared the table. I looked down at the quay. It was night now and all the street performers and buskers were in full swing.

There was always a small crowd around each of them listening and watching their talent. The favorite was the young man that blew fire from his pursed lips. He caught the most coins on the street around him.

Leslie looked as I watched him. "I know him," she said as she sipped at her drink. "He's from Australia too."

"Were you with him?" I asked curiously.

"No way," she said. "He has syphilis. He's had it since he was in Sydney."

"How do you know that?"

"He was one of seven of us that came here," she said. "We found out when his girlfriend died in the clinic here."

"Where are the rest of your friends?" I asked.

"Gone," she said. "I'm the only one that stayed here. I'd spend my life on a windsurf. This is the best place in Europe to be."

"Don't you ever want to go home?" I asked.

"I have nothing there," she said. "My father took off when I was a kid. My mother found another man. But I was not happy with them because he was always trying to get into my knickers. Finally, I took off with Charles and the gang. After we got here everyone split, and Charles got the hots for some French girl and took off."

"Why is the firemaker still here?" I asked.

"French doctors clear him for treatments here at the clinic. Besides, Sam believes that the fire will burn the syphilis out of his system. But I see him. He's going. He's as skinny as a stick. In Sydney he weighed almost two hundred pounds."

I shook my head. "I'm sorry for him." I gave her a hundred franc note. "Give it to him."

She looked at me for a moment, then turned and went down the gangplank. I watched her give him the money. She spoke to him for a few moments. He looked up at me and waved his hand to me.

I waved back. Then Leslie came back up the gangplank. "He thanked you very much," she said.

"It's okay," I said.

"May I have another vodka tonic?" she asked.

"You'll be smashed," I said.

"I don't care," she said. "Whenever I talk to Sam, I get depressed."

"You can have a drink," I said, pressing the service button again. "Where are you staying now?"

Avis brought the vodka tonic before I even had to ask for it. "Thank you," I said to her before turning back to Leslie.

"Where are you staying?"

"I have a bunk at the hostel," she said. "It's nice and clean and they have showers. It cost only five francs a night."

"That's not bad," I said. I opened my wallet and gave her five hundred francs.

"That's too much," she said. "If I went into the hostel with this much money, someone would steal it." She thought for a moment. "Will you be here for a week?"

"I think so," I said.

"Then maybe you could give me fifty or a hundred francs a day. That would be better."

"Okay," I said. She gave me back the five hundred franc note and I gave her a hundred franc note.

"Mr. Robbins," a woman's voice came up from the quay.

I looked down. "Mme. la Baronne," I said, standing up.

"May I come aboard?" she asked.

"Of course," I answered.

She came aboard. She was taller than I had originally thought. Maybe an inch or two taller than myself.

"Welcome aboard."

She smiled at me and then looked over at Leslie. "Your daughter?" she asked curiously.

I laughed. "No, she is a friend. She teaches windsurfing." I gestured to Leslie. "Leslie, may I introduce you to the Baronne de Guilame."

Leslie held out her hand. "I am happy to meet you, Mme. Baronne."

Dominique shook Leslie's hand. French style, once up, once down. "I am also happy to meet you, Leslie."

I turned to Dominique. "Please sit and have a drink with us. What would you enjoy?"

Dominique answered, "Champagne. Everything else makes me drunk and silly."

I pressed the button. "A bottle of champagne," I told Avis. Then I turned back to Dominique. "Have you had a nice dinner?"

"As usual. L'Escale's food is good but boring. Wally takes dinner there every night."

Avis returned and set a bucket with ice on the table. She held the champagne bottle in her other hand. She set a champagne glass in front of each person. She then popped the cork with expertise and filled our glasses.

Dominique tasted her champagne as she watched Avis return to the cabin. "She is a pretty girl," she said.

Leslie laughed. "If you think she's pretty, you should see Cathy, the cook. Harold's girls on the boat are famous for being the most beautiful crew in the South of France."

Dominique looked at me. "Do you hire girls because they are pretty or because they are competent?"

"I hire them for the job they are supposed to do," I said. "Pretty is a bonus."

Dominique looked at Leslie. "And isn't she too young to be your petite amie?"

I reached for Leslie's hand. She was beginning to feel uncomfortable. Her world was not like Dominique's. Her world was young and simple. "She is beautiful, of course, and I would not be unhappy if she were my petite amie. But she is attached with a very bright young man."

Leslie looked at me as she placed down her drink. "But, I am also a bit late. I promised to meet my friends at the disco."

I looked at her as she stood up. "You will see me tomorrow?" I asked.

She kissed my cheek. "I'll be here." She then turned to Dominique. "Bon soir, Madame. I am sorry that you did not enjoy your dinner. I had a lovely time on the boat with Harold," she said and scooted off the boat.

I smiled at Dominique. "You are not very nice."

"I said nothing," she said, filling her glass.

"She is a sweet child in a strange world and you are a bitch," I said.

"Do you want me to get off the boat?" she asked.

"You can suit yourself," I said to her. "I don't like having guests of mine feeling uncomfortable."

She took another glass of champagne before speaking. "You're angry," she said. "Would you like to spank me? I have no panties on under my dress. You can take me down to your cabin. I'm sure you have a leather belt. And it will make you feel better."

I laughed. "And would it make you feel better?"

She smiled seductively. "I'd love it."

I stared at her for a moment. She was beautiful and intriguing. It was crazy, but I was here to work. Then I smiled and did my Napoleonic gesture. "No, not tonight, Dominique."

She laughed and finished her champagne. "There will be another time," she said as she rose and kissed my cheek and walked across the deck and down the gangplank. She turned and gestured with her hand and disappeared into the crowd.

I sat there for a while and smoked a cigarette. Avis came on the deck. "Is it alright to clear the table?"

"Of course," I said. Then I thought for a moment. "Wake me at seven-thirty in the morning," I said. "I'll have breakfast at eight and I'll get to work as soon as I have eaten."

It was after nine o'clock in the morning before I had written to the point in the script where Marja came out of jail and was met at the prison gates by her attorney who had arranged her parole. I had already started my second pack of Lucky Strikes. I leaned back and stared at the pages. I hoped they were good. It felt like it was moving and that's what a writer always wants to feel. But you never know if it's good or bad.

I heard a voice from the deck steps. "Harold?" I turned and looked up from the dining salon through the upper salon. Dominique's face peered down the steps. Before I could speak, she said breathlessly, "I am sorry to intrude, but I would like to invite you to lunch."

I looked at her. "I'm working."

"Work or not, you have to eat," she said. "I have my own car and a reservation at my favorite restaurant on the hill behind the village."

"No, thank you," I said. "I'm afraid it will take too much time."

"Ninety minutes. Here and back, I promise. The patron used to be my chef in Paris. I have already ordered the menu," she said.

"I don't know," I answered. "I am on a deadline."

"I'll be back at one o'clock," she said. "If you don't come there will be nothing lost." Then she disappeared from the staircase.

I took out another cigarette. Ken appeared and flipped his Zippo. "Thank you," I said.

He had a smile on his face. "Are you going with the Baroness?"

"Not a Baroness, that's English. French is Baronne," I said.

"The French always have their own way," he said. "But, I think she wants to rape you."

I began to laugh. "I should be that lucky," I said. "All she asked me for was lunch."

Ken smiled. "But are you going with her?"

"Jesus," I said. "I have no privacy on this boat."

"I'm the Captain," he smiled again. "I have to know every-thing that's going on. This is my ship."

"Fuck you," I said. "I have to get back to work."

"But, you are going to lunch with her?"

I didn't answer.

Ken went back down to the galley. I could hear his voice as he spoke to the others. "Mr. Robbins will be going out for lunch."

Marja was a great person to write about. It was a natural. I felt as if I were telling a story of someone I knew. A real girl. The pages flew and I was almost halfway through the story when I heard Dominique's voice from the opened deck door.

"Harold," she said in her faint accent. "I am waiting for you."

I looked at my watch. She was exactly on time. One o'clock P.M. I glanced down at the pages again. I had had a good morning's work. "Give me a moment to wash up," I called to her. "I'll be right with you."

Her car was a small Peugeot. We arrived at a discreet small restaurant in one of the rolling hills behind St. Tropez. She tooted her car horn as we drove up. The restaurant had only twelve tables. As we walked in I noticed that only one of the tables had a tablecloth and service of silver and glasses for two.

The patron, a tall, bald-headed man, greeted us warmly. He smiled at Dominique, kissed her hand and said, "Mme. la Baronne."

She smiled at him. "Charles," she said. "It has been a long time."

"Too long, Madame," he concurred as he led us to the table.

"And Therese?" Dominique asked.

"She is doing well, Madame," he nodded. "Thank you, Ma-dame." Then his face split into a large smile. "I have made your favorite dishes. Escargot. Then I have prepared a Crown Roast of Lamb. For dessert, chocolate cake and fresh whipped cream. And I

have been able to find the same Burgundy that you used in your cellar in Paris."

"You stole it," she laughed. "Phillipe would kill you if he knew."

"But I knew, Madame, there would come a time when you would be here with us. What would you have me serve, that awful Cote de Provence that all the restaurants have here in St. Tropez?"

"Thank you, Charles, for your thoughtfulness," she smiled looking at him. "Charles, my friend, Harold Robbins, the American author."

He bowed to me. "It is my honor, sir. I have one of your novels. The Carpetbaggers."

"Thank you, Charles," I said.

He turned and went into the building. I looked at Dominique. "I don't see any other customers. Business is slow if we are the only ones here."

She laughed. "He has no problems. He is normally closed at luncheon, but he opened for me when I called."

"You've got clout," I said to her and laughed.

"Clout?" she asked. "What does that mean?"

I laughed again. "You are a very important lady."

And then lunch began. Charles was right. It was superb. I was so full by the end of the meal I didn't think I could get up from the table. I looked at my watch. I couldn't believe it. It was five o'clock. I stared at her. "Jesus! I blew the whole afternoon!"

I called Charles. "L' addition, sil vous plait."

Charles shook his head. "It's not for you, Monsieur. You are the guest of Mme. la Baronne."

I looked at Dominique. "That's ridiculous. The check should be mine. After all, you introduced me to a beautiful restaurant and we've had a wonderful afternoon."

"Don't be silly," she said. "This is France. I invited you to lunch. And besides, I'm richer than you are."

I started to laugh. She was right. It is France and she was probably richer than I. And what the hell! She is a real bitch.

"Okay," I said. "But, you still have to get me back to the boat. I've got work to do."

"Oh, I am so sorry," she said. "Charles had gone to get us our car, but he was unable to start the motor. He is trying to find someone to help fix it."

"Can we get a taxi?" I asked.

"This is St. Tropez," she said. "There are only two taxis in town and they only work at the hotels. The only taxi we can get is in St. Raphael across the peninsula from here. This is their busy time. I doubt if we could get them to come up here."

I turned to Charles. "Do you have a car we can borrow?"

"No, Monsieur. All I have is a horse and wagon. It is not strong enough to take you down into town. But, there is no need to worry. I have a lovely guest room that I can loan you."

I had been had. I turned to Dominique. "You are really a bitch. I think he might have a few small horsewhips in that guest room for you?"

"Of course," she smiled. "After all, we are in the country."

"Honey," I smiled at her. "I'm going to sit here at the table until some customers show up for dinner in a car. Then I'll get back to town. I told you, I'm on a deadline."

She stared at me. "Don't you like me?"

I smiled. "I love you. But I have to work."

"You would stay here if the windsurfer was with you," she spoke petulantly.

"You're beginning to sound like my wife. She doesn't believe that I am here to work, either. She always thinks I am screwing around."

"Isn't that true?" she laughed.

"Not when I'm working," I said. I held up my hand. "Charles, may I have a Scotch on the rocks, please."

He nodded and placed the drink on the table for me. "Thank you," I said.

He looked at Dominique and then at me. "We have several customers arriving around seven. I am sure that one of them will give you a lift into town."

Dominique smiled at me. "Champagne," she said to Charles. "Not a bottle, just a coupe."

It was eight o'clock by the time we returned to the yacht. I gave two hundred francs to the driver of the car who had given us a lift. He gave me a "merci" and returned to his patron at the restaurant. Dominique walked up the gangplank with me.

Leslie and Ken were standing on the deck.

"We began to worry about you," Leslie said. "Ken told me that you would be back after lunch, around three-ish."

I smiled. "We were in the hills when her car died."

Ken nodded. "Things like that always happen."

"Yep," I said. "I think we all need a drink."

Ken looked at me. "What about dinner? Cathy's prepared some of your favorite dishes."

"Is there enough for Leslie and the Baronne?" I asked.

"Cathy always has enough," he assured me.

"I can't eat," Dominique said. "I'm satiated and exhausted."

"I'm sorry," I said. "Thank you for the luncheon. It really was delicious."

She turned to Leslie. "Are you staying for dinner?"

Leslie smiled. "I never miss an invitation for dinner."

Dominique still looked at her. "Then you will stay on after dinner?"

Leslie again smiled. "If Harold asks me. That's another thing I never turn down if I have an invitation."

"But, Harold said that he would be working after dinner," Dominique said.

Leslie just nodded. "I can sleep until he's finished working."

Dominique smiled. "Then bon soir, ma petite," she said and went off the boat.

Leslie looked at me. "She's a tough lady."

"Yes," I said. "And a very interesting one."

I worked after dinner until midnight and then went down into my cabin. Leslie was naked, fast asleep on the single bed across from the double bed on the other side of the cabin. I stretched out in my Jockeys and disappeared into another world where Dominique had gone.

I felt my shoulder being shaken. I opened my eyes. Dominique was bending over me. I looked across the cabin at the single bed. Leslie was gone. "What the hell is the matter with you? Couldn't you see that I was sleeping?" I snapped.

"It was after ten clock," she said. "Ken told me that you wanted to start working early."

"Did he tell you to come down here?" I asked.

"I didn't ask him," she said. "I just came down to wake you up."

"How did you know that I wasn't fucking Leslie?" I asked. "What would you have done then?"

"I would watch and applaud," she laughed. "But Ken told me that she had left for the beach at eight o'clock this morning."

She sat down on the single bed. She looked at me. "Did you have sex with Leslie last night?"

"None of your business," I said, standing up and going to the bathroom. "Besides, what difference does it make to you?"

She came across the cabin and looked right into my eyes. At the same time she slipped one hand down the front of my Jockeys and cupped my balls. She kissed me and spoke softly. "I want to have a real affair with you, not just a fuck."

I could feel myself growing hard. Then I lifted her hand away. "Dominique," I said. "I have things to do. Maybe we will have something at another time."

"Maybe then I will not have the time," she said.

"C'est la vie," I said and went into the bathroom and closed the door behind me.

When I returned to the cabin, she was gone. I felt her scent. It was real and I could feel her. Then I saw a small note on my pillow.

"Chéri, Harold. There will be a time. We will have it. And it will be right for both of us. Avec amour, Dominique."

I smiled. I didn't believe I would ever see her again. Especially after Wally told me that she had returned to Paris. I stayed on the yacht in St. Tro. until I finished the script for the television sequel to 79 Park Avenue. *I was able to return to Cannes for Adréana's sixth birthday party. It was a beautiful party and I would not have missed it for the world. I received the money promised for writing the sequel.*

But, there was a disappointment. Lesley Ann Warren, who had played the lead in the original mini-series, decided that she would not play that character again. Despite pleading by Univeral and the producers, she remained adamant. She was determined to be a star on the big screen, not on television.

Bob Weston and I tried to get Universal to sign another actress for the part. But they refused. They were happy to pay the money and forget it.

In September, Grace and Adréana returned to Los Angeles so that Adréana could begin school.

I stayed in Le Cannet to start work on a new novel, The Betsy.

The telephone rang. "Harold," a familiar voice spoke.

"Yes, Dominique," I said.

*A*nother girlfriend?" I asked.

He smiled happily. "You better believe it. Jesus, Dominique was into everything, S and M, golden showers." He looked up at me. "Do you know what that is?"

"Sure. I read Harold Robbins novels," I answered impishly,

wondering if this was really about Dominique or he was just trying it out for "shock value."

He ignored my comment and continued to talk about Dominique. "She's a *baronne*. It's the French spelling. *B-a-r-o-n-n-e*. She had a hell of a life." He started to laugh. "When I started seeing Linda, Grace and Dominique got crazy and started plotting how to get Linda out of the picture."

"Is Linda going to France with you?" I asked.

"Yeah, for a couple of weeks," he said.

I shook my head and laughed. "Nothing slows you down, does it?"

CHAPTER FORTY

On the morning of Adréana's birthday in July during the following summer Harold called from Paris after appearing on the French talk show. "I'm taking the Concorde to New York and then a flight from New York to LA. It's a surprise for Adréana."

"That's so exciting, Harold. She'll be so happy. We've been decorating for her party all morning. She's having all of her friends over. The cook is making a birthday cake and food enough for twenty or thirty people."

"Don't let her know we're coming."

"I won't. How will you get here in time?"

"Concorde's only three hours to New York from here, and from New York to LA is five hours."

"Have a good trip," I said, and hung up. I had missed Harold over the summer. I had tried to keep my feelings for him stifled, but it was impossible. I knew I was in love with him.

At 5:00 P.M. the doorbell to the gates rang. The guard announced the arrival. Adréana and I were standing in the kitchen

214   JANN ROBBINS

when she realized it was her mother and father. Her face lit up and we both ran out to the driveway.

Harold made the birthday party a special memory for his daughter. He mixed and mingled with her friends, danced with Adréana, and made sure everyone was having a good time.

He called me up to his study after the party that night. When I closed the door he hugged me and kissed me. "I'm not going back to France; I'm staying here."

I kissed him back this time. Over the past several months I realized how much I cared for him. I loved him more than he should ever know. But, at that moment I didn't care if our relationship lasted one hour, one year, or a lifetime. I was his.

"You're my baby."

"I missed you," I said. We looked at each other and I knew we would never be apart. I wanted to melt into his heart, as three years of emotion, love, passion, and care had come down to this one moment.

"We belong together, angel," he said, holding me tightly.

My heart was pounding. I had longed to hear those words and I knew they were true. The words were real and I believed him.

That night we made a commitment in our hearts and we became lovers on every level. I wanted to stay in this moment forever.

"What are we going to do, Harold?" I asked. I knew the many obstacles ahead of us.

"Don't worry. It'll all work out."

Of course, I knew it was crazy and foolish and from an outsider's point of view probably wrong. I loved Harold, adored him, and cherished him. He was right; "we were meant for each other."

A friend of mine once told me, "When you find the kind of love that you and Harold have, you have everything. Material things don't matter; nothing matters. You've touched love and that's everything." I knew with Harold I touched love in every moment. I had everything.

CHAPTER FORTY-ONE

TWO YEARS LATER

When I woke up on Christmas morning, lying next to Harold, he was awake and smiling at me, holding a jewelry box with a bow on the top. "Merry Christmas, shiksa," he kidded.

My eyes widened as he opened the box for me. A Rolex. Gold with a lapis lazuli face. It was beautiful. Magnificent. I heard the sound of Etta James's recording of "At Last" coming from the family room.

"We've got lox, bagels, and cream cheese waiting," he said, and wrapped the watch around my wrist.

Still half-asleep, I felt like I must be in a dream. I pulled him back to me and kissed him. "I love you, Harold. I'm the luckiest girl in the world."

"You are my baby!" he said, and kissed me.

He took my hand when we got to the family room and we danced, just holding each other. Each time we danced it was still a thrill for me.

Each night since our affair began was as exciting as the first. All of the emotions and passions exploded into this strange and wonderful relationship. The disappointments of the past, unmet needs, lost dreams and hopes all seemed to be erased when we were together. I knew each moment could be our last, and there were nagging questions in my heart of how long would it last? Was there a future? Or would I just fall by the wayside as so many others had? I didn't know and probably Harold didn't know. We had the moment, and for us that was all that mattered.

When I felt his arms around me each night and he looked at me like it was the first time he had ever been in love, I knew I would never leave this man. Right now, he was my dream and I was his.

When we fell asleep each night, his last whispers to me were, "We will never be apart, sweetheart." I had never felt so safe or so loved.

Chapter Forty-Two

*H*arold held my hand as we sat next to each other at the family room table. He kissed the palm of my hand and rubbed my leg affectionately as he dictated the story of *Empire* into the microrecorder. He had been hired by Fox Television to write a series for the new network.

"You know, darling," he said to me after turning off the recorder. "We have to be grateful." He looked at me with pure wonder in his eyes. "It was only a couple of years ago when I couldn't speak and had to use this recorder to exercise my speech. Today, I'm dictating a story. None of it would be if it hadn't been for you. You walked into my life and changed everything."

"Harold, it's all your hard work. I supported you, but you did the work. And I'm very grateful for you." I leaned over and kissed him.

After we finished our croissants that morning, David Chandler arrived to work on the development of a new series idea for 20th Century Fox, *Empire*. This television piece was a drama series about a conglomerate starring Frank Sinatra. He was promised as the lead character but would only appear in the weekly series once a month. He would play a CEO with three high-powered vice presidents under him who would carry the individual stories on the other weeks of the month.

Harold had been hired to write a two-hour script for the debut of the series, scheduled for the fall of the coming year. Harold had hired David to assist us since David had once been a television writer and knew the form better than Harold. In fact, David had been the lead writer of *Harold Robbins' The Survivors*, America's first nighttime soap opera, which aired on ABC in the sixties, starring Lana Turner and George Hamilton.

Harold would create the story for *Empire* and I was in charge of developing the characters for the show. David would put it all together in television format.

"I don't really think that Frank will star in this, but what the hell, Fox is paying for it!" Harold said.

"Why would he want to?" David asked. "He has plenty of money."

Both Harold and David had been friends with Frank Sinatra in the past years. David had to pass Sinatra's inspection years earlier when he married his wife, Rita, who was a close friend of Frank's.

"He's got the same problem I have, cash flow," Harold said, and sighed. "He's got a one-hundred-thousand-dollar nut to crack each month just to keep his houses going. But he'll be all right; his records will sell till the end of time. I haven't seen him since his birthday a few years ago in Vegas. But I don't think he'll ever star in this piece; Frank never keeps his fucking word. So whatever he said to the Fox people is bullshit."

David shrugged. "He can write his own ticket, Harold."

"Why do you say he doesn't keep his word, Harold?" I asked.

"He told me he owed me one, anything I ever wanted was mine, after I helped him get a reading for the role in *The Joker Is Wild*. I was still living in New York at the time. This movie and Oscar got his acting career back on track. Later, when I asked him to star in

Where Love Has Gone, he said he couldn't do it because he was friends with Lana. Everyone thought the story was about Lana Turner's daughter murdering Johnny Stompanato. Christ, even Lana didn't think it was about her. Cocksucker!"

David chuckled. "Didn't you own a plane with Sammy Davis and Frank?"

"For about a year in the seventies. They nearly broke me flying all their friends all over the country. We split everything a third. I flew on it once and I think it cost me a hundred grand!"

CHAPTER FORTY-THREE

*H*arold was very anxious to break into the television market in the mid-eighties. Harold Robbins International had moved onto the 20th Century Fox lot with Bob Weston remaining as the president of the company. Harold was hoping to turn one of his novels into a dramatic series or make a continuing miniseries showcase for his books that had not yet been made into movies. He had been fascinated with the television market since *The Survivors*.

He told the story of how *The Survivors* was born many times to the press: "Gene Schwam and I arrived at the Plaza Hotel in Manhattan for the meeting with ABC. Barry Diller and Marty Starger were the 'suits' at the network. The suits at that time had taken bets on how much I would spend during the trip."

If Gene was at the table during the interview he would continue the story in his own words: "There was not a suite big enough for Harold; he ended up using three suites that joined together and totaled eight thousand dollars per night. The first thing Harold did was order champagne, Dom Perignon, and beluga caviar. He ended up spending even more than Barry Diller and Marty Starger had bet on."

"When I went into the meeting with them," Harold would pick up the story at this point, "I had no idea what story I was going to pitch, but I did have a leading lady to offer that would change the way actors looked at television. Lana Turner had agreed to play the leading role. She was a big screen star at the time and most movie actors shunned television. If she played the small screen it would change things for everyone. I had dated Lana for a while in the fifties, and later in the sixties I had an office at 9200 Sunset next to her new husband. I offered her husband a partnership with me if the series was bought by ABC."

"Did her husband know you had an affair with Lana?" the reporter would usually ask.

"That was years before. What's a fuck between friends?

"After the meeting started that morning I stared out the window of the office and looked down onto the street. I saw a Rolls-Royce. I took a bite of my lox, bagel, and cream cheese and a swig of coffee to wash it down and I started the story.

" 'It starts when a beautiful Rolls-Royce convertible pulls up and a knockout blonde puts her leg on the curb. That's all we see until a very handsome man takes her hand,' and I continued to ad-lib the story. The patriarch of the family dies within the first weeks of the series and the grandchildren start to fight for control of the millions that had been left to them.

"The room was so quiet you could hear a pin drop by the time I finished.

"Power, sex, deceit, and wealth: the four ingredients to a successful story!" Harold said, looking at David and me. Harold took a puff on his cigarette and continued.

"Before I left I put the icing on the cake. 'By the way, gentlemen, Lana Turner is the knockout blonde.' You could almost hear a gasp from the suits."

By the time he and Gene returned to the Plaza there was a green light for the project. Only the contracts remained to be drawn up.

Harold had other irons in the fire that would take him across the continent in search of his next book before the contracts were drawn up. He also had a rule: Never start work on a project until you see the money. Two and one-half months later, the contracts were at last drawn up and signed. The money was deposited in the bank. The network wanted Harold to write the story he told them in their offices while he was in New York. Harold took the money but had no recollection of the story he had told them. Thousands of stories had raced through his mind since that time. But the quintessential storyteller sat down and wrote the story bible for *Harold Robbins' The Survivors*, starring Lana Turner, George Hamilton, and Ralph Bellamy. The network was lavishing a huge publicity campaign on the project. Harold Robbins's name was the draw and there were billboards across the country with Lana Turner in life-size proportions. Harold Robbins and the *Survivors* title was emblazoned boldly across the board.

Television ran on ratings, not on books shipped and sold. The ratings were read overnight after the debut. These ratings could determine a failed or hit series. In the first segment of the program Harold had developed a crisis situation where the grandfather, played by Ralph Bellamy, a well-known character actor of the time, was near death and would within the next six segments die. This would catapult the heirs to battle over the money left to them in the will.

The network took their overnight ratings after the first three segments and discovered the audience loved the grandfather, Ralph Bellamy. The word came down from the executive offices to keep Ralph Bellamy. This changed everything in the structure of the ongoing story. There could be no tension between the heirs, and the battle over the money had disappeared. After fifteen weeks the show was canceled.

CHAPTER FORTY-FOUR

COCKTAILS AT SEVEN, DINNER AT EIGHT, PASS THE BOMBSHELLS

*H*arold was sitting at the table in the family room making a list of names when I walked in the door after running some morning errands.

I smiled happily at him. "What's the list?"

He looked at me and smiled, patting my derriere as I made my way to the chair next to him. "You've got an ass like Marilyn Monroe," he said, and leaned over and kissed that part of my anatomy before I sat down.

I was thrilled he loved my ass. Years later, he would honor my derriere in an interview with *Esquire* magazine.

"I'll take that as a compliment as long as you like it," I answered, and kissed him.

"We're having a dinner party on Friday. I've called Gérard at L'Orangerie and told him ten or twelve of us would be there for dinner about eight or eight thirty."

Gérard Ferrie was the owner of L'Orangerie restaurant in Los Angeles. It was a five-star restaurant. Harold had helped Gérard relocate in LA after frequenting his restaurant and becoming friends with him in the South of France.

"Who are our guests?"

"What about Tony Martin and Cyd Charisse, Eileen and Norman Kreiss, David and Rita Chandler, Bill and Helen Rosen, Gene and Myrna, you and I?"

These were Harold's closest friends. They were people whom he and Grace went to dinner with when they were in town together. I was curious about why he had chosen to have this dinner party.

"Sounds fun, I've never been to L'Orangerie," I said. Today I was just as happy to eat tuna out of a can as long as I was with Harold. There were no boundaries to my feelings for him.

He pulled me toward him after he had seen that look of contentment on my face. "You're great; you love everything and I love you."

"All the time, anywhere, everywhere, I love you."

"Call Michael and tell him to bring up some clothes. I want you to have something new to wear on Friday!"

Michael and Maggie were clothing designers at a shop called Metropolis on Santa Monica Boulevard. I had shopped at the store since I arrived in LA. It was a hot, trendy dress shop and I loved the designs and so did Harold. Michael Roche was Maggie's assistant who later opened his own boutique on Sunset called Addictions. His designs were always a sensation at the American Music Awards, and he once made a dress of platinum American Express cards for Appolonia, one of Prince's protégés.

That afternoon Michael arrived with his assistant and a rack of clothing that he brought upstairs to the family room. Harold had a great eye for fashion and great taste about how a woman should dress. He knew what was flattering and took a great interest in finding the right thing for me to wear.

I modeled each dress. He checked out each one as I walked around the room and nodded his approval. I felt like I was in a scene from *The Carpetbaggers* and Jonas Cord had come to life, but I wasn't ready for what happened next.

"Give me all of them, Michael!" Harold said after I had tried on five dresses.

I was stunned and excited. Of course I wanted them all, but wasn't it too expensive! I could hear Paul Gitlin's voice in my head: *"Quit spending so goddamn much money."*

"Harold, I don't need all of them," I said.

"Sure, you do. We'll be going lots of places to wear them," he said, and grinned.

Michael, of course, saw dollar signs and was thrilled.

Again, I felt I was the luckiest girl in the world! I had to keep pinching myself to know if all this was real.

"You're my baby," Harold said, and kissed me.

I was speechless. "Thank you" seemed inadequate. It was not only the gifts that I loved; it was also the abandon with which he gave and how much fun he had with his generosity. I would see it magnified a thousand times during our life together.

When our guests arrived on the following Friday evening Harold and I were downstairs at the bar waiting for them. As each of the ladies arrived they were dressed beautifully, and the men wore ties and sport jackets. The room had abundant fresh flowers and soft lighting as we all chatted and talked.

After about thirty minutes of cocktail conversation, Tony Martin looked at Harold and me sitting beside each other behind the bar. "Okay, Harold, all of us want to know." He motioned around the room at Harold's friends. "Grace has been gone a long time; Jann is here; what's going on?"

I held my breath and tried not to change expressions. This was definitely something Harold should answer. Even I was curious about his answer. Again he brought the house down.

Harold looked up at Tony and smiled. "I'm teaching Grace how to become a divorcée!"

Harold's provocative statement had stunned the audience. No one asked any more questions, and fortunately the waiter came in with fresh hors d'oeuvres.

When I looked up at the guests they were all staring and wondering what that meant. I could see the unspoken question written in their expressions: *Was he kidding or was he serious?*

On the way to L'Orangerie, Harold and I were leading the string of cars to the restaurant in the blue Corniche. Harold inadvertently ran a red light at the corner of Benedict Canyon and Sunset, a heavily traveled intersection. Unfortunately, there was a motorcycle policeman nearby, and Harold saw the flashing red lights in his rearview mirrors.

As the policeman got off of his motorcycle and came to the window, the others in our caravan pulled up behind the Corniche, creating a traffic jam.

"May I see your driver's license, sir?" the policeman said, watching the cars pull up behind his motorcycle. "Who are those people?"

"I'm taking some people to dinner," Harold answered. "Are you hungry?"

The officer didn't respond. I had already taken Harold's driver's license out of his wallet and Harold handed it to the officer.

The officer stayed official as he looked at the name. "You're Harold Robbins . . . the writer, sir?"

"Yes, Officer. I'm Harold Robbins."

The officer started to laugh. "My wife's a big fan of your books."

"Is she? She's too young to read my books!" Harold said.

This seemed to please the officer as he walked back to his car with Harold's driver's license. When the officer came back to the window he tore off a ticket. "I'm going to give you a warning, Mr. Robbins."

He handed Harold the ticket and Harold handed it to me.

"I'd like to send your wife a book if I may," Harold said politely.

"She would like that, I'm sure." The officer smiled.

"Officer," Harold said respectfully. "Give Jann an address where I can send your wife a book. I'll send her my newest one," Harold offered.

I quickly got a pen and paper from my purse and the officer gave us the address and we were off to the restaurant.

The rest of the evening was what wishes and dreams are made of, all beautiful, all delicious, and I was treated as though I belonged. I was in Harold's world now and I was Harold's world.

CHAPTER FORTY-FIVE

V alentine's Day was always a special day for Harold and me.
Since the beginning of our relationship we celebrated that
occasion as our special day. It was like Christmas, New Year's,
birthdays, and Thanksgiving all rolled into one intimate day made
for us.

I had been shopping for a couple of weeks compiling fourteen
small meaningful gifts for Harold, a tradition I had created for our
day.

He had a collection of teddy bears from Ireland and England; a
hot pink teddy bear named Mansfield given to him by a young aspir-
ing actress who hoped someday to be as popular as Jayne Mansfield;
and a teddy bear in a toga called Romeo that was a gift from our
friends Jean Kasem, of *Cheers* television sitcom fame, and her husband, the legendary American Top 40 DJ Casey Kasem.

I had found a teddy bear made from pewter in England holding
barbells and sporting a mustache, teddy bear salt- and pepper shakers, teddy bear Belgian chocolates, a writing pen in clear Lucite to

which I added a miniature teddy bear toggle to the top, a heart-shaped key chain, a poem of love from *The Prophet*, jockey shorts with hearts, chocolate-covered Oreo cookies from Armitage Street in Chicago, "My Funny Valentine" on tape by Sinatra, Tony Bennett, Julie London, and several other artists, a toy red sports car, a package of Red Hot candy hearts, a red T-shirt imprinted on the front "Be MY Valentine," a small book on the history of Valentine's Day, and a pop art red heart drawing on paper with "ooh-la-la" emblazoned across the heart.

We planned a special dinner of lamb chops, fresh asparagus, potato pancakes (crispy and almost paper thin, Harold's favorite, made by our Polish cook, Tad). At the end of dinner the cook presented us with a heart-shaped chocolate cake with chocolate icing, dark chocolate ice cream, and whipped cream dollops on top with guess what! Shavings of chocolate!

After dinner Harold and I went up to the family room and he turned on his boom box and put a tape in of some of his favorite music. He made audiotapes frequently that had his favorite songs on them. This one happened to be love songs.

When we walked into the bedroom the muted lighting beneath the bed softly lit the room. He started to laugh when he saw the gifts piled high on the bed with a big red shiny heart on top. Together we opened each one and I told him silly reasons about choosing each gift.

"You never asked about your Valentine's gift," he said, and pulled out a box.

"My valentine gift is you. I thought roses and being together all day was enough," I said.

"I'm going to make you a promise," he said with a sly look. "We're going to get married on Valentine's Day. Just relax; it will happen."

A rush of emotion filled my heart, mixed with fear. What did he mean? When?

"What about Grace?"

"Grace is making her own choices. She'll be leaving, honey. I'm not rich enough." He laughed and pulled me to him.

I didn't want to ask any more questions. I wanted to believe in that promise. Who could sleep after this? Valentine's Day was perfect.

CHAPTER FORTY-SIX

HIT THE PANIC BUTTON . . . NOW WHAT?

We finished *Empire* in the middle of March and we were all convinced it would make a great television series. Who better to bring the corporate boardroom and bedroom to the small screen than the red-hot sizzling Harold Robbins? Bob Weston presented the script to Glen Larson, who was producing the series for Fox. The check for one hundred thousand dollars would be written after approval. The sooner the better, since there was always pressure coming from Paul about the ever-present debts. Harold was pushed once again to the edge financially.

On the Friday evening we completed *Empire*, Harold invited two friends to go to dinner with us at his favorite soul food restaurant, Maurice's Snak and Chat. Harold once again dropped into his Harlem vernacular, using the word "axed" whenever possible. We ate the finest soul food in LA. Ribs, collard greens, fried potatoes, corn on the cob, and hot peach cobbler for dessert! Lou Rawls, who was also in the restaurant that night, sat down with us and we all had a great time remembering old-time soul hits that had soul-food names in the lyrics.

"I had great soul food when I lived in Harlem," Harold told Lou. "They use more grease in 'soul food' than they do in Jewish recipes." He laughed. "The only difference is the matzo will lie in your stomach for a week."

"I thought heartburn was something you had after every meal when I was growing up," Lou joked.

Harold laughed one of those laughs that started at his toes and he couldn't stop. He was happy and entertained by everyone, including Maurice, the owner of the restaurant.

When we returned from dinner, the house was quiet downstairs since our cook had arranged for the night off. We could hear the doggies barking upstairs. When we entered the family room they rushed to meet us, and we took them out for a short walk. We walked them around the circle driveway, always on a leash since the coyotes haunted the meadow.

Later, I went downstairs to turn off the lights and lock all of the doors. I ran upstairs to my apartment to check on my cats and came back through the kitchen that led to the stairs near Harold's bathroom and bedroom.

I heard the sound of water splattering on the floor as I entered the kitchen. I gasped when I looked up and saw water pouring through the ceiling. I assumed a water pipe had broken and quickly ran up the stairs. When I turned the corner into Harold's large bathroom suite I saw him sprawled unconscious on the floor. The toilet bowl was lying on its side and water had soaked the carpeting, causing the water in the kitchen. In fact, water was still pouring out.

Everything seemed to happen in slow motion and yet only seconds passed. I kept gasping for breath, I was so frightened. I could feel the tears rolling down my cheeks as I knelt down beside him. I grabbed the panic button on the counter nearby and pressed it hard. This button was never used unless a dire emergency occurred. I had never seen it used by anyone in the house, but I was instructed that it would be quicker than dialing 911. This button notified our security company office and they notified Beverly Hills personnel.

As I continued to press the silent alarm, I grabbed the phone and hit the speed dial to locate Dr. Ablon. As I waited for the doctor, I was talking to Harold, reassuring him that everything was going to be fine. Dr. Ablon's answering service came on the line and I told them the emergency and the name of the patient. The operator wasted no time with any more questions. I held on to Harold's hand and silently prayed, trying to keep my own panic from taking control.

I waited anxiously, keeping my eye on the television monitor that stayed on the gate twenty-four hours a day. I knew the paramedics, police, and fire engines would be here any minute.

I looked down at Harold and saw he was shivering but still unconscious. I ran and grabbed a blanket with the phone still cradled near my face and covered him. I prayed and waited for help to arrive.

His breathing was labored. I ran to the corner in the bathroom where he kept his oxygen tank. I placed the nose cannula around his head and turned the oxygen to three liters. I had no idea if this was the right amount, but I had seen him do this when he was short of breath due to his emphysema, which he had been diagnosed with thirty years earlier.

Dr. Ablon's voice finally came over the phone. "Hello," he said.

I could hear music and conversation in the background.

"Ed, this is Jann Stapp." Ed had been to dinner with Harold and me many times since I started working for Harold, so he recognized my voice. "I'm calling about Harold. The paramedics are on the way. He's unconscious. I just started giving him three liters of oxygen!"

"Good," Ed answered. "I'm at a restaurant. I'm about ten minutes away."

As soon as I hung up the phone I saw the fire engine on the television monitor. I opened the gate through the phone intercom and ran downstairs to lead them up to the bathroom. In seconds the paramedics surrounded Harold and I gave them all the information I knew concerning his medications.

Slowly Harold started to regain consciousness. Dr. Ablon arrived and gave them Harold's medical history. He began talking and wanting to know what had happened as he looked into the faces of the paramedics. "Jann," he called out.

I ran to his side. "I'm here, Harold," I said, crying and hoping he was okay.

He started to move his leg and yelled out in pain. All of a sudden I was pushed out of the way and Dr. Ablon and the paramedics began working on the leg. Harold tried to sit up again, but he had excruciating pain in his leg.

The paramedics delicately moved him onto a gurney. Dr. Ablon walked across the soaked carpeting in the bathroom and looked into the toilet area. The entire toilet bowl was cracked in half. "He must have hit his hip on the toilet bowl." Dr. Ablon leaned down and turned the screw that stopped the flow of water with a very concerned look on his face.

I rode in the ambulance to UCLA Medical Center with Harold and watched the technicians take all of his vital signs continually over and over again until we arrived at the hospital. They gave him a shot to ease the pain in his leg and he started getting groggy, but he smiled at me and winked at my worried expression before we arrived at UCLA Medical Center. "Don't worry; I'll be fine."

Judy Holfer, Dr. Ablon's date from dinner, sat with me in a private waiting room at the hospital. This was her first date with the doctor and she was thrown into a chaotic situation that night. She had just moved to Los Angeles and was an executive with the May Company. Judy remained a good friend from that night forward. I'm sure I was distracted and lousy company with thoughts racing through my mind about Harold's condition.

I was afraid that night. Our world had been abruptly shattered. In fact, I thought our time together might have ended. But it only made our relationship stronger. It's funny the way love works.

CHAPTER FORTY-SEVEN

*D*r. Ablon finally came to the waiting room after what seemed an eternity. "Harold has a fractured hip and he's in a lot of pain. We still don't know why he blacked out. But he wants to see you." Ed looked very worried as he led me down the hall to the emergency room cubicle. Harold was propped up slightly on the gurney waiting to be taken to Intensive Care.

"Harold, the only reason I want you in ICU is because of your breathing problems, just a precaution. You seem to be doing fine. We're trying to find an orthopod to put you into traction. You'll be moved as soon as he gets here. No one can figure out what happened to make you pass out," Dr. Ablon said as we entered.

Harold had reached out his hand to me when I walked into the room. "Are you okay, baby?" He held me close to him. "Don't worry; everything is okay."

After Ablon had finished with his explanation of what was going to happen I turned to Harold. "Are you okay? I was so worried,

Harold," I said, and couldn't help the tears that came rolling down my cheeks.

"You saved my life, sweetheart," he said softly. "You know what that means?" he asked. "The Chinese teach you when you save someone's life you're responsible for them for the rest of their life; that means you're stuck with me." He smiled. "I love you."

"I'll be with you always," I said, and smiled, with tears in my eyes.

The nurse came in and gave Harold another shot and attached an IV line to his hand.

"What do you want me to do, Harold?"

"Call Patti and Bif to go over and tell Adréana in the morning. I don't want to frighten her by waking her up in the middle of the night. Call Paul first thing in the morning." He looked at me and I could see his eyes were filled with pain. He grimaced.

"I just want you to be okay; I love you," I whispered into his ear.

He kissed my hand. "I know," Harold answered.

The attendants came to transfer him to ICU. Dr. Ablon and Judy drove me home and came in for a while. Dr. Ablon asked about the food Harold had eaten, how he had been all day, but nothing seemed to answer the question of why he had passed out. Dr. Ablon called the hospital and ordered additional tests on Harold as we sat at the bar. I could see that he was worried.

I couldn't sleep after they left. I also couldn't go into Harold's bathroom upstairs and look at the broken toilet bowl and drenched carpet. I went upstairs through the bedroom and got the doggies. My cats, the doggies, and I spent a restless night in my apartment.

The phone rang at five o'clock the following morning. It was Harold. "Call Paul right now; he's already up." He sounded nervous.

"Harold, are you in pain?" I asked.

"Like a bitch, honey."

"Okay, I'll call him. Have they run any tests yet?" I asked.

"Everything is all fucked up here. Some guy is coming to put my leg in traction. They've been waiting for him for a few hours."

"Do you need me to bring you anything?" I asked.

"My shaving kit. It's up in the bathroom in the cabinet on the left."

"Okay."

"When will you be here?" he asked, anxiety in his voice.

"I'll come up as soon as I talk to Paul. I miss you."

"Yeah," he said through the pain. "I miss you, too."

Paul was tough. He wanted to know what Harold had done to himself. "Did it fuck up his head?" Paul asked.

"Paul, Ablon says he'll be fine; they need to find out why he passed out. There's nothing wrong with his head, but the hip is fractured. He's in a lot of pain."

"I wish he could come to the New York doctors," Paul said.

"We'll call you from the hospital and you can talk to him," I said, and hung up.

Harold remained in the hospital for more than a week, in traction. The bone was healing and he was released from the hospital using crutches. He was being given tests all day long to determine the cause of the episode. A neurologist suggested the collapse had been caused by a seizure from scar tissue formed after Harold's stroke. But since no one had witnessed the incident nothing was changed in his medications.

When he came home on the following Friday, he hopped out of the passenger side of the Corniche and was showing off with his crutches, poking me with the tip of his crutch and hopping the steps.

It reminded me of a picture he had hanging in his study of him roller-skating near the yacht at Port Canto in Cannes. He had on a floppy hat and sunglasses in the photo. Harold made it a point to have fun regardless of the circumstance, and he was doing that today. Life was to be enjoyed and he could overcome anything.

When the house had been built in 1980 a chairlift was put on the back stairs. He would have an opportunity to ride on the lift now, out of necessity, since he couldn't manage the steps with his crutches.

CHAPTER FORTY-EIGHT

*H*arold's recovery was swift and he was able to start working three days later on minor rewrites for *Empire*. The draft from a few weeks earlier that had been submitted was approved by Glen Larson and Fox.

Bob Weston called one morning several months later and told Harold that Glen Larson had reversed his decision to air *Empire* and opted to use a series he had developed for the available time slot called *Halfpint*, about a midget detective. The series ran for three weeks and was canceled.

Empire floated around in limbo for a while and was finally shelved. This was the last project that was presented by Harold Robbins International and the company was closed after the contract with Fox expired.

*E*arly one morning while we were feasting on the usual fare of lox, bagels, and cream cheese in the family room, the phone rang. "Robbins residence," I answered.

"Is Harold Robbins there?" a voice spoke into the phone.

I looked over at Harold, indicating that it was for him. He shook his head. "Mr. Robbins isn't available right now; may I take a message?" I said, looking for a pen and paper.

"Is he in town?" the man said.

I never answered a direct question about Harold's whereabouts. "May I help you with something? I'm Mr. Robbins's assistant, Jann Stapp."

The man sounded a little aggravated. "Does Mr. Robbins own a boat called *Spellbinder*?" he asked.

"Yes, he does," I said.

"Do you know where that boat is?" he asked firmly.

Now I became suspicious. Harold had walked over to my side of the table and was looking at me quizzically. "Who is this?" I asked.

"My name is Joe Maloney; I'm a private investigator. Can you tell me where the boat is?"

"Mr. Maloney, it's kept in a slip in Marina del Rey."

"No, ma'am, it's not. That boat is in Ensenada. Last night someone was trying to sell the boat for five hundred dollars," Maloney said quickly.

"Can you hold on, Mr. Maloney," I said, and put the phone on hold.

I explained to Harold what I had heard to that point and gave him the phone.

"Mr. Maloney, this is Harold Robbins. How the hell did my boat get to Ensenada?"

"Mr. Robbins, I'm sorry to be calling you under these circumstances," Maloney said. "I don't know who was trying to sell the boat last night, but I will know that by this afternoon. I needed to check with you first and see if you knew anything about this."

"As soon as you know, please call me. I'll be here all day."

"Okay, sir," he answered.

"How can I reach you, Mr. Maloney?" Harold asked, and wrote down the information.

As it turned out, Chip, an acquaintance, had stolen the boat and taken it to Ensenada, Mexico, with a group of his friends. Maloney said they ran out of money and were trying to get whatever they could for the boat. Five hundred dollars.

When Harold learned who had stolen his boat, he was angry. He called Grace in Acapulco and told her what had happened. They had a bitter discussion about Chip, whom Grace knew. I could only hear one side of the conversation, but I knew that Harold had lost patience. After he hung up the phone, he called downstairs and told the houseman to go get him some cigarettes. Harold started smoking again after stopping when he had the accident. He was fighting too many battles and the stress had gotten the best of him.

Maloney called later that afternoon and he had seen the boat. He listed the damages that had been done and he instructed us to contact the insurance company and let him work out the return of *Spellbinder*.

Several weeks later an arrangement was made for a tugboat to bring the Bayliner back. The tugboat, ironically, sank on its return to LA. *Spellbinder* was stranded for several days, idly rocking while anchored in the middle of nowhere. When *Spellbinder* finally arrived and the repairs were made, Harold wanted nothing more to do with the boat and asked his captain, Lou Medina, to find a buyer.

Several weeks later I got a call that a buyer wanted to purchase the boat for cash. They would meet me at Wells Fargo Bank with the cash, thirty-five thousand dollars. This was about half the amount that Harold had originally invested in the boat. Harold sent me with two security guards.

I walked into the bank and notified the vice president, who was aware of the transaction, that we were there waiting for the buyer. Thirty minutes and then an hour passed.

Just as I was about to leave the bank, a tall, slender blond girl approached me and introduced herself as the representative for the buyer. She handed me a black briefcase and we walked to a secluded area in the bank. I called the vice president, who then took the briefcase to another room and had the money counted and deposited into Harold's account. She then gave me a copy of the deposit slip. I thanked the buyer and left.

Two months later, the DEA called the house. *Spellbinder* had been used in a "busted" drug deal and confiscated. The story of *Spellbinder* sounded more like a Harold Robbins novel than a real-life event . . . sex, drugs, power, intrigue, corruption.

The DEA asked Harold for the names of the buyers. I had kept all the papers on the transaction and we gave them the names, which turned out to be phony. That was the sad end for the Bayliner named *Spellbinder*.

CHAPTER FORTY-NINE

I opened the Sunday *New York Times* "Book Review" section and saw *Descent from Xanadu* on the top-ten softcover bestseller list. It had taken almost three years to see the conclusion of this book.

"Harold," I said. "*Descent* is on the bestseller list!"

"That's a fucking miracle; they must have shipped pretty good," he said. "It's a fucking miracle that the book was ever finished!"

We drove down to the Polo Lounge the next morning for a publicity appointment with *Interview* magazine. This was a very elite publication at the time headed by Andy Warhol. Harold knew the audience of the magazine and he tailored his comments accordingly.

"*Life* magazine featured me in an article about how to make a million writing novels. I made all the authors crazy when I asked for millions for my work. Now they all want big advances."

The reporter sitting across the table at the Polo Lounge pulled out the article, "How to Make a Million Writing Novels," dated July 31, 1964.

"Joe Levine was the one that made the movies a success," Harold said, and reached over and looked at the cover of the *Life* magazine. "Where the hell did you find this?"

"I find everything," the reporter said.

"Yeah, Joe paid me a million for the movie rights of *The Inheritors* before I had ever written a word." He started to laugh. "He also thought I was writing the book about him and he didn't want any other producer to get his hands on it."

"Were you writing about him?"

"I always write an extrapolation of many people, but it was more about Jim Aubrey, who ran CBS, and how he got screwed. Jann and I saw him the other day jogging down Tower Grove. He looks pretty good."

"Were you jogging, Harold?" the reporter asked.

Harold gave him a skeptical look. "Are you joking? The only exercise I do is on my knees and elbows. . . . [He started gyrating his pelvis along with his elbows moving in rhythm.] When I saw him I was sitting on my ass in the Maserati Quattro porte driving out of the gates of my house."

"You are the one who made authors like 'rock stars,' aren't you?" the reporter continued his questions.

"I don't know that I was the only one; authors have always been beacons in society. From Shakespeare to Chaucer . . ." Harold paused. "Henry Miller, Irving Wallace, Mario, me. When I was fighting with Knopf, many years ago, it was about the fact that authors should have the chance to make more for their work, not just the publisher. They were throwing out crumbs to us. We were schmucks! But corporations today are merging and taking over literature. Their decisions are based on the bottom line. Publishers aren't looking for the talent; they're looking at the bottom line. The marketing is becoming like the grocery store chains and selling a brand. They'll fuck themselves eventually."

"Harold Robbins is a pretty good brand name," the reporter said.

"Movies help books become stars," Harold said. "Fourteen of my books have been made into movies. But television is what makes your name and your book a household item. Television is the most powerful medium in the world today.

"*The Survivors* was the first nighttime soap opera ever viewed by the television audience. It was produced by Grant Tinker, who used to be married to Mary Tyler Moore and was a big television producer. This was all before *Dallas* and *Dynasty* today. That's why I wrote *The Inheritors;* it was the new world around me."

"I was told the publicity for *The Inheritors* was one of the most expensive and elaborate campaigns to date in the publishing industry." The reporter pulled out some more photos. "'The World of Harold Robbins' was the advertising campaign and used to promote your first seven novels, as well as *The Inheritors*. Over fifty thousand dollars was spent in 1969 on one billboard that spanned one entire block overlooking Times Square."

Harold interrupted him, "Seven sexy covers faced the subway and every time they looked up they saw one of my covers. Sales went up. It cost a lot of money, but it worked. I went on a book tour that hit every major city in the U.S. We had an entourage of go-go girls, a rock band with a kickoff party at the Nepentha Club in New York. I invited Vince Edwards, Dr. Casey, to tour with us. I told him while we were on tour if he married Linda Foster, his girlfriend at the time, I would give him an engagement party at the Coconut Grove in LA.

"When we returned, Vince asked Linda to marry him and she said yes. We sent out over three hundred invitations and I called Bob Sadeoff at the Aladdin Hotel in Las Vegas and scheduled his 'nude go-go girls' to appear. We had lines of people waiting to get in that night. Clint Eastwood started the round of toasts and good wishes for the engagement, and on the other side of the stage the go-go girls began their strip and dance. Nobody knew they were going to be there, including Vince and Linda. It was fun."

"How many copies did they sell on the tour, Harold?"

"Three million copies, but none of the publishers will do anything like that now. Too bad, they're only hurting themselves. An author today has to keep movies, books, and new ideas running like a machine. Thirty days after the *Inheritors* press tour, the movie *Stiletto*, based on my book from 1960, was released. And I started my next book, *The Betsy*."

"How many more books are you going to write?" the reporter asked.

"I average about one every two years." Harold looked up at the ceiling, figuring in his head. "About twenty-five more books and maybe I'll be even." He erupted in laughter.

"Harold you've sold millions . . . ," the reporter said.

"And I've spent all of them . . . women, cars, houses, bullshit . . . fun."

"He buys gifts for everyone," I said. "Last Christmas we went down to my friend's store in the Rodeo Collection. She just opened and was having a hard time, so he took his friends visiting from France and a couple of my friends having lunch with us and he bought everyone a gift."

"Bribery will get you everywhere," he kidded and laughed and hugged me.

CHAPTER FIFTY

Un-break My Heart

One night, the phone rang about one thirty in the morning. Harold grabbed the telephone and answered. After a few minutes he was laughing. "What's going on?" He listened for another minute. "Come on over," he said.

I was awake when Harold turned the light on. "What's going on?" I asked.

"Get up; some people are on their way over."

"Now?" I said sleepily. "What time is it?"

"Come on," Harold said, energetic and ready to party.

Thirty minutes later when I opened the front door to a well-known restaurateur in Beverly Hills and his guests, I was shocked. I had met him on several occassions, and he greeted me with a drunken sloppy kiss, almost falling clumsily. He couldn't form his words and they were a long stream of slurs. I looked at the two girls standing behind him, one dressed in a spandex zebra-print dress and the

other in a leopard faux-fur print miniskirt and low-cut black spandex top, and both wore stiletto heels and heavy makeup. One had
jet-black hair, ratted in a nest updo, the other long, straight bleached
blond hair.

They walked around the two-story foyer and were awed by the
home. One of the girls sat down at the black baby grand and played
"Chopsticks" and was especially impressed about being in the home
of Harold Robbins, the famous author.

Harold walked into the foyer from the kitchen carrying a bottle
of champagne. He greeted everyone, and I walked behind the bar to
get some glasses off the shelf and offer drinks to the group. Our
drunk friend followed me and reached up under my dress and started
feeling my tush. I very quickly grabbed his hand and looked into his
woozy eyes. "You already have two girls, babe. Three's a crowd."

He looked at me, smiling drunkenly, and dropped his hand. I
have no idea why I was trying to be so polite.

"I picked these girls up on Sunset, Harold," he slurred. "They
wanted to meet someone famous, so I called you!" he said, and
walked over to one of the girls and pulled her top down.

Harold glanced at me, looking for my response. I looked away
from him.

After I put the glasses on the bar I walked over to Harold, who
was now standing in the back of the room. "Harold, I'm going up to
my apartment. I'll see you in the morning." He tried to persuade me
to stay, but I didn't want to be part of this scene.

I ran up the stairs to my apartment and sobbed. How stupid I
was to think that this man would somehow treat me differently than
he had every other woman in his life! I remembered all of the stories
I had been told. But I thought I was special! How naive could I be?
But again I would be shocked.

Ten minutes later Harold called me on the intercom in my
apartment. I spoke to him through my tears.

"They're gone," he said.

I didn't answer; I cried.

"Come downstairs to the bar," he said.

I rushed down the stairs. I didn't know if I was happy or angry, relieved or devastated. I was glad they were gone. I knew a mountain of grief had been lifted from my heart.

I didn't know what to say when I saw him. Suddenly I felt foolish, out of place, unsophisticated, and naive. I thought about the commitment I had made to myself when I started the relationship with Harold: Always remember who he was. Yes, I probably would end up being hurt in this relationship. And I'd better not get "carried away" with the promises and hopes. *Too late*, I thought to myself. I was carried away and I knew it. Every moment since the beginning of our affair had been almost perfect, even the struggles.

He looked up at me and I thought he was angry. *Oh, for God's sake*, I thought to myself, *this is a disaster.* And then it dawned on me. He had made the choice to stay committed to me when he asked his friends to leave.

Harold got up and walked to me and put his arms around me. "I'm hooked, baby. I'm all yours; I got rid of them. I don't want any part of anyone but you."

"Who were those girls?" I asked him finally.

"A couple of hookers he picked up on Sunset. He always has to be the 'big shot.' They wanted to go upstairs to the Jacuzzi [in Grace's bathroom], but I told him I wanted all of them out."

"Was he insulted?" I asked.

"Christ, he's so stoned he won't even remember being here. Too bad if he is, but I don't want to throw us away." He looked at me seriously. "I don't want you to ever cry again. You're mine and I'm yours. That's all that matters."

This was a big turning point in our relationship. Harold had just committed himself in a way he had never before done in any marriage or other relationship. He made a choice that night; he also wanted something more and I trusted him totally after this night. What could have been the end of our relationship became a turning point toward strength.

Chapter Fifty-One

 arold's next book already had a title, *The Storyteller*. He had started to develop the story as a semiautobiographical novel during the summer. We spent many evenings talking about what he wrote and why he wrote it.

"'All of my stories have a moral choice. The protagonist reaches the point where he has to choose his own morality and decide if he can live with it. This I believe in. We all have a life behind the curtain, and sooner or later we all have to decide how we are going to live, why we are going to pull that curtain open, and what we are going to do once the curtain falls away.'" Harold was reading the page he had just finished and handed it to me. After he finished he tore the sheet into pieces and threw it away. "Fuck it."

I went to the trash can and pulled out the pieces. "Why did you do that? Every word you write is great; don't throw it away."

"You're prejudiced!" he said, and smiled. "It's about my next book, but my research is right here." He pointed to himself. "It's about a man who is a writer and he falls in love with all these women and he races around spending money, having a good time. And then for the first time, he really is in love. I just got to get it straight in my 'cuckoo' head."

He looked off in the distance, still thinking about the idea. "We'll start working after the first of the year."

It was 1985 and Harold was again having grave financial problems. Too many expenses, too little cash. The royalties in November had been less than usual and the bills had been more than usual.

Several months later, and after he had started *The Storyteller*, I was in my apartment getting dressed for dinner downstairs with Adréana and Harold. I heard Adréana scream into the phone intercom for help and flew down the stairs as soon as I heard her frantic voice. I ran into the dining room, where she was standing and Harold was in the midst of a seizure.

"Call nine-one-one," I screamed to the cook. I held Harold's head loosely against my body. My god, I didn't know what to do. I had been told to talk in a soothing manner and stay calm when someone had a seizure. I whispered at first, telling him everything was going to be all right. The seizure subsided, and as his muscles relaxed, I continued to hold him. However, he was not conscious.

Adréana and I stood with him until the paramedics arrived and again I tracked down Dr. Ablon on the phone. This time I could tell Dr. Ablon what Adréana and I had seen.

He came out and informed us that Harold had shattered his pelvis during the seizure and would require surgery to replace his hip. Dr. Ablon had called in the head of surgery at UCLA Medical Center, Dr. Eric Johnson. The compounding problem was that Harold's emphysema would make the anesthesia for surgery dangerous and add to the many complications he faced. He would have to be put on a medication to prevent any more seizures. Harold was admitted into ICU that night and it would take more than six months to get his medicines stabilized and his hip replaced and healed. There were many setbacks from severe reactions to medications along with breathing difficulties and slow healing of the bones due to his life-long smoking habit.

We found out later the seizure was most likely caused by an anti-anxiety medication, Ativan. He had quit using the drug, cold turkey, twenty-four hours prior to the seizure. This had prompted the reaction, but at the time the doctors didn't realize this was a side effect of Ativan or that seizures could occur if the medication was abruptly stopped.

One evening after arriving at UCLA Medical Center, I walked through the door of Harold's room and he was gasping for breath. It was a Friday night and his regular doctor had already made rounds and was no longer in the hospital. One of the interns on the floor took immediate steps to get Harold to Atomic X-ray, where it was determined he had a pulmonary embolism. This is a life-threatening event and could be deadly. But Harold through quick treatment survived.

Instead of this making him downhearted about all of the complications he had encountered, it seemed to make him feel like he had a courageous control of the situation. During his lengthy hospital stay he would have setback after setback, along with continuing allergies to medications, bouts with depression. During this time his stepmother, Blanche, and longtime friend Paul Mann, a furrier in Connecticut, died. Simon & Schuster cut Harold's advances for *The Storyteller* due to the many delays. In April of that same year Harold was still in excruciating pain and had to have another surgery after X-rays showed that the femur bone in his left leg had deteriorated. He survived and overcame every obstacle.

There would be days when I would wonder if he was going to survive and then just as quickly he would make miraculous comebacks!

In June of 1986, after spending a month in the Palm Springs Desert Hospital physical rehabilitation unit, Harold arrived home. This time he was using a walker and with physical therapy he could progress to using a cane.

"You're going to have to help me learn to walk," Harold announced cheerfully. "Those fucking doctors don't know what they're talking about. They are all full of shit."

This was the way he usually referred to doctors and their predictions.

"I've outlived most of my doctors," he would usually say about any of their diagnoses when he didn't agree. "They told me I had to eat all the things I don't like. I told them the only thing I liked to eat was your pussy."

Dr. Ablon was sitting with Harold and me in his office while the nurse was taking blood from his arm. The nurse blushed, Dr. Ablon laughed, and I shook my head. I never knew what Harold might say about any part of my anatomy, but of course that's why I loved him. He was totally unpredictable and fascinating. I thought he was as perfect as he thought I was. We made a great team.

Harold looked at Dr. Ablon. "She's done physical therapy all of her life, and now she's going to get me walking!" He started trying to move his pelvis, mimicking sexual moves, and he yelped out in pain. "You gotta get rid of this pain, Ablon, so I can get back to my favorite exercises."

Harold was on his way to a full recovery. And he would laugh all the way and continue to grow in courage. But, the future would hold some trying times.

CHAPTER FIFTY-TWO

C 'mon, Harold, they gave you a half a million almost a year ago and they haven't seen a word and neither have I. That money is long gone and I can't get more until you do a hundred pages," Paul said, his voice coming through the speakerphone.

"I've been in pain, and these goddamn painkillers don't help. Christ, and the more money I get, the more it flies out the fucking window! All this medicine is expensive."

"You need to get rid of the properties; they're sucking everything dry," Paul said.

Harold stared down at the table. I started to leave and he grabbed my hand and motioned for me to stay.

"What do you think the Beverly Hills house can go for?" Paul asked.

"The market's not that great. I'll call Asher Dann. He's the top guy in Beverly Hills. I can talk to him."

"Send Grace over to France to sell the house. I talked to Jack Kevorkian [Harold's French attorney] in Paris this morning. He's looking for some buyers and he'll take care of everything. She just needs to be there to let people in. Let Bob Mayer take care of the sale in Beverly Hills, and let Oscar Obregon or whoever is still alive down in Acapulco sell that one."

"Anything else we can sell?" Harold asked glumly.

"Yeah, your fuckin' book when you get it written," Paul answered, and hung up.

"I guess that's what we'll do eventually," Harold said, and looked at me.

"Harold, would it help if you didn't have to pay me?" I asked, and walked over and put my arms around him.

"No, you need your money. Things aren't quite as bad as Paul says. We've got some royalty payments coming through. Who knows? Maybe we'll pull ourselves out of this mess."

Harold always depended on the next book, or the next movie, or the next million. In fact, he used every financial crisis as a motivation. I always knew he was ready to go to work when he went out and made a big purchase, a boat, a Rolls-Royce, a diamond ring, a house. It was his "push" to put the story on paper. The only problem was, the money was spent many times over before it arrived.

Paul Gitlin told a story that exemplified Harold's spending style. "When he was writing *The Betsy*, Herbert and I were waiting on every page. Harold was under pressure, writing with music blaring on the stereo, people walking in and out of the suite, girls in the bedroom. He was supposed to finish not in days but in hours and he had been up for more than twenty-four hours working. We were at the Hotel Elysee in Manhattan," Paul said, looking over at Harold, who was nodding and confirming the story. "Herbert was sitting right next to him as he pulled each page out of the typewriter. Herb would edit him.

"Every time Harold would take a break, he would scoop a spoon into the beluga caviar tin a couple of times, light a cigarette, and start back to work. Herbert and I would take a shot of Scotch and wait for the next page. I would ask every hour, 'What page is he on?'

Herbert would answer and Harold kept working." Paul would shake his head in awe at the scene of chaos. "All the bullshit still going on around him.

"Finally, Herbert said, 'He's finished!' Robbins got up and smiled. I applauded and told them to call the 'kid' and have him get the chilled Dom Perignon out of the refrigerator. It had been down-stairs in the kitchen for two days. We all had a glass. It was a great night. In a couple of days I worked on the numbers with the accoun-tants, the IRS, paid all of the bills, the taxes, and I told Robbins that he was finally in the black."

At this point in Paul's story, Harold would always burst out laughing. "I pulled out a picture in a magazine of an eighty-five-foot yacht and told him I had written a check for two hundred and fifty thousand dollars and it was now mine! It made them all crazy."

Later, after *The Betsy* was published, Harold's work was dubbed by a columnist writing a review on the book "compulsively read-able." They saw his work as powerful but not critically accepted, just compulsively readable: "He wasted no words and his characters don't think, they act!"

It was the formula that made his scenes, his characters, and his story fly off the page and etch themselves in the mind of the reader. No one ever forgot Jonas Cord or Dax Xenos; a whole generation of children named Jonas and Dax were spawned from the electricity of these characters on the pages of a Harold Robbins book.

Harold read this article in a newspaper as he sailed the Mediter-ranean on the eighty-five-foot yacht he purchased from the comple-tion of *The Betsy*. He had ten copies of the magazine delivered to Paul Gitlin's office.

CHAPTER FIFTY-THREE

*A*fter Paul's admonitions to get to work, *The Storyteller* was started in earnest the following week. Harold was in pain and he was uncertain about the future, but he would sit at the typewriter and work and keep moving forward. I would sometimes walk into the study and see him with sweat beading on his forehead from the pain. He would ask for painkillers only as a last resort, and eventually the painkillers would stop the creative process. It was a constant effort to balance the pain and allow him to write. It was an agonizing effort to watch.

This book began with a metaphor of his own life. It began with a semitrailer truck smashing into his main character, Joe Crown, on the 405 freeway in the opening scene of the book.

One evening after completing the first chapter Harold talked about what he felt: "I'm trying to understand the things that have happened to me and find the answers. Joe Crown will find the life he's always wanted and forget all the bullshit."

Writing was Harold's way to find freedom for his characters and in this case his own life.

A reporter for *Talk Soup* on the E! Channel once asked Harold in a video interview about an article she read where he claimed that he purged himself through his writing.

Harold answered with a deadpan expression, "Honey, the only time I purge myself is with an enema."

The poor girl, who was doing her first interview, turned crimson and the cameraman fell over laughing.

The next day Harold showed me the first page of the book:

Fear is the surrogate of pain. It comes first. You look out the rear window, then the side window. You're traveling at thirty miles an hour, in the correct lane, heading for the Wilshire turnoff on the San Diego Freeway. Everything is in order. Then you see the big trailer truck barreling alongside you, cutting in front of you from the left lane, racing you to the turnoff.

"Stupid!" I said, hitting my brakes to allow the truck to move in. It was then the fear began. The truck was still beside me. I hit the brakes even harder. The fear began clutching into my gut and throat. The trailer was tilting toward me, looming above me like a gray prehistoric monster. I turned the wheel away from it.

It appeared as if in slow motion that it was falling toward me. I think I screamed in fear. "You're going to kill me, you son of a bitch!"

The truck jackknifed, turning its six headlights, glaring and blinding. Then the fear was gone, replaced by an agony of pain, and I screamed again as a million pounds of steel tumbled down, pushing me into the dark.

"You've used the word 'fear' five times in the first page," I mentioned. I was glad it was on the page. Maybe it would help him overcome the pain, by seeing it as a companion to fear. He had overcome "fear" throughout his life and now he would overcome pain, too.

"This is something that all of us face at one time or another. None of us escape fear, but we are all trying to beat it," he said. "In the last few months I've seen that fear and pain are companions."

After grueling months of work, *The Storyteller* was completed in November of 1985. A promotional press party at the Bistro Garden kicked off the publication with all the press and celebrities in December. Jackie Collins and Irving Wallace and Harold posed for the press and celebrated amazing accomplishments. The next day the book was plastered all over Rockefeller Center, and *The Storyteller* hit the *New York Times* Best Seller List in January 1986.

In the next few years Harold would face countless financial, legal, and marital problems, from both past and current marriages. He would turn the page and close the door to his past and open his heart to a new beginning. He would make hard choices that would create a new future for him, and he would eventually find a contentment he had never before known.

CHAPTER FIFTY-FOUR

e had barely felt a tremor in the middle of the night on July 8, 1986, but the California earthquake centered close to Palm Springs had hit the resort town hard. Harold and I were scheduled to spend the weekend in Palm Springs. We turned on the television the following morning and saw the damage done at our hotel, Maxim's on Palm Canyon Drive. I picked up the phone and called the hotel to verify if they would be open.

"Yes, Mrs. Robbins," the receptionist said when I gave her the confirmation number. "We'll be open and the elevator will be working. They are already repairing the damage from the earthquake. But we'll put you on a lower floor just in case the tremors cause any more problems."

"This is Mr. Robbins's assistant," I said, correcting her reference to Mrs. Robbins. "Will the restaurant be open?"

"Yes, we have a formal dining room, a restaurant in the lobby, and an outdoor café."

"What's the temperature today?" I asked.

"It will be around one hundred and ten! The outdoor café has misters that drop the dry heat considerably."

One ten. Hot! "We'll probably have room service."

The one thing they didn't mention was the "aftershocks" that were shaking the desert every few minutes. I had not been through any earthquakes of great magnitude in California, but as soon as we arrived I realized that these aftershocks were more nerve jangling than the quake! Harold had been in earthquakes in LA and Acapulco and had no fear of them. In fact, he usually slept through them.

We had arrived in Palm Springs to search for a new home. Harold was selling all of his properties. Grace had gone to France to sell the house in Le Cannet. When we found a home that Harold felt was suitable during this visit he called Grace in France.

"Grace, we found a house with three full guesthouses. It's a small main house and you'll probably want to change some things." He paused. "We're sending Polaroid pictures to you. . . .

"Grace, we're renting it; don't call any goddamn decorators. I don't even know if it will work down here. It feels about one hundred and fourteen degrees today. Hot as hell. Who knows if we'll be able to live here? Let's try it and see."

He listened and I could hear Grace's voice through the phone.

"If you don't like it, Grace, you can leave. This is the only place we can afford to live; it's about five grand a month. Jann has looked at every goddamn house in Beverly Hills, and the rents go for ten to twenty thousand. At least any of the houses that you would live in. We don't have any choices here, Grace." He listened.

"Yes, I looked at Sidney Korshak's house and it won't work for us. This one does. There's a big master bedroom for you and your clothes and a small room across the hall for me. . . .

"Yes, the closets in the master are large." He listened to her response. "Grace, I have to go."

He hung up the phone and his face was clouded with anger.

"Harold, do you think it would be better for me to stay in Los

Angeles?" I asked. I didn't believe this arrangement was going to work. These thoughts had been nagging at me since the Beverly Hills house had been sold to producer Dino De Laurentis. I was trying to be realistic about the situation, but in my heart I knew if I had to walk away from Harold now I would be devastated. This probably made my question to him an unrealistic one. But my heart and head were not on the same plane.

"What do you mean, 'stay in LA'?" he said, looking at me.

"I mean, maybe it's time you try to make a life without me here?"

"Do you want to leave?" he asked.

"You know I don't," I answered, near tears just thinking about the absurdity of this conversation.

"I love you, and I made you a promise," he said, and put his arms around me. "You can never leave me. Who else would I dance with?"

Harold and I had been doing physical therapy in the swimming pool since his hip operation. Part of the routine we did was dancing. We did the tango, the samba, the fox-trot, the Watusi, "dirty dancing," and any other dance or move we thought of. Being buoyant in the water made Harold feel free from the pain and he could move with no restriction and made me feel like I was a professional dancer.

Chapter Fifty-Five

After we moved to Palm Springs in the fall, Jack Romanos, Irwin Applebaum, and several other Simon & Schuster executives came to Palm Springs from the LA book fair to see Harold. It was the first time Harold had met the new rising star of Simon & Schuster, Jack Romanos, who at that time was president of Pocket Books, the paperback division of S & S. He was young and energetic and it was apparent that he would be as powerful a force in the publishing industry in his time as Harold was in his own time. Jack brought marketing to a new level in the late eighties and nineties for S & S and became president while Harold was still an author with the Simon & Schuster conglomerate.

It was a very friendly four-hour lunch, with Harold telling stories on himself, his past with Simon & Schuster, and his future plans.

"My literary agency has a guy going around trying to get all my papers and notes of my original manuscripts, but there are none. I write from my head and my heart; I can't make notes or outlines.

The guy says my original manuscripts should be donated to a library so people can read them and see how I work and know the kind of person I am. I tell him that's crap; anyone who wants to know a hundred years from now what I'm like, all they have to do is read my books. I donated the manuscript to *The Carpetbaggers* to Boston University and they wanted it because they said I was the best commercial author of the century. What else does anyone need to know? I don't even know how I write the books."

"I've read all of your books, Harold," Jack said.

Harold mugged, "You're too young."

"Maybe, but I learned fast." Jack smiled back playfully. "What we always want and need from you, Harold, is your next book. The industry is changing, more competition and more demand."

"Christ, we just got *The Storyteller* off the ground, Jack," Harold said. "You cut the advances on my books and you want me to write them faster?"

"It's the way the business is now. You can never let your audience forget you," Jack said matter-of-factly.

"Don't worry, boys," Harold said with a touch of arrogance. "I'm going to live forever. I've survived two hip surgeries, a femur bone replacement, a bleeding ulcer, a bang on the head, and Jann has saved me every time." Harold took my hand. "Now that I've been through all of that I'm ready to write again. Maybe *The New Carpetbaggers*."

I could see this grabbed everyone's attention.

What none of us realized at the time was that Harold had writer's block for the first time in his life.

We were still living in Maxim's and Harold had delayed moving into the house. Grace had moved in all the furniture from three other homes and he delayed every day going to the house on 990 N. Patencio. After Jack's visit we settled into a routine of work. It wasn't working and each day Harold was looking at a blank page.

We moved to the home on Patencio and he set up his office in one of the guesthouses. He would call me to come into his office and talk about ideas, but he could not get his head into a story. The world had changed for Harold, and his mind was spinning with problems.

One of the problems with having to take painkillers for Harold was that it slowed him down and he felt it was the cause of the writer's block. We started physical therapy to help free him from his pain and lessen the use of painkillers. It seemed to only get worse with every day. He tried again to stop smoking. All of his new doctors wanted him to quit, the same as the old doctors. But quitting was easier said than done. Harold had smoked for over fifty years, almost four packs a day. He had tried to stop on many occasions but would always go back to smoking.

One night while watching television in the middle of the night he saw a "quit smoking" system he thought might work for him. It was a little electronic beeper that would notify you when it was time to have a cigarette; each day the beep would sound fewer and fewer times until you were no longer smoking. Harold loved gadgets and this method intrigued him. The day it arrived in the mail he read the directions carefully, inserted the batteries, and began his new smoking regimen. This system worked pretty successfully for several weeks. He thoroughly enjoyed hearing the beep and lighting up.

One day he called me from my office into his office. He was holding the electronic beeper, looking at it and shaking it, and putting it up to his ear.

"I think there's something wrong with this machine." He looked up at me innocently.

I took the beeper from his hand and looked at it. "What's the problem with it?"

"It's been beeping and beeping every day, but in the past few days, it just doesn't seem to be beeping anymore." He had that little mischievous look on his face.

I knew I was being had, but I played along. "Well, Harold, do you think it could be the batteries?"

"Oh no, I checked the batteries," he answered solemnly.

"What do you think is the problem?"

"Well, I just think it's broken," he said, and threw the little machine in the trash and lit up a cigarette.

Harold finally stopped smoking in 1990 after more than fifty years of smoking. The doctors said it added years to his life.

CHAPTER FIFTY-SIX

"Maybe I just can't write anymore!" Harold said in frustration. He was sitting, as he had done every day for the past several months, trying to write his novel. "I don't know what to do, darling," he said, and put his head back on his chair. "It's too goddamn hot in Palm Springs. I can't fucking breathe or think."

"Let's go to the beach," I suggested. "There's a beautiful Ritz-Carlton in Laguna."

"We will. But later. I have to figure out my fucking head."

"I think you need to write what you want to write and quit worrying about what your editors want."

"They want a bestseller and they don't care what it's about." He looked at me considering the possibility and shrugged his shoulders. "But you're right, I want to write in a new way! The world is changing; life is changing. Something's not right. People are always what I have written about. What they do when pushed into situations, how they handle their world. Now they want the formula to stay the same, like I'm a goddamn machine. How many moguls can you write about? How rich can they become? Who the fuck cares about them? I can't know what makes a bestseller; I can only write what I feel and I can't make anything stay the same. That's the big problem: I've been trying to stay the same. Now I just have to figure out where I need to go."

Within weeks and before he started, his new novel, *Spellbinder*, was optioned for a movie, with Harold being hired to write the screenplay. Even though he had not wanted to write another screenplay, he had been given the freedom to choose whom he wanted to work with on the script. He chose me. Harold and I spent the next three months writing *Spellbinder* for the screen.

"We'll watch Jimmy Swaggart; he's the best one of all of them," Harold said after he received a partial payment for the work. He had new energy with this new project.

Every Sunday night we would tune into Swaggart's sermons. We also watched movies on evangelists from *Elmer Gantry* starring Burt Lancaster to a documentary on the new "religious right."

"It's unbelievable that *Gantry* is still so good," Harold said after we viewed the movie. "If we can get a lead as good as Lancaster the movie will be a hit."

We took the structure of the book and tried to stay true to the story as much as possible. On our final day of work, with the deadline looming, we were about forty pages away from completion.

At eight o'clock on Saturday morning he began to write, determined to be finished by the end of the day. One by one, he handed me pages. I would make changes and then get his approval. There was no such thing as Final Draft or Movie Magic in 1987. At 8:00 P.M. we had finished only half-enough pages. We stopped and ordered dinner from our cook, Jose.

Harold wanted chili dogs, French fries, and Coca-Cola. This was what he called his "all-American" dinner, one that he had enjoyed since he was a kid living in Hell's Kitchen.

I thought after he ate dinner he might run out of energy, but at 3:00 A.M. he was banging away at the typewriter handing me pages and I was the one who was exhausted. I couldn't believe his energy. Writing was his cure; it lifted him out of his pain and his worries, into the world he was writing about. He looked over at me after completing a scene and saw my tired eyes.

"Harold, I don't think I can do any more," I said. "I'm exhausted."

He started laughing and kidding me that I couldn't keep up with him. And he was right; he had twice the energy and I knew he was not using drugs to keep him up. He was working on the adrenaline and excitement of creating.

"Go get a Coca-Cola and some instant coffee," he said.

"I've had coffee; it's not helping," I said.

"I guarantee this will work," he said, and I walked off toward the kitchen.

He poured the Coca-Cola into the glass, dumped two teaspoons of instant coffee in, and mixed it. No ice. He placed it in front of me.

"Drink it," he said. "All of it."

It tasted awful, bitter, but I drank it. He was right. Within ten minutes I woke up. At 5:00 A.M. he finished the screenplay, and at 8:00 A.M. I finished compiling the scenes and handed the piece to a waiting courier to be taken to Los Angeles. The deadline was noon on Sunday.

We thought the writer's block was broken.

CHAPTER FIFTY-SEVEN

arold received a phone call from Jack Romanos one morning. It was September and it had been nine months since Jack's last visit. He was coming to Palm Springs and wanted to have dinner with us. We made arrangements at our favorite restaurant, Riccio's. This restaurant was our "home away from home" only a few blocks from our house. The Riccios were our extended family. Bobby, in particular, was who Harold called on when he needed help in doing fund-raisers or special parties.

Our date with Jack and his wife, along with two of his friends from New York, was on Saturday night. Riccio's, as usual, was packed with well-known locals and visitors when we arrived.

The valets at Riccio's knew the blue Corniche convertible the minute we drove in the driveway. There were usually groups of people standing outside the restaurant waiting for a place at the bar or the dining room or for their car. Harold emerged from the car wearing his black signature Stetson, his sport coat, shirt, and scarf, and even though it was evening he was wearing his large black sunglasses. After I walked around beside him we entered the restaurant amid whispers about who we were or might be.

Alex, the valet, would continue the mystery and tell people who asked that part of Riccio's policy was never to reveal the names of celebrities who frequented the restaurant.

Once we arrived in the dining room, other patrons who recognized Harold came over to the table throughout the meal. Autograph seekers, fans, other celebrities were well aware that Harold frequented this restaurant. We often saw Ray Sharkey, a well-known actor who starred in *The Idolmaker*, Rick James, a pop-funk singing artist, and Harry Caray, the longtime announcer for the Chicago Cubs. During the season (October to May) Riccio's was packed with locals, visiting celebrities, sports legends, and the rich and famous who made this California paradise their winter playground.

"Harold, I really need this book for the Christmas lineup. Are you going to have it for me?" Jack said as we were eating dinner.

"Jack, I normally finish a book every two years."

"Times are changing. Everything is more competitive. I'm counting on it for Christmas. We did *The Storyteller* in seven days, Harold. Don't do that to me again," Jack said.

"You'll have it," Harold promised, behind his dark sunglasses.

After we finished dinner, Dimitri Arvantis, the maître d' and head sommelier, came over with a bottle of Cristal champagne and whispered in Harold's ear. I thought some girl in the restaurant had sent over a bottle of champagne for Harold. It wasn't unusual for women to flock to Harold's side, send bottles of champagne, or snuggle next to him in a restaurant booth, regardless who was sitting next to him. And it wasn't unusual for me to smile and remove them.

Harold turned to us laughing after Dimitri finished his story. "My white Pekingese, Kinky, has been sent a bottle of Cristal by two ladies who have a female Pekingese. They're trying to seduce my baby boy, Kinky!"

Only in the world of Harold Robbins would someone buy a three-hundred-dollar bottle of champagne to seduce his dog! It was after midnight when we left the restaurant, and the bottle of champagne was shared by Jack and his friends and Harold. Kinky saw a drop of champagne and Harold turned down the offer of having baby Kinkys.

"Harold, you promised the book for Christmas publication," Jack reminded him as we drove off.

I turned to Harold. "Are you going to be able to do the book for him?"

"I'll do it."

"Harold, I think he's very serious about it." I had seen a look on Jack's face when he asked. For some reason, I felt there was a lot riding on this commitment.

Adréana, Harold's daughter, was married to Jeff Greenberg on December 23, 1990.

Several months later, Grace Robbins filed for divorce from Harold after a newspaper article interview that Harold had done with the *Los Angeles Times* stated in a quote from him that he wanted to spend the rest of his life with me.

CHAPTER FIFTY-EIGHT

arold started seeing a new, highly recommended doctor, Jay Roberts, a specialist in physiatry, in Palm Springs. The doctor's pain treatments eased Harold's constant hip pain. Everything was turning around for Harold and he was becoming pain free. Jay Roberts not only helped him with the pain; he also gave Harold hope for the future and a possibility to walk. Dr. Roberts and his wife, Beverly, and their two sons, Ryan and Jason, became lifelong friends. As a doctor Jay was the very finest, a doctor who would come to our house day or night, a healer of the highest degree. He understood Harold's sense of humor and in turn became like a son to Harold.

Our first visit with Dr. Roberts went something like a comedy routine. The nurse asked Harold, "How tall are you?"

Harold was waiting for this one. "Six-two," he answered. Jay turned with a half smile and looked at him. Harold grinned. "Before I busted my hips."

Jay and the nurse laughed.

Within a month, Harold was back on crutches and sometimes able to walk with only a cane. At this point, he felt about seven feet tall! We rented a home in Laguna where we stayed for the summer and he wrote most of his next bestseller, *The Piranhas*.

It was pissing rain at eleven o'clock in the morning in front of St. Patrick's Cathedral. The police had blocked all traffic down Fifth Avenue from Fifty-fourth Street to Forty-ninth Street except buses, and they were only in a single line close to the sidewalk near Rockefeller Center across from the Cathedral. The street itself was crowded with blackened-window stretch limousines. The sidewalk and the steps leading up to the entrance of the Cathedral were jammed with television cameras, reporters, and the morbidly curious crowd that always managed to show up for death and destruction.

Inside the Cathedral all the pews were filled with black-dressed mourners, some very expensively dressed, others in threadbare black—but each looked down toward the altar to the front of the ornate gold coffin with a simple wreath of flowers at the foot. There was an expectant air as they waited to hear the mass that would be given by Cardinal Fitzsimmons. They wanted to hear what he had to say, because he had always hated the dead man.

—HAROLD ROBBINS,
THE PIRANHAS (1991)

He takes us into the funeral with a detailed description of the entire scene, bringing us into the moment. Then, in Harold Robbins fashion, the story quickly takes a turn.

The Cardinal rushed the mass. The whole thing was over in less than ten minutes. A thin, small, black-suited man began running down the center aisle, waving a gun.

I heard my Aunt Rosa scream and saw the Cardinal dive quickly down behind the altar, his robes flapping. I left the pew and went after the man, but not before he emptied his gun into my Uncle's coffin, crying loudly: "One death is not enough for traitors!"

He had his momentum in the first few pages, a trademark of each of his bestsellers.

He completed the first and second sections of the book and with money on the way he found a way to spend it. One morning after we had returned from Laguna to Palm Springs, I walked into the bedroom, thinking that Harold was probably getting dressed to go out to the office, but he was sitting on the side of the bed still in his pajamas.

"You better get dressed," he said, turning to me and smiling happily. "We're going out to lunch."

"Really. Where are we going?" I asked.

"I don't know; the Rolls-Royce salesman is taking us out," he said, and smiled again.

"What???" I said. "What Rolls-Royce salesman?"

"I just bought a new one. A new Silver Spur Rolls," he said.

"How? What do you mean?"

"They have a beautiful magnolia and cream out at Fred Smith's Rolls place, I just bought it," he announced.

I laughed with him. "Over the phone? You haven't even seen it and you bought it?"

He continued to grin and nod his head.

"Can you pay for it?" I asked, knowing that Paul Gitlin's screaming would be heard from New York to Palm Springs when Harold told him.

"Piece of cake," he answered.

About thirty minutes later, a plush, luxurious, shining magnolia-colored Rolls-Royce arrived at our front door. We included all the dogs in our celebration, piling them into the backseat and bringing our houseman along to care for the dogs while we had lunch. We went to a Japanese restaurant for lunch. A lunch was served to our houseman outside first and water bowls and snacks for the dogs. No one was ever deprived when Harold was in charge. Harold signed the papers to buy the car and he was motivated to write.

CHAPTER FIFTY-NINE

H arold, *The Piranhas* is great!" Paul said after receiving the pages of the manuscript.

"You like it?" Harold asked.

I walked into the office and Harold pointed to the telephone. I could hear Paul's voice.

"It's a great beginning. I'll send it over by messenger to Michael Korda this afternoon."

"Jann just came in; tell her what you told me. . . ."

"Hi, Paul," I said.

"It's great work, kid."

"Hey, Paul, we're going to be in the desert for Thanksgiving. Why don't you come out?"

"My fucking back is killing me. I'm going to the doctor and I may have to have surgery."

"Christ," Harold said, laughing. "We're falling apart!"

"Yeah, but we're still alive!" Paul answered.

"Paul, I wrote a check for a new Rolls."

"Robbins, you think you're rich again? Goddammit!"

"Don't worry, Paul. This book is going to be great!"

In March when Harold was finishing *The Piranhas* he was diagnosed with bronchial pneumonia, with fever running over one hundred degrees and barely able to breathe without constant oxygen support.

Dr. Roberts came to the house late one evening when Harold's breathing became labored and recommended that he be hospitalized.

"No, I have to finish this book. Whatever you can do at the hospital you can do here. I want to keep working. If I croak, it won't matter where I am."

Dr. Roberts set up a minihospital in our bedroom with IVs of antibiotics flowing into Harold's bloodstream. Harold, propped up with pillows, looked like a King dictating over his kingdom. He completed the last fifty pages of his book, listening to the characters in his head and speaking their lines as I recorded, wrote, and edited the final manuscript.

Dr. Roberts would stop by our house every night while we were working and treat the illness. There were many nights when Dr. Roberts and I both felt we might have to call the paramedics, Harold appeared so sick. But at each crisis Harold would always refuse to go to the hospital. He would somehow make a miraculous comeback in these instances. I remember Dr. Roberts holding the telephone one night getting ready to dial 911.

Harold looked up at him. "Jay, I'm fine." His breathing would get better and he was back to normal.

When I faxed the final pages in to Simon & Schuster, they had no idea of the risk and dedication that Harold had taken to meet his deadline of April 1. I only wished that I could tell them of his determination to overcome all of the obstacles, along with the courage of a lion and his commitment he felt for the company he had helped build. I don't think they ever realized the dedication and loyalty he felt from over fifty years of producing blockbuster novels.

After the book was completed, Harold spent the next two weeks in bed. We had another period of time when we could be together with each other, no interruptions. He was continually surprising me in our relationship.

"Honey, I just talked to Terry. He's on his way over with some things."

I had no idea what he was talking about. "Terry?" I asked.

"Yeah, Terry Weiner from the jewelry place," he answered. "He's bringing some things."

"What do you mean? What things?"

"Oh-h, things like an engagement ring," he said, teasing and smiling.

I stopped almost in mid-step. "You're kidding, Harold. . . . Are you kidding?"

He kept the signature mischievous grin. "Why would I kid a girl like you about a thing like that?"

"Harold, what are you doing? You're not even divorced yet," I said.

"I don't give a shit!" he said.

I ran to him and hugged him. "I love you, Harold." This man had just made all of my dreams come true. It seemed that we had been married already. I never imagined that he would go through the ritual of engagement rings.

"Quit talking about it, and show me," he said, pulling my T-shirt off.

Terry arrived a little later, with a tray of rings. Again, I felt like I was living in one of Harold's novels. We picked out a beautiful platinum 4-carat square-cut diamond. It wasn't the diamond that was important but the commitment we were making, and that meant more than a thousand diamonds.

CHAPTER SIXTY

With the publication of *The Piranhas*, there was a series of interviews. *Lifestyles of the Rich and Famous* requested to do a show with Harold and me in our home in Palm Springs. We spent two days being interviewed, driving the streets of Palm Springs in the blue Rolls-Royce Corniche, entertaining friends in our home, and lounging by the pool. It was the first interview I had done as the future wife of Harold Robbins.

Needless to say, being basically shy in front of cameras, I was apprehensive, but with Harold sitting next to me holding my hand I felt I could do anything, conquer any fear, climb any mountain.

"Harold, wouldn't it be better if you were by yourself?" I said, trying to wiggle out of an appearance. "They don't want to hear about me."

"I want you to be right next to me. You're with me now and nothing is going to change that and you're the most beautiful woman I've ever known, inside and out, and I want everyone in the world to know who you are," Harold said, and put his arms around me. "There's no one better than you in this world."

"There's no one better than you, Harold," I said, and closed my eyes, hoping that my life would always be this happy.

In June, Harold was scheduled to do a series of interviews with television, newspaper, and radio press about the publication of *The Piranhas* in Los Angeles. We stayed at a bungalow in the Beverly Hills Hotel and it was like coming home for Harold.

This would be five days of non-stop interviews scheduled for morning, afternoon, and night. At each interview Harold announced that we would be getting married, showing them the beautiful diamond ring on my finger.

"This beautiful girl has been with me since 1982 and we're going to spend the rest of our life together. She's saved my life three or four times."

"How many times have you been married?"

Harold looked at me. "This is the only Mrs. Robbins, and has been for a long time."

"Is your divorce going to cost you a bundle?" one reporter asked.

"Well, fellas," Harold said to that group of reporters in the bungalow. "I've just signed a new contract with my publisher. It's a twenty-million-dollar contract for ten books. I told them I wanted the cash up front."

It was a joke. He never said the name of the publisher and nobody caught the punch line "I wanted the cash up front." It was printed in the press. The following day Grace's attorneys were calling for confirmation of this story and actually filed for a court hearing. The divorce court judge handling the case even laughed when he saw the article. Even he could see that it was a put-on.

Several weeks later, after our houseman, Tad, saw someone taking pictures of the house, he went outside and discovered it was a photographer from the *Globe* magazine. They wanted a picture of the woman Harold Robbins was going to marry.

"You better go out and talk to them; they'll stay out there until they have a story," Harold said to me. "Tell them to call Schwam if they get shitty." He picked up the phone to call Gene.

I went outside and introduced myself.

"We'd like to talk to Mr. Robbins about his divorce?" the reporter said. "And we'd like to confirm that Mrs. Robbins caught you together naked in the pool?"

I smiled and asked them to call Gene Schwam.

"Can't we get a picture of you?" the reporter asked, wiping sweat from his face. It was stifling hot in Palm Springs and they had been standing outside for a couple of hours waiting for one of us to emerge.

"Would you like some water?" I asked.

"Oh, sure, that would be great." He looked relieved.

"I'll have some water brought to you," I said, and went back inside. "I'll be right back."

Tad brought them a thermos of water and glasses. He brought it out on a silver tray.

When I returned I had Gene Schwam's card to give to them.

"How about the picture?" the reporter asked as I handed him the card.

"Sure," I said.

While one of them was taking photos the other was firing questions.

"How long have you and Harold been together?"

"Forever," I said.

He laughed. "What did you say when Mrs. Robbins caught you together?"

"I've been Harold's assistant for years. Where has she been?"

The next week my picture was in the *Globe* with a story about the romance between Harold and me.

This would be only the beginning of rumors, spies watching our house, accusations that would put me on the pages of the *Globe* as well as the *National Enquirer*.

CHAPTER SIXTY-ONE

"ello, Robbins residence," Harold answered the phone. "Yo, Fred, what's happening? . . ."

I heard a series of "uh-huhs" and "yesses"; then Harold hung up the phone. He turned around with his sly grin. "They have something called a 'bifurcation' in California. I didn't want to say anything until I got this call. The divorce is final; property settlement will be later."

I felt a sense of relief! "Oh, Harold, I'm so glad!" But I was surprised when the next question came.

"You want to get married, pussy? On Valentine's Day?"

"Yes, yes, yes!" I screamed. It was February 7, 1992, when we received that phone call. I had seven days to plan the wedding.

We called Adréana and Jeff to tell them of our plan. They knew the devotion and love we had for each other and that we were happy. Harold invited Jeff to stand with him at the wedding. I called my best friend, Paige, and asked her to stand for me. She had been my only confidante and friend throughout my relationship with Harold and had gone through the tears, trials, moments of happiness, and she and Harold had become close friends.

o you promise to obey, to love one another, to be true to your wife?" Judge Block said with a smile as he looked at Harold. Harold and I were standing in front of the huppah taking our wedding vows seven days later.

I smiled at the last phrase. Harold raised his eyebrows.

"I put that in especially for you, Harold," Judge Block said. Our small group of guests laughed.

Harold looked at me. "I do, honey!"

I never thought this day would ever really happen. I loved and adored and cherished him and he loved and adored and cherished me. What more could anyone need? I knew he no longer had millions of dollars, and I knew he had been accustomed to more material possessions in his life and a wilder life with many women. But none of that seemed important when we were together to him or to me.

Adréana and Jeff; my niece, Dawn, and sister, Suzanne; Harold's sister, Ruth, and niece Zerrie; Dr. Jay and Beverly Roberts; and our friends from Riccio's, Bobby, Dimitri Arvantis, and Danny, attended the ceremony. Our dogs, Gypsy, Kinky, Phantom, and Zorro, strolled through the veranda as Harold and I spoke our vows to each other. After the ceremony, we were all taken, by limousine, to Riccio's for a wedding luncheon hosted by the boys at their restaurant.

The press had been notified at 12:01 after our vows at 12:00 noon that we were married. Phone calls poured into the restaurant asking for interviews. *The New York Times* called and both Harold and I talked with them. *People* magazine and the *Globe* magazine interviewed us. We sent them photos of the wedding the following day.

That evening we had a dinner party for forty more of our friends. Harold had arranged for his friend Lew Mitchell from the Orient Express gourmet Chinese restaurant in Los Angeles to cater the wedding dinner. He brought his staff to Palm Springs and created not just a dinner but an event that he and Harold had planned down to the last detail, including fireworks over the pool next to the veranda.

It was one of the happiest days of our life together.

CHAPTER SIXTY-TWO

 e were sitting in Le Basque in Manhattan at a dinner being hosted by Simon & Schuster. The table included Jack Romanos, Carolyn Reidy, and other dignitaries. Jack had suggested to Harold that Simon & Schuster find somebody to help him write his books. Jack explained he needed a book a year on the shelf. The subject was brought up as delicately as possible, but how do you tell the world's bestselling author that they can't wait for him? They needed product! Harold, of course, didn't like the idea. But he told Jack he would think about it.

Later that night, Harold told me what Jack proposed.

"There won't be any more great books written if they put deadlines on creativity! I know Jack is doing the best he can, but they'll destroy me. Publishing has become the grocery store business today. Pretty soon they'll raise the prices on books and then slash the prices like a bargain basement. It's going to put everything out of reach for the 'common man' and they'll lose a whole generation of readers.

"I know I can't write books as fast as I used to. I wish I could, but

I know that every one of the books I've written, whether it took two years or five years, has been on the bestseller list." He shook his head, not understanding anything in his world now.

1995 — THREE YEARS LATER

Harold was walking down the hallway early one morning on his crutches with a determined look on his face, removing every photograph of himself and his past from the gallery filling the wall on each side from ceiling to floor.

"What are you doing?" I asked, standing at the opposite end of the hall. I was still half-asleep, holding a steaming cup of coffee.

"I'm taking down these pictures. It's all bullshit. This whole fuckin' life is nothing but bullshit!" He looked down at the framed photos he had stacked on the table in the hall. "It's fuckin' bullshit!" He continued to remove the photos. "Get me some painkillers; my legs are killing me!"

I ran and got some water and his painkillers. He woke up every morning after a restless night with pain, and last night had been especially emotional and physically painful for him.

I handed him the painkillers and glass of water. His hands were shaking as he took them.

He looked at the photograph of the World of Harold Robbins display in Times Square from 1969 that monopolized every billboard in the Square. He placed it facedown.

"Harold, everything you've done in your life is successful. You have made a mark in this world that is unmatched and it hasn't stopped. I don't care what Paul says or Simon and Schuster or Mario Puzo or Stephen King or your ex-wives or the IRS! Your life is not what 'they' say or do but what you have done and are doing. You have faced twenty-four-hour-a-day pain and you are happy in spite of it and you continue to work. We struggle to pay the bills and keep a roof over our heads, but we have each other and we love each day we spend together. Our time is so precious."

He looked at me, listening.

"You are the most wonderful man that ever lived, and that's all that matters," I continued, feeling my voice become stronger each moment, and yet I wanted to cry out to someone, to anyone, to please help him. I hated to see his discouragement.

I loved and adored him. I would give my life for him and I wished I could shoulder his burden of pain. I would gladly trade places with him. I knew at this very moment in his life he was facing what none of us would like to face.

"The world has passed me by," he said, and cried. Tears rolled down his cheeks.

I felt searing pain in my own heart that he felt in those words. I could feel tears running down my cheeks. Why couldn't I take this pain for him? He had been forgotten by his publisher of his past, and his future had come to a dead end. But I knew he was the most courageous man, the strongest man, I had ever known. In fact, there was no one who would ever compare to him.

Harold had written a letter to his attorney that morning that ended their lifelong relationship of agent and author:

THE CLONING OF HAROLD ROBBINS

Harold Robbins is an American writer who has written 20 more or less successful best-sellers.

One day in New York there was a meeting of four important literary surgeons. Jack, the President of the publishing company, Bill, the editor of the paperback book department, Mike, the editor of the hardback division, and Chuck, his assistant also an editor.

They had a meeting at which time they agreed that Harold would take too long to write a novel since they needed a Robbins book each year for the next four years. So they proposed to Paul that Harold agree to accept the money for each year and they will select another writer to write the novels. And the first novel they want to have written and published will be the sequel to The

Carpetbaggers, probably the most well known of the best-sellers in Robbins' library.

Stupidly, Robbins agreed with the offer despite having no control over the work and for a lower sum of money than he had previously been paid.

Unfortunately the outlines that were sent to Robbins were nothing like Robbins' work or style.

Harold Robbins had cloned into a monster that would destroy his reputation.

I saw tears form in his eyes when he finished removing the pictures. "I don't give a shit about the past. It was all bullshit, a waste! Grace, Lillian, the friends, the cocksuckers who publish my books. I've worked my whole fuckin' life and all I have to show for it is bullshit!"

"I know, Harold, it seems like that now, but you've experienced the best in life and you are a great writer; you haven't wasted anything! You went through a lot of wives to find me and I love you and I know you love me," I said, smiling, trying to lighten the situation. "We have everything, Harold. Don't let anyone take that away." I ran to him, fell to my knees, and hugged him.

"Why do you think I want to get rid of all this shit?" he asked, looking at the stack of photos. "You are the only good thing that's ever been in my life. I'm just sorry I can't give you the life you deserve. We are fuckin' busted! I hate all this shit coming down on you."

"So what?" I looked up at him and smiled. "All I want is you. You've made every day of my life since I met you an adventure."

He smiled back at me. His frustration and anger disappeared.

Harold Robbins, the world's number-one bestselling author since the beginning of his career, was working today without a contract. He had gotten out of the hospital yesterday after being hospitalized in Intensive Care for seven days. The doctors ran tests and treated him but couldn't determine why he was unable to keep any food down for those seven days. What was wrong with him? They didn't know.

I knew. His entire life had been shaken. A man who had written so many bestselling novels and sold more books than any other author had no reason to write. I also knew that he would find his way back to his writing. I reminded him in his own words that echoed in my thoughts: "A writer writes! That's what you do."

CHAPTER SIXTY-THREE

*T*his is the first time I haven't had a contract since I was at Universal," Harold said. "I've got every fucking asshole on my back for money and I have no answers."

"Don't worry, Harold. You can write what you want," I said. "I know it'll be great!"

"Everybody wants me to write an autobiography," he said.

"Instant bestseller," I encouraged him.

"How am I going to remember everything?" he asked.

"Remember we have those tapes. But it's okay if you forget some of the girls' names," I kidded him.

He began to write his autobiography that day.

PROLOGUE
(AFTER THE TROPIC OF CANCER . . . BY HAROLD ROBBINS)

It's Tuesday, January 2, 1996. This year I will be 80 years old. I sit here at my IBM typewriter and try to figure out how I can tell the story of my life. Not easy. I don't really know if it's real life or just another story. Maybe it's all the same to a writer. My life, it seems to me, is a story much like any other. After all, I wrote and became Harold Robbins. With each new character, a new man, but in reality very much another man. I became many men. Francis Kane, Johnny Edge, Danny Fisher, Jonas Cord, Nevada Smith, Jed Stevens, Angelo Perino and many more. But, it doesn't matter. I am those men and they are me.

Each day he would return to his typewriter. The pain in his hip was constant, and unknown to us at the time, the hip socket area had become infected. In order to endure the pain he took four or five painkillers a day. His progress was slow, but he was determined.

I placed his fan letters, which had continued to come in every day since I had known him, on his desk near his typewriter. He enjoyed reading what his readers had to say. Many sent books to be signed, cards to be autographed, and letters of appreciation.

He read the letters each morning and signed each book and card.

"I'm glad they still fuckin' remember me." He picked up a letter and read: "'Dear Mr. Robbins, where are you? When are you writing another book?'"

The phone rang and I answered. "Oh my God!" I said as our banker explained that we had no money in our account. I hung up the phone as Harold stared at me, wondering what had happened.

"Harold, the IRS has just frozen our bank account!"

He called Paul. "Harold, you didn't have the money to make the payments. You know the IRS; they do what they want to do. I'll call and talk to them."

We had economized in every way we could, sold all but one car just to keep up with the physical therapy bills, doctor bills, and pharmaceutical bills necessary to keep Harold out of pain.

That night we had only twenty dollars in cash left and no food in the kitchen. We went to the grocery store nearby and Harold and

I shopped for our "last supper"! We came out with four small lamb rib chops, asparagus, and baked potatoes and dog food and cat food. We went home and together prepared the meal; we laughed as Harold instructed me how to prepare the asparagus and baked potatoes; we grilled the lamb chops, seasoned them, each task being done with love and humor. We both feared tomorrow, but tonight was ours and not the IRS or anyone else could take that away. It was the most romantic, delicious meal we ever shared.

"I've never had so many problems, but I've never been happier in my life," Harold said that night as we sat at our magnificent beveled glass table.

Together we felt nothing could stop us.

It took over a month, but the IRS released the lien on our account after a payment had been made. In the meantime, we went to our friends across the street, Mike and Bob Pollock, and borrowed money to live on.

Harold put aside his autobiography and began to work on a novel. He picked up the phone and called Gene Winick, his agent, to ask him to try to get him a contract with a new publisher. Harold told Gene the story idea for his new book, which he had titled *Wishing Well*.

"It's loosely based on the Perrier family in France. Their lifestyle in the South of France, the story about how all this water business began back in the 1800s and how the Perriers marry only for inheritance purposes. How they started the billion-dollar water business and now we have all these designer waters." Harold had typed this out and handed it to me. "Send this to Gene Winick; he's been talking to Bob Gleason at Forge Publishing. I think they'll like this story."

I walked over to the fax machine and dialed in Gene's number. Harold had returned to McIntosh & Otis Literary Agency after Gene purchased the company and he had left Paul Gitlin.

A month later, Bob Gleason, executive editor for Forge Books, flew out to Palm Springs to meet with Harold.

"Goddammit, Bob, I've got a lot of books left in me and I'm going to stop these painkillers. I'll take Tylenol. I'm going to write a hell of a book!"

Several weeks later Gene Winick called. He had just received the contract to publish *Wishing Well*. The title was later changed to *The Predators* for Tor/Forge Publishing, a Tom Doherty imprint.

"I feel like I'm coming home, Gene. Tom was at Simon and Schuster in the good days of publishing. And Bob cut his writing and editing teeth with Herbert Alexander. Herbert was the best editor I've ever had. This is going to be a new beginning; I feel it."

Harold turned to me with a look of excitement and expectation, transformed into a twenty-one-year-old character named Jerry Cooper on the way to the greatest adventure of his life. "You hear that, sweetheart? Everything is going to be okay," he said, and pulled himself out of his chair. With the music playing in the background we danced for the first time in a long time. "Always remember, you're my favorite dancer!"

Epilogue

W riting *The Predators* was a labor of love, a renewal for Harold Robbins. It was also the antidote to his excruciating pain. Sitting at his typewriter, he lifted himself into the world of his story. I would often watch as he created, weaving his words of magic onto the page. He was completely conscious of only one thing, his story, forming the words of the characters, whispering what they were saying, as he typed, two-finger style, his words onto the page. The dogs could be barking, doorbells ringing, and other events clamoring throughout a day, but he was in the world of Jerry Cooper, the war, the love affair with Giselle the dancer, from hustling stolen jeeps to building an empire.

There were days when Harold looked pale and wan as he struggled to get to the typewriter, but his characters and his story led him to the seat of creativity that lives in a writer's thoughts and he felt new again.

When friends and fellow authors would drop by to visit, they often commented to Harold that they could see the pain on his face, but they could also see renewed energy and the excitement about his book.

Harold had found the creative sparks of renewal he hadn't known since the early days of his career, before the trappings of fame and fortune.

Each time he would talk with his editor, Bob Gleason, Harold would have new ideas, new plots for ongoing books. Each evening at dinner, he would talk about the work he had done during the day. Almost in awe, he talked about how the story kept moving in directions he had never imagined. He felt he was being driven by a stronger force, a love for his life, his craft, and his future.

On his last day of writing *The Predators* he had gone to work early. Nine A.M. He stopped for lunch and dinner and he was very quiet that day. At eleven o'clock that evening he turned and looked at me sitting at the desk behind him.

"It's done," he said, and smiled. "I did it. I didn't know it would be finished tonight." He was as surprised as me.

He picked up the phone and called our close friends Admiral Bill Narva and his wife, Rose. They were at our house in fifteen minutes. It had been a tradition since Harold had written his first novel to celebrate the completion of each new book with a bottle of Dom Perignon, and later the date of completion and the name of the book were written on the label and framed. On this particular occasion, Harold had chosen 1992 Dom Perignon Rosé.

The following morning he called Bob Gleason and talked with him about the ending of *The Predators*, the next book, and the many books Harold wanted to write.

Thirty days later Harold underwent emergency hip surgery. During his rehabilitation he was visited by Gene Winick, his agent, with his wife, Ina, and Bob Gleason on a Saturday afternoon. Harold had arranged for the conference room, normally used by the doctors, to receive his guests. He also persuaded the nurses and orderlies to have refreshments and cold drinks served.

The afternoon was spent talking about copy for the *Predators* book cover and concept. For that reason, Harold talked in depth to Bob about his transition from *Never Love a Stranger* and *A Stone for Danny Fisher* to *The Carpetbaggers.*

"When I was in the financial department at Universal, Howard Hughes wanted us to sell him some movie theaters. I was in charge of the deal. It never went through, but I got to know Hughes. He changed the whole way I looked at fiction and life. A pioneer in aviation, filmmaking, and the Las Vegas casino business, he was the ultimate role model for my rags-to-riches Danny Fisher–type hero. When I explained my new vision to Alfred Knopf, he was horrified. When I explained it to Herb Alexander, he was mesmerized. Herbert understood my vision, my financial needs, and we made history. That's how the world changes."

Harold's answer to Bob gave him a new understanding of *The Predators.* Harold had combined both worlds in this one epic novel.

The Predators was arguably the most creative period of Harold's life. He not only wrote a fine novel to rank with *Danny Fisher* and *The Carpetbaggers,* he besieged me, night and day, with ideas and plots for all the other novels he planned on writing. I believe that was the happiest period of Harold's life.

—BOB GLEASON, EXECUTIVE EDITOR,
TOR/FORGE

As I watched Harold excitedly discuss his work, talk about new ideas, I knew that Harold Robbins would live forever. Amazingly, he had overcome the pain and his use of painkillers to write possibly one of the finest novels of his career.

On October 14, 1997, Harold Robbins made his transition from this world. He was on to the next life, the next book, the next adventure. But here, where we are, he lives forever in the hearts he left behind.

I will always have my hand in Harold's and feel his presence with every beat of my heart. I will cherish and grow from what he taught me about life, love, compassion, and generosity. He is my prayer of love.

The Predators was published on May 21, 1998 . . . Harold's birthday.

THE NEW YORK TIMES MAGAZINE, JANUARY 4, 1998

The Lives They Lived: Harold Robbins; Smutty Plots, Clean Prose b. 1916

Serious writers feared Harold Robbins. He had nothing to do with literature. He drove a Rolls-Royce and sailed a yacht. He was a prose machine, a futuristic piston, pumping out lucrative sentences. He ignored the critics. Words, for him, were sexual commodities. "All writers are whores," Robbins opined. Alexander Pope might have agreed. Both were masters of closure, of sentences that end, and make their endings known. Robbins's material is smutty but his prose is clean. Simple, speedy and efficient, his sentences demonstrate, in a parodic fashion, what Roland Barthes called "writing degree zero." They seem transparent but in fact are opaque bonbons, coldly functional fetishes, absurdly themselves. In "Where Love Has Gone," Robbins wrote, "She took a Wash'N Dri from the package her mother had sent her and tore the foil wrapper." In "The Adventurers," he wrote, "Sue Ann stuffed another chocolate into her mouth and rose from the chaise lounge." Such bland utterances are so fake, they're real. They have a quiet, mercenary dignity. Their refusal of insight makes them as modern as neon, or Niagara Falls.

—WAYNE KOESTENBAUM

If there is nothing else evident in my work, for myself there is only one thing that stands out. I am a people writer. Because people, with all their hopes and dreams, greed and ambitions, strength and weakness, love and hate, are all that interest me.

—HAROLD ROBBINS